The Best of
BRITAIN
for
CHILDREN

The Best of
BRITAIN
for
CHILDREN

Deborah Jaffé
&
Sue McAlpine

DIAL
PRESS

ACKNOWLEDGEMENTS
The authors would like to thank Terry Bloxham for her
painstaking research; the Ballantyne, Carnegie, Duff-
Porritt, Goudge, Maltin, McAlpine, McCreadie, Stephens
and Walker families and Mary MacDonell for their
comments; Liz Elkind for her hospitality; Richard and
Margot Walker for proof reading; Monica Considine and
John King for word processing and technical advice; John
Parker for introducing us to one another; the many site
attendants and publicity officers, sources of invaluable
information and help and George Kessler and David
McAlpine for their support.

This book first published in 1993

ISBN 0-7110-2142-2

Published by Dial Press.
Dial Press is an imprint of Ian Allan Publishing, Addlestone, Surrey.

Printed in England.

CONTENTS

INTRODUCTION

Here is a personal anthology of the best places in Britain for children. We hope you will have as much fun exploring them as we did. You can choose from castles, palaces, stately homes, underground caves, railways, mines, farms, science centres and museums.

We can help you deal with such august institutions as the British Museum; we can take you along Hadrian's Wall or up Snowdon; we can guide you round HMS *Victory,* onto the simulated flight deck of Concorde, down the mine-shaft of Big Pit, onto the battlements of Corfe Castle and across the water to St Michael's Mount. You can go back in time to experience the sights, smells and sounds of a Viking homestead, a vast Tudor kitchen, a World War 1 trench. You can steer your children round the hands-on, interactive experiences of science centres or the rope bridges and scrambling nets of adventure playgrounds. We can introduce your babies, toddlers and teenagers to dinosaurs, robots, shire horses, flamingoes, movie stars and miners. Your children can find out what astronauts eat in space, see exactly how a zoetrope works, how many bones a diplodocus has, and a myriad of other facts and observations.

If you thought that museums were stuffy places filled with dusty exhibits in glass cases in distant, empty rooms hung with the musty air of long neglect, then be prepared to have your eyes opened. Changes are happening so fast in the world of museums that they now have a huge variety of activities and events for children of all ages and inclinations. Nobody has to whisper or behave as though they were at the funeral of a distant cousin; exclamations of delight need not be embarrassing intrusions; warders or attendants should not be disapproving or intimidating.

Museums need not be indigestible. In fact, taken in small bites they can turn out to be delicious. We hope all this will open out wide vistas, stimulate different ways of thinking, inspire creativity and awaken new perspectives. Enjoyment comes first but learning will seep in gradually, like osmosis. So start your children at an early age on a journey of discovery and they might suddenly, somewhere come across something which might change their whole lives.

Symbols Used in Entries
O opening times
£ admission charges
P parking
🚌 public transport
♿ access for pushchair and wheelchair users and facilities for those with other disabilities
✕ restaurant, cafe, picnic area

NT National Trust
EH English Heritage

Opening times and admission charges are correct at the time of going to press, however there may be occasional variations. We suggest you phone to check these and also to verify any Christmas or other holiday arrangements.

Many sites offer a reduced rate for groups of visitors, usually of ten or more, we suggest you arrange this beforehand. Some places, which are closed in winter, will open for a pre-arranged group booking.

PLANNING THE VISIT
Think about the ages, interests and physical abilities of your children. If you have a baby in a pushchair or a toddler, a trek up the windswept, rock-hewn steps of Tintagel Castle would be rather taxing but a visit to a Wildfowl and Wetlands Centre could be great fun for everyone. An older child may be doing a

Young visitors enjoy some hands-on postal experience at 'Eureka' in Halifax.

articular project at school or have a
een interest in a specific subject, like
ostume or steam trains, so a visit to
ne of the many specialist museum
ollections or railways would be
nvaluable.

A concentration span of one hour
eems appropriate for a lot of children
nd many of the places we have chosen
an be visited within this time.
bviously you can spend longer and
evisit sites as often as you want.
lowever, some places, like the open-air
nuseums at Beamish and Dudley, need
full day's visit.

As a parent you may shy away from
aking your children to a military
nuseum, but these are excellent places
o explain to children the horrors of war,
ne history of flight, telecommunications,
isguise, camouflage and much more.

All the places we have included
relcome children. Staff are friendly and
sed to children enjoying themselves,
ut please keep an eye on your roaming
oddler or more boisterous children
those energies may not be so greatly
ppreciated. We have often found it
ppropriate to split up as a group. One
dult can take older children to the parts
nat really interest them, whilst another
ccompanies the younger ones to more
ppropriate places like the playground
or special rides. Many of the sites hold
hildren's exhibitions and holiday or
veekend workshops as well as hands-
on exhibits, simulators, quizzes, videos,
omputer data bases and activity
heets. Some places have their own
ducation departments where staff are
amiliar with the requirements of the
Iational Curriculum. It is often worth
elephoning for details of what is on
eforehand. Many sites have excellent
ccess for children and adults in
vheelchairs enabling them to visit the
vhole site. There are lots of facilities for
eople with visual and hearing
lifficulties. Museums have hands-on
exhibitions, where you are expected to
ouch exhibits and the Yorkshire
Sculpture Park has a tactile sculpture
rail through the grounds. It is a good
dea to telephone beforehand to check
he facilities and to arrange for help,
vhich many places offer, if you need it.

Let your children go at their pace
juiding them gently round, encouraging
hem to point things out to each other.
We often play I-Spy while looking at
aintings, or we imagine what life was
ke living twelve to two rooms or
iscuss the relative sizes of dinosaurs.

Take notebooks and felt pens with

you as sitting down and drawing what
you see is an excellent way to have a
rest and can be a good focus to a
distracted child as well as a souvenir of
your visit. Photography is allowed in
many places so take your camera. We
have found that the shop, (at the end of
the visit), is a great attraction to
children. To avoid great debates about
pocket money, loans and expenditure,
why not let them buy one postcard or
something of particular interest relating
to the visit. Do not be put off by the
weather, especially if rain is ruining your
holiday. Go off to the nearest museum
and spend a dry and fascinating time
indoors. Torrential rain nearly ruined a
day in Dorchester, but we discovered
wonderful treasures in the County
Museum and forgot about the outside
world. However we could only visit
Hadrian's Wall in the rain but, dressed
in boots and anoraks, we still had a
great time.

Check opening times before you plan
your visit, especially in autumn and
winter in rural areas, where many sites
are closed. If you are planning a mid-
week trip on a railway, ring to find out if
it is open. Our children were very
disappointed to find one Monday
morning that the train only ran at
weekends. Some places are closed on
Sunday, others on Monday and others
open only in the afternoon.

There is masses to see and do in
Britain, so find out what is happening
locally and make use of it. Ruined
abbeys and castles lead to great
dramatic play; cathedrals and churches
can be inspiring, point out vaulted
ceilings, stained glass, pews, carvings
and towers. Nature reserves and city
farms are full of live animals; local
museums often give fascinating insights
into the development of local geology,
industries and economies; arts centres
may run holiday workshops for children
and small theatres often have special
Saturday morning performances.

If you decide to go to London use
public transport as driving in the inner
city is a nightmare and parking is very
expensive. Public transport can be an
adventure and there are various one
day and weekly passes combining the
tube, buses and BR Network South
East. Under fives travel free of charge.

A Family Railcard from British Rail is
a good investment if you are planning to
travel by rail a lot.

We hope you enjoy visiting the sites
as much as we did and wish you luck in
your adventures.

AVON

American Museum in Britain
Claverton Manor
Bath BA2 7BD
Avon
0225 460503

○ 27 March-7 November, 2-5pm every day except Monday. Grounds open 1pm-6pm Tuesday-Sunday. Bank Holiday Sunday and Monday 11am-5pm.

£ Adult £4.50, Child £2.50, Under Five free, OAP £4.00 for galleries and museum. Grounds only-Adult £1.50, Child £1.00. Disabled free into the museum and galleries, £1.50 for grounds

P on site

A36 or Bathwick Hill, Bath

to 1/3 of rooms only

café

I first came here as an inexperienced tourist guide to a group of elderly Americans, who loved it. Years later I came back with my children who loved it too. I would recommend it as a marvellous place for grandparents to take grandchildren.

Make sure you see the Conestoga wagon, the Observation Platform on a railroad car and the replica tepee, before you follow the route through the house. Ask the museum herbalist for information about herbs in the Herb Shop and admire the extraordinary collection of bandboxes in the Milliner's. Inside are a series of furnished rooms brought from houses in America and reconstructed at Claverton Manor.

Stationed in each room, poised to sally forth on a detailed description, are the most enthusiastic and eager museum attendants I have yet encountered. The first one will tell you everything you would ever need to know about the Keeping Room, with its great oak table and Bible laid open for a reading by its Puritan owners. In the blue-green panelled living room from Lee, New Hampshire, is a large folding bed. In the Borning Room, used in time of childbirth or illness, there are stocking stretchers and a wig stand. The child's bed can easily be trundled out from beneath the four-poster. Further on are beautiful quilts with names such as Log Cabin and Grandmother's Flower Garden. The stencilled bedroom is well known; its delicate stencils were done by a travelling stenciller from powder paint mixed with skimmed milk. Look out for the miniature bed.

Downstairs is Charles W. Morgan's cabin from the last of the great Yankee whaling ships; with a bed that pivots and so remains level when the vessel rolls, and a very cramped 'captain's convenience'. Intrepid visitors can venture on to the Virgin Lands west of the Mississippi, along the Santa Fe and Oregon Trails to encounter cowboys and Indians, the Gold Rush and the Wells Fargo. An inviting smell encourages you into Conkey's Tavern where the fire is lit and gingerbread awaits freshly baked in the beehive oven by an even more enthusiastic member of the museum staff! The gingerbread will whet your appetite for the delicious, home-made George Washington cake or the Connecticut Snickerdoodle in the café.

On the way home my American visitors launched into their family histories. I was inspired to keep my things tidy in Shaker boxes and wondered how I could hang my chairs on the wall while hoovering. The children were keen to practise stencilling and patchwork: the start of two new crazes in our household. Perhaps it was all thanks to the conscientious attendants!

Bath Industrial Heritage Centre
Julian Road
Bath BA1 2PH
Avon
0225 318348

○ Easter-1 November 10am-5pm every day.
2 November-Easter 10am-5pm weekends only.

£ Adult £2.80, Child £1.60, Under Five free, OAP £1.60, Family Ticket £7.50

P nearby

buses from city centre

pushchair access, wheelchairs users should ring in advance

café

Unlike everywhere else in Bath, you might be the only people wandering around this extraordinary place. This cluttered, ramshackle museum is full of wonders.

The contents of Mr Jonathan Burdett Bowler's ironmongery and brass foundry were transferred, lock, stock and barrel, from their original premises in Corn Street, when a clearance order was served as the whole area was due to be demolished. Now everything is back in place in an 18th century Royal

A fine selection of Mr Bowler's wares from the Bath Industrial Heritage Centre.

ennis court, itself once in danger of emolition.

It is almost as though the rescuers of owler's family business were guided y his ghost. Everything is indeed back place, but lying piled higgledy-iggledy with nothing ever thrown away ut put down anywhere just as it might ave been. The atmosphere itself is still ere. You get this strange sensation nat the clerk of the works, with the days akings neatly tallied in the ledger, has viped his pen clean, pushed back his hair, turned down the gas, put on his at and coat and gone home for the ight. Time is suspended.

So it is with the mineral water factory ffice downstairs where Bowler's aughters kept the books, paid the mployees and received orders for rinks. The brush is still sitting in the lue pot, waiting for work pasting labels n bottles, to be continued next norning. There are huge glass jars filled ith coloured potions, heaps of spices, iles of corks and strange recipes for rinks such as Twaddle and Bath 'unch. Try some out from the soda untain upstairs.

Bowler's foundry seems to have een the kind of place where you could o and ask for a brass screw to fit a "1/4in hole. He would rummage around the back for a bit and soon return with vhat you wanted. Now you buy your ntrance ticket from the same counter nat Mr Bowler sold his spare parts, its helves still cluttered with gas mantles, andbells and candlesnuffers. You will ave no difficulty in transporting yourself ack a hundred years with Mr. Bowler at our side ready to do his best for one of is regular customers.

Museum of Costume
Assembly Rooms
Bennett Street
Bath BA1 2QH
Avon
0225 461111

○ 1 March-31 October, Monday-Saturday
9.30am-6pm, Sunday 10am-6pm.
1 November-28 February, Monday-Saturday
10am-5pm, Sunday 11am-5pm.
Closed 25, 26 December.

£ Adult £2.50, Child £1.40, Under Eight free,
OAP £2.50.
Bath residents and schools free.
Special combined ticket available for
Roman Baths and Museum of Costume.

P city car parks

⇔ BR Bath Spa, Coach station 15 minutes walk.
City bus service.

♿ yes

✗

In the Museum of Costume, on the lower floors of Bath's Assembly Rooms, you can find out what went in and out of fashion over the last four hundred years, from the late 16th century to the present day.

These are fashionable and expensive clothes, worn only for special occasions and then kept carefully in trunks and wardrobes. Museums usually have more of those kind of clothes in their collections as everyday or working ones become worn out. The displays here are changed every year as costumes are vulnerable and can be damaged by light and humidity. The collection is huge and will always demonstrate how styles, shapes and fashions change. Spend time looking at the early costumes of the 16th and 17th centuries as they are very rare and usually seen only in paintings or drawings. Look out for richly embroidered 18th century coats and

A brocaded silk dress of 1833 from the Museum of Costume.

Roman Baths Museum
Pump Room
Abbey Churchyard
Bath BA1 1LZ
Avon
0225 461111 ext 2785

O 1 March-31 October 9am-6pm.
   August 9am-6pm & 8-10pm.
   1 November-28 February 9am-5pm, Sunday
   10am-5pm
£ Adult £4.00, Child £2.00, Under Eight free.
   Ticket includes entrance to Museum of
   Costume.
P city car parks
BR and bus stations 5 minutes walk away
& yes
✕ restaurant

waistcoats, fans and canes, hats and hairstyles; powder compacts and jewellery. Children will enjoy the room settings from the elegant figures in the 18th century drawing room to a 19th century maid in the bathroom. See how shapes change. Look at the silk-brocaded coat dresses of the 18th century, supported on basket-like hoops or 'panniers' worn beneath the gown and widening it to a ridiculous, almost grotesque, extent. In the early 19th century the fashion swung the other way with dresses made of light fabrics, hanging loosely from high waists and then back again to the crinolines and bustles of the mid and late 19th century. Compare these with the straight, short dresses of the 1920s, the 1950s 'New Look' and so on.

Catch sight of a glimpse of ladies' ankles around 1810 before hemlines came right down for over a hundred years until the 1920s when daring 'flappers' shingled their hair and showed their knees. Throughout the Victorian era it was considered indecent to show your ankles; legs were referred to as 'limbs'.

Find out why wigs went out of fashion, why women wore ten petticoats at a time and what it was like to wear stuffed birds, animals and even beetles on your hat or around your neck. This is a specialised museum, but it tells you much about human vanity and life styles. It also makes you think about your own clothes, which ones you keep and which ones you give away and why. Ask your children which of their clothes they would like to donate to future displays at the Museum of Costume. Perhaps, however, the well worn jeans and trainers, will be of more interest than the best dresses.

Even if you cannot go of a winter weekend and have to jostle along with the crowds at the height of the season, a visit to the Roman Baths Museum will stay in children's memories for a long time. Despite its huge number of visitors it still manages to vibrate with an intensely exciting and extraordinary atmosphere.

This was once the Roman city of Aquae Sulis where a hot mineral spring gushes out of the ground at a rate of two hundred and fifty thousand gallons a day. Round it the Romans built a luxurious bathing suite and a classical temple dedicated to the goddess Minerva.

Unless you have very small children, we recommend you join a guided tour round the Baths, but wander through the rest of the museum at your own pace. Look out for the Gorgon's head, once part of the Temple facade. Find the lead curse, coins and jewellery thrown into the sacred spring as offerings to the gods. Look out for what remains of the Temple, the sacrificial altar and head of Minerva.

When you reach the sacred spring overflow, tell your children to listen to the sound of the water, smell the air, look at the colour of the stone, feel the steam. None of this can have changed over two thousand years. It is not hard to imagine the Romans here. You can walk on the very stones that their bare feet would have trod, you can feel the temperature of the water as it flows from the spring into the Great Bath, you can look at the hypocaust and the cold plunges. Throw in a coin, as they must have done, and make your own wish.

Upstairs in the 18th century Pump Room you can taste the spa water, look down on the King's Bath, and imagine the undiscovered wealth that lies beneath your feet.

On the way home you can decide which of your treasured possessions you might throw in to the sacred spring, and why.

Blaise Castle House Museum
Henbury
Bristol BS10 7QS
0272 506789

O Saturday-Wednesday 10am-1pm, 2-5pm.
£ free
P on site
🚌 bus from city centre
♿ ground floor only
✗ picnic area

The name derives from St Blaise, a popular medieval saint, but the house was designed in 1795 for the Hartford family with gardens landscaped by Humphry Repton. Before you go in, rush round the park and catch a glimpse of the sham castle on the hill beyond and the thatched dairy behind the museum. Sometimes there are butter and cream making demonstrations here. Inside the museum are dolls' houses (some used to instruct children in domestic duties), model soldiers, a fort with its ramparts manned by Grenadier Guards and all sorts of toys and games. Look out specially for a child's tub cart driven by a pony or goat and a child's Dandy-gig, driven by pulling and pushing a lever. Also a metal Slipper Bath, shaped like a shoe; you wriggled inside it until only your head was visible.

Bristol City Museum and Art Gallery
Queen's Road
Bristol BS8 1RL
0272 223571

O 10am-5pm every day
£ Adult £2.00, £1.00 after 4.15pm, Under Sixteen free, OAP £2.00, £1.00 after 4.15pm
Day Ticket £3.00 includes entry to other Bristol museums
P Berkeley Place
🚇 BR Templemeads. Bus 8, 9
♿ to most parts
✗ restaurant

According to a colleague, ex-member of staff here and proud mother of a then two year old, the Bristol City Museum and Art Gallery holds unexpected delights for toddlers. At the front door an attendant will instantly appear and help you with your pushchair (and, of course, wheelchairs), lend you toddler steps for better viewing and smile resignedly as your child runs across the hall shouting gleefully or climbs, with intrepid first steps, the Terrazzo marble staircase. Here is a challenge for early walkers and an exciting echoing space for children who want to make a bit of a noise. The museum also claims to have the most 'commodious baby-care room in the country' with a rocking chair and sympathetic notices to nappy changing parents.

Most popular with children are stuffed animals; in particular Alfred the

The central hall of the Bristol City Museum, complete with flying machine!

Gorilla. A hippopotamus and a rhinoceros confront each other in a vast glass case along with an aardvark, a tiger, a kakapo and a dodo. In the Egyptology galleries are mummies, including a stuffed crocodile, and displays with X-rays showing skeletons within their wrappings. Look out for a replica burial chamber, and the museum's greatest treasure, the carved reliefs from the palace of Ashurnasirpal II at Nimrud. In the Geology Gallery there are coral reefs full of shells and sponges, a scintillating display of minerals, a model of archaeopteryx, the earliest bird with the teeth, claws and bony tails of a reptile and the feathers and wings of a bird. Don't miss the skeleton of the Giant Irish deer and the two hundred million year old Ichthyosaur.

If you are local, join the Magnet Club, for a whole range of exciting activities at the weekends and holidays; membership is free.

Bristol Industrial Museum
Princes Wharf
City Docks
Bristol BS1 4RN
0272 251470

O Saturday-Wednesday 10am-1pm, 2-5pm
£ Adult £2.00, Child Free, OAP £2.00,
   Day Ticket-visit more than one Bristol museum
   in one day £3.00
P on site
🚌 buses from city centre
& yes
✗

This museum is inside the last surviving transit shed in Bristol City Docks, alongside a floating harbour where the world's oldest tug, *Mayflower,* 1861, is moored. If you turn up on a summer weekend she will take you on a trip round the City Docks. Failing that you can see the Fairbairn Steam Crane in action or climb aboard the steam railway for a trip round the Harbour. Brunel's *Great Western* steamship was built on this site in 1837 and his SS *Great Britain* in 1843 in the dry dock where she is now exhibited at Great Western Dock in Gas Ferry Road (see below).

Among the large vehicles on the ground floor is the world's first touring caravan, the Wanderer, built in 1880 for Dr W. Gordon Stables. He took a coachman and a valet with him on every trip, but always left his wife behind. Peer inside to see its rich mahogany

furnishings. Look out for the Grenville Steam Carriage, the world's oldest self-propelled passenger carrying road vehicle, still in good working condition. Upstairs there is a full-size engineering mock-up of the flight deck of a Concorde supersonic airliner and a 1947 helicopter.

If your children have friendly feelings towards cars and aircraft then this is a museum for them. They can also come in free!

SS *Great Britain*
Great Western Dock
Gas Ferry Road
Bristol BS1 6TY
0272 260680

O Summer 10am-6pm
   Winter 10am-5pm. Times change with the
   change of clock.
   Closed 24, 25 December.
£ Adult £2.90, Child £1.90, Under Five free,
   OAP £1.90
P nearby Pay and Display
🚌 bus 511. Ferry summer only
& limited
✗ café and picnic area

The SS *Great Britain* was designed by and built for Brunel in 1843 at the dry dock, now the site of Bristol Industrial Museum. Older children, interested in shipbuilding, may well enjoy a visit to this historic ship.

The SS *Great Britain.*

The Exploratory lives up to its claim of encouraging 'hands on' participation.

The Exploratory
Bristol Old Station
Temple Meads
Bristol BS1 6QU
0272 252008
Information Line 0272 225944

O 10am-5pm every day except Christmas week
£ Adult £3.75, Child £2.50,
　Under Three free,
　OAP £2.50
　Family Ticket £11.50
P weekdays at Temple Way.
　Daily at Temple Gate House & Station car park.
🚉 BR Bristol Temple Meads station. Bus routes.
♿ yes
✗ café and picnic area.

'Please do touch the exhibits'.
So says the Exploratory's leaflet, and that is exactly what you can do in this excellent hands-on science centre. Whether you are four or a hundred and four, whether you are just learning to read or are a genius scientist, you can discover 'serious' scientific principles with very little effort and tremendous enjoyment.

There are a hundred and fifty exhibits or plores as they call them. There is no set tour; you can explore whatever meets your eye. You can rush, as many do, or stay with one plore for a bit until you really have the hang of it. The Exploratory's pilots can help if you have any difficulties. They'll put you in the right direction but won't give you any quick answers.

How do magnets work? Why are sunsets red? How do aeroplanes fly? Why not try and find out some of the answers? Look out for illusions and ghostly shapes; experiment with 3-D vision, mirrors and reflections, holograms, colour and light. See your shadow still outlined on the wall after you've left. Find out about sound with whisper dishes, echo devices and sound waves made visible with gas flames. Swirl the water in 'whirlpool bottles' to make a vortex and see how water escapes down a bath plug hole.

Put your hand into a 'tornado' and feel the swirling motion of a current of air. Walk over a suspension bridge; pull pulleys and levers to lift objects much heavier than yourself. Look out for the beach balls that hover in the air, a swivel chair that starts to spin when you sit on it holding a gyroscope, a harmonograph that draws an infinite variety of patterns. Spin on a momentum platform and ride a bike fast enough to make enough pedal power to work a television camera.

The temporary exhibitions are worth travelling some distance for so find out what is on before you come. Bring plenty of money because the shop is full of potential Christmas presents!

BEDFORDSHIRE

The Shuttleworth Collection
Old Warden Aerodrome
Near Biggleswade SG18 9ER
Bedfordshire.
0767 627288

○ 1 April-31 October 10am-5pm,
   last admission 4pm.
   1 November-31 March 10am-4pm,
   last admission 3pm.
£ Adult £4.00, Child £2.50, Under Five free,
   OAP £2.50.
   Flying Display Days and special events are extra.
🅿 on site
🚉 BR Biggleswade
♿ yes
🍴 restaurant and picnic area

Come to the Shuttleworth Collection and find out about the history of aeroplane flight. There are some very old craft here including a Bleriot 1909 plane, World War 1 fighters, 1920s de Havillands, a Gloster Gladiator of the 1930s and a World War 2 Spitfire. You may recognise some of the planes from the starring parts they have had in films whilst you can climb aboard others and look into the engines.

This is one of the oldest collections of aircraft and was begun by a motor racing driver, Richard Ormonde Shuttleworth, in 1932 when he bought a DH60 Moth and piloted it himself. Becoming an aircraft enthusiast he amassed quite a collection but was killed in an RAF flying training accident in 1940. A trust was formed in his

memory and the Shuttleworth Collection, as it is today, is the result.

Richard Ormonde Shuttleworth's early purchases are still here for you to see. The 1930s and 1940s have been so carefully preserved that even Monsieur Poirot would be happy. There are demonstrations and many aircraft are flown in the summer months (ring for details). Occasionally Shuttleworth's 1898 Panhard Levassor car is brought out; it was with this vehicle that he won the London-Brighton rally in 1928. There are other veteran and vintage cars here too.

Most of the collection is indoors, so the weather is not a problem. There is an adventure playground and the restaurant offers an intriguing children's menu of Skyliner and Spitfire Sandwiches and Flying Hot Dogs.

A 1910 Bristol Boxkite (*below*) and a Hawker Hind light bomber from the 1930s (*bottom*), both taking part in a flying display at the Shuttleworth Collection.

14

BERKSHIRE

Windsor Castle

Windsor
Berkshire SL4 1NJ
0753 868286. Visitors with disabilities
ring ext. 2235.
Information Line 0753 831118.

○ Open every day from 10.30am closing at
various times.
The State Apartments are closed when the
Royal Family is in residence.
Ring the Information Line for details.

£ State Apartments: Adult £4.00, Child £1.50,
OAP £2.50. Gallery: Adult £2.00, Child £1.00,
OAP £1.50. Royal Mews: Adult £1.60, Child
£0.80, OAP £1.40.

🅿 town centre car parks

🚉 BR Windsor Riverside

♿ most of the Castle is accessible to wheelchairs,
though it is best to ring beforehand. Access is
limited for pushchairs which have to be left
outside the State Apartments.

✗ no

The Princesses Elizabeth and Margaret in
unfamiliar guise - part of the exhibition on the
royal family's own pantomimes.

For over nine hundred years a castle
has stood, majestically, on the hill at
Windsor, It dominates the town, which
has grown up outside its walls. It is both
a royal palace and a fortress, an
important venue for state ceremonies
and a much loved home.

In the fire, of November 1992, we
were able to see the fragility of much of
the fabric of this ancient building as well
as the works of art and antiquities inside
it. Television cameras showed
unforgettable pictures of huge carpets,
valuable paintings, beautiful vases and
furniture being loaded onto army trucks
whilst flames billowed through the roofs
and towers behind. Fire apart, Windsor
is an important royal home to visit. This
is not a ruined castle where you can
play games and pretend to be kings and
queens, but a famous tourist site, full of
visitors from all over the world. Young
children might find the formality tedious,
so we recommend a visit for older
children and adults.

As you walk through the gates of this
royal enclave look for the soldiers on
sentry duty. We always try to make
them smile, but their training is so
thorough, that they never do. Walk up
the sweeping drive into the austere St
George's Chapel, where ten monarchs
are buried. Built by King Edward IV in
1475, this is a fine example of late
medieval architecture.

Further up the driveway, and in the
castle proper, are the State Apartments,
much of which were damaged by the
fire. Through special glass windows you
can see the wrecked and devastated
rooms and compare them to the
splendour of those unaffected. From
different vantage points you can see the
progress of clearing St George's Hall
and watch archaeologists sift through
debris and ash, searching for pieces of
metal, plaster and wood all of which
may give clues useful to the renovation.
Eventually, when enough information

Returning one of the carpets saved from the fire.

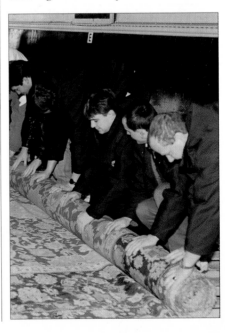

has been amassed, decisions will be made as to how best to rebuild the gutted hall. Look at the photographs of it before the fire, and the huge table which stretched along its full length and was used for grand state banquets.

In the Waterloo Chamber find the Pantomime Murals which have never been seen by the public before. These sixteen murals were painted in 1944, by 15 year old Claude Whatham, for the production of 'Old Mother Red Riding Boots' starring Princesses Elizabeth and Margaret, then aged eighteen and fourteen years. Discover the history of royal pantomime in the photographs and original programmes on display.

The rest of your tour around the State Apartments will take you into such august rooms as the Garter Throne Room, used by the Queen to install Knights of the Order of the Garter; the King's State Bedchamber, used by Charles II and since as a 'guest' room; the King's Drawing Room; the King's Dressing Room and Queen's Drawing Room.

No visit to Windsor would be complete without seeing Queen Mary's Dolls' House. This must be the most perfect miniature palace in existence. It was designed by Sir Edwin Lutyens and presented to Queen Mary in 1923 as a symbol of national goodwill. Outside look over the castle walls at the splendid views of Berkshire, Eton College and Windsor Great Park. Make your way down the driveway to the Exhibition of the Queen's Presents and Royal Carriages outside the main gate.

Royalty and Empire
Windsor Central Station
Thames Street
Windsor
Berkshire SL4 1PJ
0753 857837

○ 9.30m - 5.30pm April - September.
  9.30am - 4.30pm October - March.
  Closed 25 December.
£ Adult £3.95, Child £2.45, OAP £2.95,
  Family ticket £10.50.
P Town centre car parks
BR Windsor Riverside
♿ Most areas accessable

See how Queen Victoria arrived at Windsor. Cross the road, from the Castle to the Railway Station and look at the life-size, wax figures, military band and royal train which evoke this grand event. You can see the 'Queen' sitting in the waiting room, then look through the windows of her luxurious train and finally inspect the guard.

Two views from the Royalty and Empire displays. Queen Victoria approaching her carriage and in the Waiting Room with the Prince and Princess of Wales (later Edward VII).

CAMBRIDGESHIRE

Imperial War Museum
Duxford Airfield
Duxford
Cambridge CB2 4QR
0223 835000

Mid March-24 October 10am-6pm every day.
25 October-Mid March 10am-4pm every day.
Adult £5.80, Child £2.90, Under Five free,
OAP £4.00, FamilyTicket £16.00
on site
Cambridge
yes
restaurant and picnic area

The Imperial War Museum (see page 58) houses its large military machinery at Duxford Airfield. In a series of hangars there is a fascinating collection of military and civilian aircraft, tanks and vehicles. On Bank Holidays you can see Duxford from the air or take a train ride around the site. There are air displays throughout the year. Lots of surprises are in store for the visitor.

Concorde is an obvious attraction, you can climb aboard it and pretend to be, supersonic, half way across the Atlantic. Those with strong stomachs will want a ride in the Tornado simulator, for which there is an extra charge. Find the *Jesse Lumb* lifeboat and midget submarine. In the Land Warfare Exhibition you can see vehicles from the collection, being demonstrated in a special arena.

In Hangar 4 sound and lighting effects recreate a World War 1 'Dawn Patrol' with a Bristol Fighter and an RE8 biplane. Duxford Airfield was a fighter base for the US 8th Air Force in World War 2. It was from here that Douglas Bader led his squadrons of Hurricanes and Spitfires in the Battle of Britain. You can see a reconstruction of the Operations Room used during the battle; inside you will hear the sound of a bombing raid and notice the old telecommunications systems.

Many of the craft are being restored and preserved and you are able to watch this happen in hangars and workshops. There is lots to do and see here; use the transport system to get around the site and let your children loose on the adventure playground. Most of the exhibits are under cover in the hangars so you can visit in the rain!

Below: A restored Spitfire on one of the Duxford taxiways.
Bottom: Duxford's Battle of Britain era Operations Room has also been brought back to its original condition.

CHESHIRE

The Grosvenor Museum
27 Grosvenor Street
Chester CH1 2DD
Cheshire
0244 321616

O Monday-Saturday 10.30am-5pm,
   Sunday 2-5pm
£ free
P Little Roodee car park
🚌 buses from city centre
♿ no. Pushchairs must be left in the entrance hall
✗ no

For the Romans, Deva was a remote garrison on the western edge of their Empire. For Charles 1, Chester was fiercely Loyalist but the Battle of Rowton Moor nearby was a disastrous defeat for the Royalists during the Civil War. Chester is now a pleasant city to explore on foot, inside its defensive wall and along its historic roads. Go to the Grosvenor Museum if you need to know about the Romans and their army. There is an imposing life-size model of a 1st century AD legionary with cingulum, caligae, gladius, pilum and pugio. What are they? There is rare Roman glass, amphorae and glossy red Samian ware from Gaul. All self-respecting Romans used it as their best dinner set. Mass produced on an industrial scale there was a choice of designs with fruit and flowers, classical myths, hunting scenes or gladiatorial combat.

What happened to the young man with a badly set broken leg whose skeleton was found down a well? Was he thrown down or did he fall in?

Follow the passage through to the Georgian House. Look for the Victorian chemist's sign with coloured lettering to distinguish between human and animal medicines. Useful to stop illiterate farmers from dosing their cattle with Oriental Tooth Paste. Room settings are always welcome to the weary museum visitor, especially a young one. These are well worth lingering over. So is the Natural History Gallery half way up the main staircase.

The giant ammonite is too big to miss but you might not see the Dusky Knot-Grass Dagger Moth camouflaged on a bit of lichen or the Narrow Bordered Bee-Hawk Moth pretending to be a bumble-bee. The best bluff of all belongs to the Chinese Character Moth whose main means of survival is its successful disguise as a piece of bird mess.

The Nursery from the period house at the Grosvenor Museum

Chester Toy and Doll Museum
3 Lower Bridge Street
Chester CH1 1RS
244 346297

Monday-Saturday 10am-5pm. Sunday
12 noon-4pm.
Closed 24, 25, 26 December, 1 January.
Adults £1.50, Child 70p, Under Five free,
OAP 70p, Family Ticket £3.20
city centre car parks
close to bus stations
no
no

A tiny museum packed with tinplate
toys, cars, dolls, bears, games, boats,
puppets and a huge collection of
Matchbox toys. A juke box filled with
fifties and sixties 45rpm records for
parents with tendencies to nostalgia.
You'll need a handful of coins for this as
well as the 'What the Butler Saw' slot
machines on the staircase.

The Boat Museum
Dockyard Road
Ellesmere Port
South Wirral L65 4EF
Cheshire
051 355 5017

April - October 10am-5pm every day.
November - March 11am-4pm closed Friday.
Adult £4.00, Child £2.70, Under Five free,
OAP £3.00, Family
Ticket £12.50.
on site
C3 bus from Birkenhead and Chester.
yes
café and picnic area

It is hard to imagine living with all your
family in the tiny cabin of a narrow boat,
which has to be negotiated and pulled
by horse, with its cargo up and down
this country's canals. Here at Ellesmere
Port's Boat Museum you are free to
clamber across the boats moored in the
upper basin, balance along their narrow
sides, duck under the tiller and squeeze
into the six by eight feet cabins. This
was home to the canal men, their wives
and children. Here are the brightly
painted designs, the ribboned plates,
the lace edgings, the horse brasses. Try
and imagine fitting all your family's
possessions into these tiny cupboards.
There are two narrow beds. No wonder
much of the time was spent up on top.

In the dock's buildings you will find
the forge, where Les, the blacksmith,
will make you a tiny, lucky horseshoe,
and stables where you can greet the

Brightly painted canal boats feature at the
Boat Museum.

horses. Hauling the boats was hard
work, but a good horse knew exactly
when to stop and start so that, for
example, a boat could drift neatly into
the lock. In the Toll House you can find
out what cargoes were carried and
where tolls were paid. In the Island
Warehouse look out for good
reconstructions of workshops such as
the rope workshop with its large,
knotted bolts of rope. Look out for the
icebreakers, rocked from side to side by
gangs of men holding onto a rail,
stretching along the middle of the boat.
In the tunnel section you can see how
the men lay on their backs and 'walked'
the boats along with their feet on the
roof of the tunnel.

Visit the cottages in Porters Row.
There used to be twelve of them, built
for £780 in 1835. They are fitted out to
show front rooms and back kitchens of
the 1840s, 1900s, 1930s and 1950s.
Meet the 'owner' of one of the cottages
who will enthusiastically recommend
you visit her outside lavatory. Do you
long for the 'luxury of a clean shirt'?
Then use Sunlight Soap, says one of
the hoardings outside.

The lock fills and empties and there
are boats on the move. You can take
short trips up the Shropshire Canal,
round the docks, watch ocean-going
vessels pass by on the Manchester
Ship Canal and look across the Mersey
Estuary. Watch restorers at work in the
boat repair workshops, volunteers and
canal enthusiasts all helping to make
this fascinating museum a living,
working environment.

Jodrell Bank Science Centre and Arboretum

Lower Withington
Macclesfield SK11 9DL
Cheshire
0477 71339

○ Easter-31 October 10.30am-5.30pm every day.
1 November-Easter 12 noon-5pm weekends only.
Closed 25 December.

£ Adult £3.20, Child £1.80, Under Five free,
OAP £2.40, Family Ticket £10.00.
Season Tickets Adult £9.00, Child £5.00,
OAP £7.00, Family £20.00

🅿 on site

🚉 BR Goostrey 2 miles, no bus

♿ yes

✗ café and picnic area

Driving towards Jodrell Bank you catch tantalising glimpses of the Lovell Radio Telescope. It seems like a typically elusive UFO on the horizon and is just as impressive when you finally reach the science centre. It is the second largest, fully steerable radio telescope in the world and is as big as the dome on St Paul's Cathedral. It tracked the Sputnik in the early days of space exploration. It is a listed 'building'.

We found Jodrell Bank a very friendly place, not too daunting or demanding, a smaller, and certainly less crowded version of the Launch Pad at the Science Museum.

We got close up to an astronaut and found how his suit is made and what he eats in space. We looked at holograms and prisms, we sent the earth round the sun in the gravity hollow, we tried out the gyro wheel and chair, we saw ourselves into infinity in the mirror and shook our own hands, we whispered

The giant array of the large radio telescope at Jodrell Bank.

messages via the sound reflectors and we met the talking head of Sir Isaac Newton who explained some knotty scientific problems to us.

The Planetarium Show (under fives not admitted) was greeted with enthusiasm by two normally disenchanted young teenagers. We boarded a space ship and were launched into the solar system to go where no one has ever gone before. We pressed buttons to vote whether we wanted to land on the moon, get closer to the rings of Saturn, a world of gas and ice or explore beyond. In December you can see the sky as it was over Bethlehem two thousand years ago as the Wise Men or astronomers of the time saw it.

We bought packets of Astronaut's ice cream and had a picnic in the Arboretum. The Environmental Discovery Centre here has nature trails which explore the woods.

At work on the water wheel at the Quarry Bank Mill.

Quarry Bank Mill and Styal Country Park (NT)

Styal SK9 4LA
Cheshire
0625 527468

1 April-30 September 11am-6pm, last admission 4.30pm every day.
1 October-31 March 11am-5pm Tuesday-Sunday, last admission 3.30pm.
NT Members and Friends of QBM free. NT members may have to pay for special events. Mill and Apprentice House: Adult £4.25, Child £3.00, OAP/Concession £3.00, Family Ticket £12.50.
Mill only: Adult £3.30, Child £2.40, OAP/Concession £2.40, Family £9.50
on site
BR Styal ½ mile
Not upstairs in the Apprentice House
restaurant

This is Samuel Greg's cotton mill, built in 1784 in a ravine cut by the drop in the River Bollin so that water power could be readily harnessed. It was one of the earliest enterprises to take full advantage of Arkwright's water frame and Crompton's spinning mule, revolutionary machines which could do the work of hundreds of handspinners at many times their speed.

We first crossed a high walkway over the main courtyard and wandered through room after room of this seemingly endless mill. Some rooms had the studied silence of a quiet, country museum, others, such as the weaving sheds, were deafeningly noisy from the frenzied action of the looms, with their leather thongs whipping the shuttles through the warp. Even the museum staff who worked here had a glazed expression, oblivious to visitors, as they moved through a forest of rollers and levers, from one machine to another. We imagined these rooms a century ago, full of adults and children, working long shifts and prone to terrible injuries.

We watched demonstrations of spinning and hand weaving, we learnt about bleaching, printing and dyeing, we followed the fortunes of four generations of the Greg family and we finally descended to the huge watermill and admired an eccentric waterpowered sculpture.

We had heard so much about the Apprentice House at Styal that we were eager to see it ourselves. Only thirty people can visit at a time so make sure you book when you first arrive.

Apprentice children, usually paupers from the parish workhouse or from the orphanage, were cheap and ideal workers. For each one the parish provided four guineas and two sets of clothing. Eighty children, from eight to eighteen, were packed into this house, working a twelve hour day with school on Sundays, insisted upon by Hannah Greg.

We were taken through the house by the manageress in a neat print dress, apron and bonnet, who treated us fairly peremptorily, as though we were her recalcitrant charges. We scratched on slates by a smoking fire in the schoolroom; we were shown the rows of box beds with straw palliasses, each for a pair of children; we learnt about the house diet of thin porridge and potato pies, boiled pork and cabbage on Sundays; we looked at the herbs, purges and powders for children's ailments and were offered a measured dose of brimstone and treacle. No one took up the offer!

We drew back in horror at the real leeches swimming in an earthenware jar. Punishments were described with self-righteous rigour, two days solitary confinement in the dark, sitting on the floor of a tiny attic room, working overtime at the mill so missing out the rudimentary schooling and, for the runaways, worst of all as far as the two girls with me were concerned, was having your hair crudely shorn off.

Groups of children can come here as 1830s apprentices. They are dressed in white bonnets and aprons or black jerkins, breeches and caps and are taken through a day of wood chopping, carting coal, hoeing the garden, scrubbing the floor, mending shirts, wielding dolly-pegs, kow-towing to the Misses Greg, eating porridge and washing up their pewter plates and wooden spoons in the pump in the yard. They stop short at using the earth closet.

Others can join in on summer weekends, spring cleaning, learning to spin or weave, hunting for treasure or joining spooky Hallowe'en trails round the Mill or buying Christmas presents from Samuel Greg's Emporium.

Catalyst. The Museum of the Chemical Industry
Mersey Road
Widnes
Cheshire WA8 0DF
051 420 1121

O Tuesday-Sunday, Bank Holiday Monday
  10am-5pm.
  Closed 24, 25, 26 December, 1 January.
£ Adult £2.25, Child £1.50, Under Five free,
  OAP £1.75 Family Ticket £6.75
P nearby
BR Runcorn, bus Runcorn - Widnes
yes
café

Catalyst is a new and exciting museum about the chemical industry and its effects on every day life. It examines the past and present of the industry and appeals to people of all ages especially

Visitors enjoying one of the interactive exhibits at Catalyst.

children from seven upwards. There is an indoor play area for them. Catalyst aims to be fun whilst at the same time being educational. There are occasiona holiday workshops for children.

Go to the Observatory by the all-glass external hydraulic lift and find yourself high above the River Mersey in an amazing floor to ceiling glass gallery. Here with remote control video cameras you can get a bird's eye view of the industry as well as exploring its past with video games and computers.

'Scientrific' lets you explore the ways in which chemicals are manufactured and the products they create. Here you will find exhibits on process control, chemical engineering, materials technology and health care. Try your skill at moving a 'chemical' from a storage tank to a reactor vessel on the giant hands-on Pumps Pipes and Valves exhibit. You can examine the low friction properties of PTFE as well as compare synthetic materials with natural ones.

The building itself is of historic interest. It was originally part of a 19th century alkali works and overlooks the River Mersey and St Helens Canal.

Future exhibits are being planned so when you go you will no doubt find more fascinating displays on the role of the chemical industry in the environment, feed production, health care, transport and leisure activities.

CLEVELAND

Captain Cook Birthplace Museum
Stewart Park
Marton
Middlesborough TS7 8AS
Cleveland
0642 311211

○ Summer and Bank Holidays 10am-5.30pm.
Winter 9am-4pm, closed Monday.
Adult £1.20, Child 60p, Under Five free,
OAP 60p, Family Ticket £3.00
🅿 nearby. On Site for the Disabled
🚉 BR Marton. Buses from Middlesborough
♿ yes
✕ restaurant and picnic area.

Captain Cook was born in Marton in
1729 and this museum is full of things
about him and his voyages of
exploration. Shops and Whitby
Quayside, from where he sailed, have
been reconstructed, complete with
atmospheric sounds of church bells, sea
gulls and horses' hoofs on cobbled
streets. There are displays about
navigation, a wonderful sextant, octant
and compass, as well as a model of
Cook's ship *Endeavour*. Cook's
voyages are not forgotten, with artefacts
from many of the lands he visited:
Tahiti, Australia, New Zealand and
Canada. Outside the museum is a large
totem pole given by the people of
Vancouver and based on designs by
Nootka Indians. There are masks,
carvings and music from the Australian
Aborigines and New Zealand Maoris.
You will also find drums, maces, fans
and combs from the Pacific Islands. In
the conservatory you will see thousands
of plants from Australia and the Pacific
Islands. This is a museum for anyone
involved with traders and explorers at
school and for older children interested
in ethnography.

Outside, wander round Stewart Park
with its aviary and tiny zoo.

Preston Hall Museum
Yarm Road
Stockton-on-Tees
Cleveland
0642 781184

○ Easter-30 September, 10am-6pm,
last admission 5.30pm, every day.
October-Easter 10am-4.30pm, last admission
4pm, every day.
Closed 25, 26 December, 1 January,
Good Friday.
£ Free
🅿 on site pay and display
🚉 BR Eaglescliffe 1 mile. Bus Stockton-Yarm.
♿ pushchairs must be left in the conservatory.
Wheelchair access.
✕ café and picnic area in park

The niece and nephew of a friend, live
in Stockton-on-Tees, and spend a lot of
time at Preston Hall. The varied
collection includes a headman's axe,
maces, swords, daggers and armour.
There are numerous snuff boxes made
out of various materials and in a host of
different shapes. An interesting
selection of children's and men's
clothing forms the centrepiece of the
displays in the Costume Gallery.

One of the two most popular
attractions is the outdoor, reconstructed
Victorian Street, along which there is a
schoolroom and an enticing selection of
recreated shops including a
dressmaker, hatter, taxidermist,
blacksmith, grocer and chemist.

The attic houses the other attraction;
a treasure trove of children's toys and
games. Look for the monkey automaton
and Mr Punch amongst the more
familiar train sets, dolls, farms, books
and board games.

The main building at Preston Hall.

CORNWALL

National Museum of Gypsy Caravans
Trereife Park
Penzance TR20 8TJ
Cornwall
0736 62750

O April-October 10.30am-5.30pm
£ Adult £3.00, Child £1.25, Under Five free
OAP £1.25
P on site
bus, Lands End Road
yes
restaurant and picnic area.

Three friends aged from eight to fifteen years spent an exciting afternoon here, the eldest was still talking about it months later. The Romanies and the freedom of their nomadic lifestyle have a certain fascination for us city dwellers. They first came to Britain in the 15th century and it was thought, at that time, that they were descended from the Ancient Egyptians. So they were called Gypsies, a corruption of Egyptian. But their lives here have not been easy; for centuries they have been persecuted and often killed by local inhabitants. Although we associate them with their beautifully painted caravans, until the 19th century their homes were tents.

My friends found out about the language and crafts of the Romanies and the harshness of their lives. They saw various gypsy caravans, some were very simple road carts and others splendid Victorian creations with delicate painting along the side. I am told the carriage ride through Trereife Park was great fun.

Left: A young visitor at Trereife Park.
Below: The Museum is also an active equestrian centre.

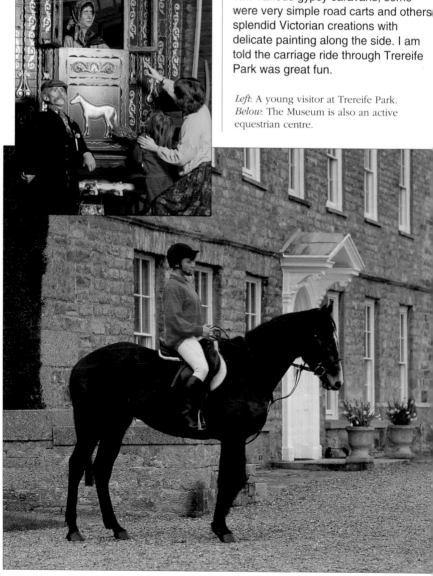

Tintagel Castle (EH)
intagel PL34 0AA
ornwall
840 770328

○ 1 April-30 September 10am-6pm.
1 October-31 March 10am-4pm every day.
EH Members free. Adult £2.00, Child £1.00,
Under Five free, OAP £1.50.

🅿 nearby in village

🚋 BR Bodmin Parkway. Fry's Bus Service from
Wadebridge

♿ no

✕ nearby

Location: the castle is on Tintagel Head,
half a mile along a track from the
village, no vehicles allowed. We came
here on a wild and windy day in March.
The children were very reluctant to get
out of the car and we had to steer them
firmly past the souvenir shops and bribe
them with promises of food and drink
before they agreed to walk down the
track towards the coast and ruins of
Tintagel Castle. (There is a Land Rover
service at the height of the season.)

They were impressed when we told
them that King Arthur was born here.
King Uther Pendragon, with the help of
Merlin, crept into Tintagel Castle at
night and seduced the unsuspecting
Igerna, who assumed it was her
husband. It is just a piece of romantic
fiction but it helped three lazy teenagers
and two small children up steep paths,
through archways, up and down flights
of rock cut steps, along the edge of the
cliff and up on to the top of the summit
plateau where they all went wild!

At last they began to take an interest
in their surroundings, speculating about
the mysterious remains of buildings,
asking questions about past and future
excavations, about Cornwall's ancient
kings and medieval earls, about Celtic
Christians. Did the Romans come here?
Who lies in these graves? We found a
cave where the flat slate floor was
marked with strange round hollows and
we could make out the names and
initials of much earlier visitors.

We were all fascinated by the shape
of the cliff face, the isthmus joining this
island of slate and volcanic rock to the
mainland and Merlin's cave that goes
right through the neck of the island. A
thousand years ago this neck was much
broader and higher but there have been
many landslides, for sea, wind and rain
are constantly playing a part in
changing the face of the cliff. The
possibility of falling rocks and tidal
waves added to the fun!

Other places to visit here are the early
12th century Tintagel Church, dedicated
to St Materiana and King Arthur's Great
Halls in the centre of Tintagel where
Robert Powell will tell you the story of
King Arthur in an 'electronic theatre'.
Launceston and Okehampton Castles
are also in this area.

The coastline between Tintagel and
Boscastle must be one of the most
historic and dramatic in Britain. Parts of
it are very much on the tourist beat,
parts for intrepid explorers and parts for
locals who know its hidden paths to
seemingly inaccessible beaches and
other places. At Rocky Valley there are
labyrinth pattern carvings; at Trethery a
holy well and Roman milestone; at
Trevalga puffins hang out near Long
Island; at Bossiney 'Elephant Rock' with
his trunk in the sand. Get hold of a
leaflet called 'Tintagel and the
Coastline' which tells you everything.

St.Michael's Mount (NT)
Marazion
Near Penzance TR17 0HT
Cornwall
0736 710507

○ 1 April-31 October, Monday-Friday
10.30am-5.30pm, last admission 4.45pm.
1 November-31 March, Monday, Wednesday
and Friday. Open most weekends in season.
Guided tours or free flow as tide, weather
and circumstance permit.

£ NT Members free. Adult £3.00, Child £1.45,
Under Five free, OAP £3.00, Family Ticket £8.00

🅿 on mainland

🚋 BR Penzance 3 miles then Penzance - Falmouth
bus

♿ no

✕ restaurant 1 April-31 October

Getting there by boat at high tide and
returning on foot across the causeway at
low tide endows a place with a certain
mystery, which we certainly felt when we
were there. Here was once a Benedictine
chapel established by Edward the
Confessor inspired perhaps by the holy
Mont St Michel on a tiny island off the
coast of Normandy. St Michael's Mount
here, is now a spectacular 14th century
castle high up on a rock looking out over
Land's End and the Lizard. We stepped
out of our boat right onto Queen
Victoria's footstep, caught for ever in a
brass plaque. We climbed the cobbled
pathways, up to the castle where we
roamed through the rooms and looked
out through windows where once others
had waited for the Spanish Armada. We
also had a delicious lunch there.

CUMBRIA

The Beatrix Potter Gallery (NT)
Main Street
Hawkshead
Ambleside
Cumbria LA22 ONS
05394 36355

O 1 April-31 October, Monday-Friday and
   Bank Holiday Sundays 10.30am-4.30pm,
   last admission 4pm.
   Closed in the winter.
£ NT Members free, Adult £2.40, Child £1.20,
   Under Five free, OAP £2.40.
P car park nearby in Hawkshead
▄▄infrequent bus service from Ambleside
♿ no
✗ no

You cannot visit the Lake District
without being reminded of Beatrix
Potter. The landscape constantly brings
back recollections of her paintings and it
is difficult to escape the huge amount of
memorabilia dedicated to her
characters.

This tiny museum which takes about
thirty minutes to go round, is for the true
Beatrix Potter fan. It is housed in the
former office of her husband, William
Heelis, a solicitor; the interior remains
unaltered since he practised there from
1900-1954. You will find a collection of
Potter's original drawings and
illustrations for her books as well as a
display about her life as an author,
writer and farmer. A gem for the
enthusiast of five years and over.

Hadrian's Wall.
If you are in Cumbria, try to visit
Hadrian's Wall which crosses England
from Solway to Wallsend.
Please refer to page 99 for
our experiences at
this fascinating
place which is
worth visiting.

Rexel Cumberland Pencil Museum and Exhibition Centre
Southey Works
Greta Bridge
Keswick
Cumbria CA12 5NG
07687 73626

O 9.30am-4pm every day.
   Closed 25, 26 December, 1 January.
£ Adult £2.00, Child £1.00, Under five free,
   OAP £1.00, Family Ticket £4.50
P on site
▄▄bus nearby
♿ yes
✗ no

It is not by accident that all those boxes
of Lakeland and Derwent coloured
pencils come from the Lake District. At
this small museum in Keswick, you will
find the origins of this industry closely
linked to the discovery of graphite
nearby in Borrowdale in 1500. The
manufacture of pencils in Britain started
here first as a cottage industry and then
in the 1830s, as the Cumberland Pencil
Company.

You enter the museum through a
reproduction graphite mine complete
with old machinery and see the ways in
which the first pencils were made.
There is a display of calligraphy as well
as the history of packaging, wartime
pencils and current manufacturing
processes. Children are encouraged to
draw in a special activity area next to
the longest pencil in the world.

The beautifully restored delivery van at the
Pencil Museum.

DERBYSHIRE

National Tramway Museum
rich
Matlock DE4 5DP
Derbyshire
773 852565

○ Easter -30 September, Monday-Friday 10am-
5.30pm, Saturday and Sunday 10am-6.30pm
Weekends and half term weekdays in October.
Closed some Fridays in September.
Adult £4.20, Child £2.40, Under Four free,
OAP £3.50, Family Ticket £10.90.
on site
bus East Midlands 135, 140 to museum
yes except into trams
restaurant and picnic area.

You will find out everything you would
ever need to know about trams at this
open-air museum. More than forty
horse-drawn, steam powered and
electric tram cars built between 1873
and 1953 are to be found here. Using
old pennies as your currency you can
buy tickets and have as many rides as
you want. Take the trams along cobbled
Main Street from the bridge to the
terminus, go on a two mile scenic tram
ride past the substation and a lead
mining display with views of the
Derwent Valley. In the exhibition hall
you will find all kinds of trams, single
and double decker, open topped and
others with roofs on. Look at the
electricity supplies, the driving posts at
each end of the tram, the beautiful
lighting and woodwork, the seats —
very different from today's buses. There
is a tram depot and workshop too. Let
off your own steam at the playground
and have a picnic by the bandstand.
There are often extra events happening
so check in advance. All great fun.

Two of the National Tramway Museum's
impressive fleet pass the Victorian bandstand
on the site.

Museum of Childhood (NT)
Sudbury Hall
Sudbury DE6 5HT
Derbyshire
0283 585305

○ 1 April-31 October 12 noon-5.30pm every day.
November-Christmas Saturday and Sunday
only 12 noon-4pm
£ NT Members free, Adult £2.00, Child £1.00,
Under Five free
P nearby
BR Uttoxeter or Burton-on-Trent. Bus every
hour Uttoxeter - Burton-on-Trent.
to most parts
café and picnic area.

Give your children the opportunity to
compare their lives, homes, toys and
clothes with those of children from the
19th and 20th centuries.

Peer in at dolls' houses, climb a
chimney, crawl along a mine tunnel,
open a door to Mrs Tiggywinkle and a
family of mice in a tiny mousehole in the
skirting board. Enjoy the games and
toys in the Childhood Fantasy area.

In the Victorian Day Nursery, where
the governess rules, look out for dolls,
puzzles, a train set, (perhaps the most
modern toy of its time) a baby walker
and high chair. On the top of the
cupboard, a Noah's Ark, kept specially
for Sunday use. In the Night Nursery,
where Nanny ruled, look out for
mourning clothes and small boys'
dresses. In the parlour a giant chess set
to play with, along the corridor gas
masks and ration books for children of
World War 2. In the Victorian
schoolroom, slates, abacus, dunces'
caps and cane.

Housed in the 19th century wing of a
beautiful 17th century house, this is one
of the National Trust's properties very
much aware of children's needs.

DEVON

Exeter Maritime Museum
The Haven
Exeter
Devon EX2 8DT
0392 58075

○ 1 April-30 September 10am-5pm every day.
1 October-31 March 10am-4pm, weekends only
£ Adult £3.80, Child/Student £2.20, Under Five
free, OAP £2.90, Family Ticket £10.20
🅿 on site
🚌 Matford Park and Ride
♿ to 70% of the museum
✗ restaurant and nearby picnic area

Even if you are a landlubber this museum, awash with boats, will fascinate you. Situated in old warehouses on both sides of the Exeter Canal, the oldest in Britain, Exeter Maritime Museum is very popular with children. There are boats, large and small, from all over the world and you can even climb aboard some of them. Laze out on the decks, cling to the outriggers, move the sails, reef in the jib, pull ropes and jam them in the cleats and turn yourselves into sailors. The display based on Henry VIII's flagship, *The Great Harry*, has tremendous scope for pirate games. The entrance fee entitles you to two free rides across the canal on the floating bridge.

Whilst there is an indoor exhibition area many boats are moored outside on the canal. Here you will find *Bertha*, a dredger built in 1844 to work on Bridgewater Dock; she is the oldest working steam boat in the world. You

can climb aboard *Keying II* a Chinese junk, and *St Canute*, a Danish working fire fighting and ice breaking tug.

If you thought that Jason and the Golden Fleece was only a Greek legend then prepare to be mistaken. In Exeter you can see the *Argo* built by Tim Severin and sailed by him and twenty strong Argonauts to retrace Jason's voyage from Greece to the Black Sea, where they found that fleeces are still fastened to the bottom of streams to catch tiny pieces of gold.

The fascination and the romance of the sea is examined in the 'Cruel Sea' exhibition where famous survivors of ordeals and incidents at sea like Captain Bligh and Vietnamese Boat People are documented.

Cookworthy Museum
The Old Grammar School
108 Fore Street
Kingsbridge
Devon TQ7 1AW
0548 853235

○ 1 April-30 September Monday-Saturday
10am-5pm.
October 10.30am-4pm.
Closed November-March except for groups of
12 or more by appointment.
£ Adult £1.70, Child 70p, Under Five free,
OAP 90p, Family Ticket £3.50.
🅿 nearby
🚌 bus routes from Plymouth, Dartmouth and
Totnes.
♿ to parts of the museum
✗ picnic area on site.

If you are in South Devon the Cookworthy Museum is well worth a visit. All children, even the under fives, will find something fascinating here. Exhibits are well displayed and labelled at child height. Children are encouraged to touch exhibits throughout the museum. There are pencils and crayons to use in the drawers of the kitchen table.

From the street the museum seems tiny but it is packed full of things relating to the history and everyday life of Kingsbridge. The original building was built in 1671 as the Grammar School; various additions have been made over the centuries. The museum is named after William Cookworthy, born in Kingsbridge in 1705; an apothecary by profession he became the first English

Visitors happily browsing around the Exeter Maritime Museum.

maker of porcelain. There are coins and notes from the Kingsbridge Bank; local industries such as rope-making and iron tools; a dolls' house; clothes and photographs donated by local people. In the Cookworthy Room you can get a feel of what it was like to be a schoolboy in the time of Charles II. Look for the boys' initials, inscribed over generations, on the oak panels. The pharmacy has been reconstructed here and was originally the local chemist's shop run by a descendant of Cookworthy. Sit and draw at the table in the school kitchen. Outside, in the garden, you will find a large collection of farm machinery including cider presses, ploughs, carts and hand tools, many of which can be touched.

Craftspeople run workshops here when the museum is open; a thatcher was due to arrive the day we visited.

Overbecks Museum (NT)

Salcombe
Devon TQ8 8LW
0548 842893

○ 1April-31 October 11am-5.30pm.
Last admission 5pm.
£ NT Members free. Adult £3.40, Child £1.50, Under Five free, OAP £3.40. Also includes admission to the house, garden and estate walks.
🅿 small car park
🚉 ferry from Salcombe to Bolt Head
♿ unsuitable
✕ café and picnic area

Secret doors, ghosts and tropical gardens abound at Overbecks. The museum is small but set in a wonderful garden high on the hills above Salcombe with stunning views over the estuary. It is well worth planning to spend an afternoon up here at the museum and roaming around the gardens. Make the outing even more adventurous by taking the passenger ferry from Salcombe to Bolt Head and walking up the hill. Palm, olive and banana trees all grow in the gardens which benefit from unusually mild weather.

Staff in the museum are friendly and welcoming to children. There are quizzes and colouring sheets for them. More important, however, are the clues they have to find in order to discover the secret door, small enough only for them to climb through and into a hoard of old toys and dolls' houses. Fred, the friendly ghost, also lives here and must be found.

Morwellham Quay
The Morwhellham and Tamar Valley Trust
Morwellham
Tavistock PL19 8LJ
Devon
0822 832766

○ 1 April-31 October, every day 10am-5.30pm, last admission 3.30pm.
1 November-31 March 10am-4.30pm, last admission 2.30pm.
Closed Christmas Week.
£ Adult £6.50, Child £4.50, Under Five free, OAP £5.50 Reduced prices in winter.
🅿 on site
🚉 BR Gunnislake. Bus Station Tavistock, then taxi
♿ limited
✕ restaurant and picnic area

Morwellham Quay was once the greatest copper port in the British Empire, a busy and thriving industry around which many people's lives revolved. Then, out of dereliction and desertion, came an open-air museum. If you go there now you are taken back to the year 1868, when the mine was last worked, to experience the living past. You will meet quay workers, miners and servant girls, all dressed in period costume. Ask them questions and they will answer 'in role'. At the Lime Burner's cottage, children too can dress up and feel part of the scene.

Follow the Red Trail to the port and quays and the Blue to Morwellham Farm and the Tavistock Canal. Above all, nerve yourself (the fainthearted will need extra encouragement) to board the riverside tramway and plunge underground, right through the hill and along the old George and Charlotte Copper Mine. No imagination is needed to bring alive the appalling conditions down there.

Down at the dock and on the quays you can meet the blacksmith, the chandler and the cooper. Compare the relatively luxurious assayer's cottage, filled with bottles and equipment to test the ores, with the miners' one roomed cottages where twelve children slept in sacks on the floor.

In the port you will find barges, where you can talk to the sailor on board the last of the Tamar-built ketches. At the farm, friendly Shire horses are willing to take you on a wagon ride along the Duke of Bedford's own carriageway. In the museum you can use equipment to smash rocks or find copper and pyrites in piles of rubble, like panning for gold.

DORSET

Corfe Castle (NT)
The Square
Corfe Castle
Wareham
Dorset BH20 5EZ
0929 481294

○ 8 February-31 October 10am-5.30pm,
  or dusk if earlier, every day
  1 November- 7 February 12 noon-3.30pm
  Saturday and Sunday.
£ NT Members free, Adult £2.80, Child £1.40,
  Under Five free, OAP £2.80
🅿 nearby in West Street
🚌 Wareham-Swanage bus route
♿ difficult in castle itself.
✕ restaurant and coffee shop

The ruins of Corfe Castle can be seen
from miles around, standing
triumphantly in a gap in the Purbeck
Hills and are the focal point in this
beautiful Dorset village, standing at one
end of the main street. Children are
enthralled by it. Seeing it from afar,
coming closer then walking up the
grassy-banks, through the keep and
under the portcullis, climbing amongst
the ruins of what was once a motte and
bailey castle. Playing games, finding out
what the castle's inhabitants did, what
they could see, where the enemy were
and trying to figure out what bits are left
are all fascinating activities; even four
year olds can participate. The climb is
not too steep. Our three and four year
olds managed without having to be
carried but we did have to keep a close
eye on the eager climber at the top. On
a clear day the views around are
breathtaking.

For more than six hundred years the
castle was in use. Its defensive site
guards the main route through the
Purbeck Hills and Dorset from the sea.
William the Conqueror began the
building of the present castle and
through the Middle Ages many kings of
England spent time here. However,
during the Civil War, most of Dorset was
controlled by Parliament except for
Corfe which remained loyal to the
Crown. Lady Banks, the then owner
managed to build a garrison and there
followed a six week attack on the Castle
by Parliamentary forces. The castle
survived and became the one Royalist
stronghold between Exeter and London.
A second, more successful siege took
place in 1646 and the garrison

capitulated. Parliament then wanted the
castle demolished and instructed
sappers to undermine towers and finish
it off with explosives. Their work is what
we see today, this wonderful ruin with
beautiful sculptural forms weathering
into the Purbeck landscape.

Back in the village there is plenty to
do. Find the Town Hall, the smallest in
the country, in West Street and walk
into what must be the tiniest museum in
Britain (entrance free). Children love
this eccentric and eclectic collection of
local history, from dinosaur footprints to
gas masks.

Opposite, the Model Village is very
popular with younger children. The
whole of Corfe has been reconstructed
here in miniature, in local stone,
complete with bride and groom at the
church door, wedding music inside and
the castle as it would have been. Have
lots of one pence coins to throw into the
stream running in the moat. Be
prepared for a stint in the town stocks
as your children delight at turning you
into a villain.

If you have the energy follow the trail
around the village. A nice relaxation, for
children and parents, is tea in the
garden of the National Trust café
looking up at the castle.

The Dinosaur Museum
Icen Way
Dorchester
Dorset DT1 1EW
0305 269880

○ 9.30am-5.30pm every day
  Closed 24, 25, 26 December
£ Adult £2.95, Child £1.95, Under Four free,
  OAP £2.50, Student with card £2.50,
  Family ticket £8.95
🅿 nearby BR Dorchester West. Buses from
  Bournemouth, Salisbury and Exeter
♿ access to ground floor only.
✕ no

If your children are at the dinosaur
stage then this museum is certainly for
them. Here they can see life-size
reconstructions of Tyrannosaurus Rex,
Triceratops and Corythosaurus who,
after having lived peacefully for one
hundred and fifty million years, became
extinct quite suddenly sixty five million
years ago. You can put your hands into
boxes to find out what a dinosaur might
have felt like. There are fossils and

The usual collection of fascinated youngsters gathered round a dinosaur!

skeletons as well as dinosaur footprints. You can see skulls of sabre tooth tigers and mammoths in a display about animals since the dinosaur. There is another life size reconstruction of a Triceratops in the outdoor play area. Dinosaurs enthrall most children, filling them with ideas for drawings and play.

Dorset County Museum

High West Street
Dorchester
Dorset DT1 1XA
0305 262735

O 10am-5pm Monday-Saturday
£ Adult £2.00, Child £1.00, OAP £1.00
P town car park
BR Dorchester South, Dorchester West. Buses from Bournemouth, Salisbury and Exeter
access on ground floor only.
no

This is a well laid out museum with a great variety of things to interest children aged five and upwards. Start downstairs with the Roman mosaic pavement and its head of the god Oceanus dating from the 4th century AD. Go into the Bygones Gallery, which is like an over-filled garden shed bursting with farming implements, horse saddles and brasses, a wooden privy from a 19th century Dorset cottage, complete with a drawer to collect the waste; always fascinating to children, and a

mask to put over a bad tempered bull to stop him chasing people.

Upstairs, in the Archaeology Gallery, there are skeletons from the Iron Age. Find examples of Dorset wildlife now and in Dinosaur times, well displayed and labelled at child height, in the Natural History and Geology Galleries. Look out for the Dorset Ichthyosaur, a carnivorous dolphin-like reptile which lived in warm seas one hundred and ninety two million years ago.

Look over the balcony rail of the Victorian Gallery and see the Hall beneath. Look around at the building, at its iron work, light and space. It was built in 1883 by G. R. Crickmay to whom Thomas Hardy was articled as an architect before becoming a novelist. In this gallery you will find a hand-operated fire engine, a 19th century wooden Noah's ark and musical instruments. In the Victorian Hall, downstairs, find Dorchester's town stocks and Roman stone coffins. Older children and adults will be interested in the reconstruction of Thomas Hardy's study at the far end.

As you are leaving the hall spend a moment looking at the delightful 19th century dolls' house in the foyer. This is a lively and stimulating museum with just the right amount of things to see.

Poole Harbour, Brownsea Island and Poole Quay

This is one of the largest natural harbours in the world. It is magical to watch huge, cross channel ferries and cargo ships gallantly making their way through the mass of pleasure craft, yachts and dinghies, with the occasional pilot launch bobbing on the water. At the mouth of the harbour is the quirky Sandbanks to Swanage car ferry which runs on chains and seems to plough through every other vessel's path. It is amazing that no boat ever sinks. A wonderful summer's day of adventures can be spent around the harbour, at Studland Beach with its fine sand, on Brownsea Island and at Poole Quay. If you have no time to visit all, then just one will be worth it.

If you are arriving from the Studland side, park your car in one of the bays along the beach. It costs around £1.00 to park for the whole day. Take the ferry, as foot passengers, to Sandbanks; this is all on deck so even on a hot day it can get chilly. When you disembark turn immediately left and take one of the many ferries to Poole Quay via Brownsea Island. Coming from Sandbanks take the ferry here, or from Poole Quay if you are in Poole, to Brownsea Island.

Brownsea Island is open in the summer months only and there is a landing fee so allow time for your visit; it is not worth going at the end of the afternoon. Chug across the harbour to Brownsea, which is the first stop; either get off here or go on to Poole Quay and the Waterfront Museum and Scalpen's Court.

Brownsea Island (NT)
Poole Harbour
Dorset BH15 1EE
0202 707744

○ 1 April-10 October, 10am-8pm or dusk, whichever is earlier.
Check the times of opening and the last ferry.
£ NT Members free, Adult £2.00, Child £1.00, OAP £2.00, Family Ticket £5.00
🅿 at Studland, Sandbanks, Poole Quay. No cars are allowed on the island.
🚌 Sandbanks-Poole Quay Ferry. BR Poole ½m from Poole Quay. Bus 150 from Bournemouth, 152 from Poole, 12 Yellow from Christchurch.
♿ yes, all ferries will assist wheelchair users.
✗ restaurant and picnic area
Parties wishing to have a guided tour should contact the Warden, Dorset Trust for Nature Conservation 0202 709445.

From the harbour, Brownsea looks like fantasy land, belying its very real and varied history. This five hundred acre island has been vital to the defence of Poole and the Dorset hinterland for centuries. With Corfe Castle it formed part of Henry VIII's defensive strategy, along the south coast, against Spanish invasion. Over the centuries it has had many owners and now belongs to the National Trust. The Customs House, originally built in an attempt to stop smuggling, which was prevalent along this coast, still stands. In Edwardian times Brownsea was a place of splendour and style when the wealthy van Raalte family owned it and hosted lavish house parties whilst having a feudal attitude towards the treatment of their staff.

In 1907 one Major General Robert Baden-Powell was given permission, by the van Raaltes, to bring a group of boys from diverse social backgrounds, including Eton and London's East End, to camp on the island. From this beginning the worldwide scouting and guiding movement was born. There is a permanent exhibition on Baden-Powell at Brownsea in the Waterfront Museum.

Before the National Trust took over Brownsea it was owned by a recluse, Mrs Mary Bonham Christie, who let nature take its course and inadvertently created a marvellous habitat for wildlife which has been preserved. Cormorants curlews and spotted redshanks live on the lagoon, red squirrels in the woods and Sika deer on the heathlands.

During World War 2 Brownsea became a refugee centre for those arriving from Europe via the Channel. They were taken from here to the mainland. You can still walk along the quay and see the cottages, church and customs house which have been built over the centuries.

Follow the track round to St Andre's Bay and find the ghost village of Maryland, built in the last century by Colonel Waugh who failed in his attempt to turn the island into a pottery centre.

Early Boy Scouts At Brownsea island

Waterfront Museum

**High Street
Poole BH15 1BW
Dorset
0202 683138**

○ 1 March-31 October, Monday-Saturday 10am-5pm, Sunday 2 -5pm.
1 November-28 February Saturday 10am-5pm, Sunday 2-5pm.
£ Adult £1.95, Child £1.25, Under Five free, OAP £1.75, Family Ticket £5.00. Includes admission to Scaplen's Court Museum next door.
🅿 town centre car parks and Quay
🚌 Sandbanks-Poole Quay Ferry, buses to Poole Quay.
♿ to most parts
✗ café

Arriving by ferry from Sandbanks and Brownsea Island you will see the actual working port of Poole with huge loads of cargo on the quayside. Avoid the amusement arcades and aim for the Waterfront Museum.

Housed in the medieval town cellars and 18th century Oakley's Mill, the Waterfront Museum is a great adventure for children. It is devoted to the varied history of Poole from the Iron Age to the 20th century. There is a good education department and on the top floor a constantly changing, hands-on exhibition area; ask at reception for details. It was about light and reflection when we were there. We all found the distorting mirrors very funny.

There is a good lift to each floor and as you make your way up, the history of Poole begins to unravel itself. Stroll through the Victorian Street on the ground floor, into the chemist's shop, and pub, then past the undertaker. Upstairs to the 'Smuggler's Tale' and the raid on Poole Customs House. Smugglers were common along this coastline, also at Lulworth Cove, and a source of great excitement and wonder for children.

There is a reconstruction of an Iron Age log boat found in Studland Bay in 'Plunge into the Past'. Here you can also see a life-size model of an underwater diver exploring the Studland Bay wreck, which is older than the *Mary Rose*; and listen to the sub-aqua sounds. Shipbuilding and pottery are two of Poole's famous crafts; videos and photographs show the lives of the working people.

On the fourth floor there is an extensive exhibition on Baden-Powell and the beginnings of Scouting on Brownsea Island. So exciting was our visit to the Waterfront that our children of four and five and a half years, had to be dragged away to lunch and demanded to return again in the afternoon. There is a lot to do here for children of all ages.

Scaplen's Court Museum of Domestic Life

**High Street
Poole BH15 1BW
Dorset**

○ 1 March-31 October, Monday-Saturday 10am-5pm, Sunday 2-5pm.
1 November-28 February, Saturday 10-5pm, Sunday 2-5pm
£ Adult 75p, Child 30p.
🅿 town and quay car parks
🚌 Sandbanks-Poole Quay ferry, buses to Poole Quay
♿ to most areas
✗ no

Do find a little time to spend wandering around this medieval merchant's house and courtyard. On the ground floor is a large, working, Victorian kitchen where regular cooking sessions take place (ring for details). There is a bread oven and a wonderful array of utensils. To my children's surprise, many were not dissimilar to those we use today. Upstairs is a schoolroom, with a teacher's and children's desks; lift the lids to see what they kept in them. Go into the nursery to see the toys and games; many seem very familiar, although made of wood instead of plastic

If you are exhausted, find your way to the ferry and enjoy a ride across the harbour.

The Victorian Kitchen at Scaplen's Court.

Tank Museum
Bovington Camp
Wareham BH20 6JG
Dorset
0929 403329/403463

○ 10am-5pm every day except for 10 days
at Christmas

£ Adult £4.00, Child £2.00, Under Five free,
OAP £2.00, Family Ticket £8.00. Includes
admission to Costume Collection and
T. E. Lawrence Exhibition.

🅿 on site

🚉 BR Wool

♿ yes and special audio tours.

🍴 restaurant and picnic area

A visit to the Tank Museum is an excellent way for children to learn about the experience of war and its effects on individuals. Our five year old was fascinated by the tanks and armoured vehicles and the people who operated them. You can not only see tanks but climb into many of them as well as going in a tank simulator. Staff are very friendly and helpful. The museum is situated in Bovington Camp; the main hangar was built in 1939 for the Allenby Barracks so you really do get the feeling of roughness and cold. There is nothing glossy here. Start with the Roman chariots, armoured knights on horseback and a model of a tank designed by Leonardo da Vinci. Essential to a tank are the needs for protection, mobility and firepower. The combination of these and a tractor's ability to move over rough terrain provided the beginning of the tank as we now know it.

Go into the World War 1 Hall and see how the modern tank was first used on a mass scale. From the outside they seem strong and impenetrable but look inside and see how basic and terrifying the conditions were. We never think about the young men who were shut up here for hours at a time. Their only communication with base, in World War 1, was a basket of homing pigeons. As you climb in and out you realise how short of space they would be; it is difficult for an adult to stand and as you peer through the slits you really do feel you are inside a mobile castle or fortress. Tanks are no place for the scared or claustrophobic.

Look at the mock-up battlefield with bombs and blasts. In the World War 2 hangar you can see large and small tanks, Allied tanks and German tanks; camouflaged tanks painted green, brown/beige and even white for winter,

A World War II Sherman tank on display outside the Tank Museum.

to meet the needs of the climatic conditions and terrain of the different fronts. Look at the names and insignia painted on them.

There is a large display, with tanks and videos, on the Gulf War which many children can remember; my young daughter informed me she had already seen it on television. Look at the Allied tanks and Iraqi ones, made in China of Russian design. The sand coloured paint is now peeling off the Allied vehicles, revealing their original green beneath.

Throughout the museum, there are examples of transporters, amphibious tanks, armoured cars, different guns and ammunition as well as new developments in tank design and technology. Look at the names and huge animal faces painted on some of them. Be prepared for the side attractions, such as the electronically controlled, miniature tanks to manoeuvre and the simulator, all requiring extra cash. There are change machines on the walls as you go round. The simulator is not for the travel-sick but it does give an excellent illusion of a tank in motion preparing for attack.

Don't miss the small display cases, they are as important as the vehicles and contain collections of medals and uniforms, World War 1 tank shaped teapots, ration packs for the soldiers in

The tanks, photographs of women at war, down the mines or in the munitions factories on the home front. Look out for the medical corps and the field hospital.

Perhaps the most chilling reminder of the role of the tank is the small white vehicle at the entrance bearing the bold letters UN, all too familiar on our television screens in footage of the war torn former Yugoslavia.

Be prepared for questions about the past. Why do we have wars? what were grandparents doing? and much more from your children. Even though I was rather hesitant to take my daughters here I regard our visit as an excellent introduction into learning about war, its futility and inevitability. This is not about glory and winning; it is about human beings. Everything is very immediate. What better way to learn?

Priest's House Museum

23-27 High Street
Wimborne Minster
Dorset BH21 1HR
0202 882533

O 1 April-31 October Monday-Saturday 10.30am-
   4.30pm, Sunday 2-4.30pm
   Closed 28 July.
   1 November-Christmas weekends and
   Christmas season only.
£ Adult £1.50, Child 50p, Under Five free,
   OAP £1.00, Season Ticket £5.00
P town car parks
BR Poole or Bournemouth, bus 132,133
ground floor and garden only
café and picnic area

We visited Priest's House on a disappointing autumn day having found that most other museums and holiday attractions, in Dorset, were closed for the winter. Happily, Priest's House was open and we received a very warm welcome. Questionnaires were

The working kitchen at the Priest's House.

immediately given to the children and as we went round we found them very useful and comprehensible, even for our five and a half year old. The staff, mainly volunteers, were very friendly and could not wait to talk and tell us about Priest's House; it turned out many of them are grandmothers and used to children's questions and noise.

From the street, Priest's House looks like an old shop, its bow windows filled with all kinds of objects. These are not for sale, but part of the collection. The Entrance Hall used to be part of a courtyard but was filled in in the 18th century. Try to find out where you are standing from the model. The ironmonger's shop, on one side of the hall, is a reconstruction of the one run here by the Coles family from 1872-1960. Look at the objects and compare them with the versions we have today.

In the Stationer's Shop and Parlour you will see panelling on the walls and behind it parts of the original stonework. Upstairs find the skeleton of the dead cat, toys and games in the nursery and displays of archaeology. Come back downstairs and go into the working Victorian kitchen, with its range, kitchen table, rag rug and various utensils. See at close hand how thatch is made and then look at the blacksmith in his forge.

Spend time in the long, narrow garden with its unusual plants and a mulberry tree reputed to be two hundred years old. There are lots of interesting places to sit; at the very bottom of the garden is a small shelter decorated with Roman tiles excavated at Tarrant Hinton villa. This is a lovely, small museum and well worth the visit if you are near by. There is a Saturday club for children; the long waiting-list means you must book well in advance.

COUNTY DURHAM

Beamish, The North of England Open Air Museum
Beamish
County Durham DH9 0RG
0207 231811

○ 1 April-31 October 10am-5pm every day,
last admission 3pm.
10 July-4 September 10am-6pm, last
admission 4pm.
1 November-31 March 10am-4pm,
last admission 3pm.
Closed Monday and Friday.
Closed 20-25 December inclusive and
1 January

£ Summer: Adult £5.99, Child £3.99,
Under Five free, OAP £3.99.
Extended Summer Opening: Adult £6.99,
Child £3.99, Under Five free, OAP £3.99.
Winter: Adult £2.99, Child £1.99,
Under Five free, OAP £1.99.

P on site

🚌 buses from Durham, Newcastle and
Sunderland.

♿ some first floor areas inaccessible to
wheelchairs.

✕ café and picnic area

Lessons 1913 style in the school room at
Beamish.

Beamish is a vast open-air museum of
life before 1913 in a coal mining area.
Buildings have been brought here from
surrounding areas and there is a tram
and bus system to get you around the
site. Children of all ages and adults find
this a fascinating place; there is so
much to do and see that it is well worth
allowing a whole day for your visit.
There is masses of open space for
children to run around and to have a
picnic. It is probably best to take a
buggy for slow walkers!

There are four main areas to visit
and it is up to you which order you go
in. The Colliery Village with its row of
miners' cottages, chapel, school and pit;
The Town with the larger, smarter
houses of the professionals, the Co-op,
printer and café; The Railway Station
with steam trains and The Farm with
live animals.

The transport system is a delight in
itself with trams and trolley buses, bells
and conductors. Our five year old made
sure she rode on everything.

The separate developments of the
working classes, coming from the local
rural community, and the educated
professionals are clearly shown at
Beamish. The Town is a relatively
sophisticated place; look at the plaques,

by the front doors, to see who the
residents are, the music teacher, the
dentist, the solicitor. Their houses are
large and you can go inside to see the
smart parlour, the nursery with its cradle
and board games. Gape at the ghastly
drills, old chair and spitoon in the
dentist's surgery. Peep into the room
next door to see the dentures being
made. It was a father's wedding gift to
make sure his daughter had a good
fitting set of false teeth thus ensuring his
future son-in-law would not be faced
with large dental bills for ever decaying
teeth.

Go across the road to the large Co-
op shop. The Co-operative movement
began in Rochdale about one hundred
miles further south, and spread
throughout the north of England. It
enabled the working classes to get
quality goods and a share of the profits,
and prided itself on catering to every
need from the cradle to the grave
including insurance and funeral
services. I was surprised to remember
our 'divvy' number and the glee at
collecting it periodically. When we were
at this Co-op the friendly sales assistant
was trying to persuade us to buy an
ounce of sennapods to keep us regular
as well as a new liquid coffee (Camp).
The shop is full from floor to ceiling of
every grocery item you would want,
ham shanks and vegetables. Go to the
drapery department to see corsets,
collars, hats, shoes, cottons and cloth.
Clanking around the ceiling is a
wonderful Lamson-Paragon cash
system connecting each department
with the central office. In the hardware
department you will find baskets,

Above: Street scene at the centre of Beamish's award-winning town displays.

Above: The scene inside the traditional Co-op drapery shop at Beamish.

crockery, enamel tins, candles, brooms and tin baths. Only the middle classes had bathrooms, the rest filled up a tin bath with water and bathed by the kitchen range. Look at the £sd pricing system.

If you need a break go upstairs to the dingy café with oilcloths on tables placed in neat rows. Glance at the headlines from 1913 at the Newspaper Office over the road. Eighty years on, it is familiar reading, warning of 'crisis in the Balkans'; World War 1 started in Sarajevo. Upstairs is the office of the local newspaper with linotype and automatic presses.

You may hear the sound of the brass band coming from the bandstand or treat your children to rides at the old

fairground. Try and get the old boat swings to work or ride the flying chairs. We later discovered that our grandma once ventured, behind her mother's back, for a 'forbidden ride' on the boat swings only to be made sick by the motion.

The railway was vital to transport coal from the collieries and Beamish station is complete with steam trains, goods sheds and the station yard. Find *Locomotion* No 1, a replica of the original *Locomotion* built by George Stephenson in 1825 for the Stockton and Darlington Railway. The Coal Merchant's office dates from 1900 and comes from Hexham.

Take the tram to the Colliery Village and experience the toughness of working class life. The Board School with its smell of disinfectant, two large classrooms, open coal fires and teachers. There were sixty children in each classroom, class 1 five to eleven year olds and class 2 eleven to fourteen year olds. The school would close if there was an epidemic of measles. You can sit at the desks and write on the slates. Our children spent ages here and retold it all to their grandma afterwards. They were amazed at the number of children, the copperplate script on the board, the fire, the desks with lids and the slates. Do talk to the teacher who is extremely helpful about the history of education in this area. At the age of fourteen children left school, most of the boys went to work in the pit and many of the girls into domestic service. Find the chart on the wall which shows how women were employed; millions were in domestic service. In the playground you can try your hand with the metal hoop. Grandma used to excel at this, we were hopeless.

Nip into the chapel and listen to the sermon extolling the virtues of hard work. What a cold building and uncomfortable pews!

Opposite spend time going through the front gardens of the miners' cottages and peeping into the tiny rooms. The gardens are full of ducks and hens or cabbages. You might find a miner's wife sewing. Ask her how many children she has, sixteen maybe, all of whom sleep upstairs in the one tiny attic. The parent's bed is in the front parlour and the back room has the range and a large table. Outside, across the yard is the privy. Coal was mined here, at Beamish, and you can go into the drift mine to see the conditions in which the men worked. Hard hats must be worn. Look at the notices pinned up outside the manager's office; the pit is still checked daily for poisonous gases.

From the village take the tram or bus to Home Farm with its exhibitions of farming practice, herds of cows and sties of pigs; there were lots of piglets

when we were there. Go through the yard of ducks and geese and cross the road (watch out for cars) and into the farmhouse with its range and demonstrations of rag rug making. See butter and cheese being made in the pristine dairy; you can even buy some of the local varieties.

If you have done all this your family should be exhausted but stimulated after a very exciting day out. Make your way back to the main entrance savouring the smell of burning coal fires on the way.

Inside one of Beamish's pit cottages.

ESSEX

Mark Hall Cycle Museum and Gardens
Muskham Road
Harlow CM17 0AB
Essex
0279 439680

O Monday-Thursday 10am-5pm, Sunday closed 1-2 pm
£ free
P on site
🚌 bus nearby
♿ yes
✗ no

Housed in the converted stable block of Mark Hall Manor, this collection of bicycles was started by John Collins in 1948. His family have been in the business since the beginnings of bicycle history. Among the bicycles in the museum, both strange and familiar,

you can see the hobby horse of 1818, the boneshaker, several pennyfarthings (you'll soon see why they were suitable for men in skin-tight trousers) and multi-seaters from the tandem to the quintuplet. There is an unusual collection of contemporary photographs which give an insight into the difficulties of women bicycling in long skirts, and the often extraordinary functions of the bicycle in wartime. Look out for the very amusing Dunlop collection of models, rather like three dimensional cartoons.

Spacious, airy, well-lit and displayed at child level, this is an exciting museum for both cyclists and non-cyclists and certainly worth a visit. Behind the museum are three walled-gardens of the manor house, the largest has been divided into sections to become rose, cottage, kitchen and herbaceous gardens.

GLOUCESTERSHIRE

Corinium Museum
Park Street
Cirencester GL7 2BX
Gloucestershire
0285 655611

○ 1 April-31 October, Monday-Saturday
10am-5.30pm, Sunday 2-5.30pm.
1 November-31 March Tuesday-Saturday
10am-5pm, Sunday 2-5pm.
Closed between Christmas and New Year

£ Adult £1.25, Child 75p, Under Five free,
OAP £1.00.

◨ no

🚌 BR Kemble 2 miles, infrequent bus service

♿ yes, award winning facilities.
Pushchairs no problem

✗ picnic area by the parish church

The museum reflects many important aspects of this part of the Cotswolds, but it is most famous for its Roman antiquities. The mosaics here are incredible. There is a life-size reconstruction of a mosaicist's workshop in which the craftsman is shown cutting up pieces of marble into small bits known as tesserae. See if you can find a hare nibbling a plant in one of the mosaics. The Four Seasons mosaic was discovered in 1849 in Dyer Street, Cirencester and is now the floor for the triclinium, or dining room with its Roman sofa and basketwork chair. In the kitchen is a raised stone hearth, quern stone for grinding corn and pots filled with Roman delicacies such as stuffed dormice and snails fattened on milk. Outside is a Roman Garden. A useful museum for anybody 'doing' the Romans and welcoming to children of all ages; there is even a room to feed babies in privacy.

The National Waterways Museum
Llanthony Warehouse
Gloucester Docks
Gloucester GL1 2EH
Gloucestershire
0452 307009

○ 10am-6pm every day summer time
10am-5pm every day winter time
(hours change with the clocks).
Closed Christmas Day

£ Adult £3.95, Child £2.95, Under Five free,
OAP £2.95, Family Ticket £9.50, Season Ticket-
Friend's Association £8.00

◨ on site

🚌 BR Gloucester 15 minutes away.
Bus stop nearby

♿ yes

✗ café and picnic area

The National Waterways Museum is laid out in a huge warehouse, once a great corn store, in Gloucester's Victorian dockland. It tells the story of canals using a good mixture of the latest museum devices to lure you and your children round the exhibits. As in any

Gloucester Docks and the Waterways Museum.

worthwhile museum, the learning process is effortless. There are sacks, barrels, packing cases, ropes and pulleys, weighing machines, alongside audio-visual equipment (one video screen tidily stowed away in a British Waterways tea chest) life-size figures, archive film and sound recordings. The graphic panels are worth more than just a glance. They ask questions and invite opinions; some are even operated by cog machinery and so make reading more fun. Look out for the original spiral chute which slid loaded sacks of grain from the top to the ground floor. Watch out for 'live' rats and 'dead' pigeons to show the state the building was reduced to before it was transformed into a museum.

Outside in Llanthony Yard, there is a busy canal maintenance yard with craftsmen at work in the Engineer's workshop, blacksmiths at the forge and shire horses and carts in the stables. You can have a go at complicated knot-tying or painting a narrow boat design. On the canal you can climb aboard a barge, squeeze inside a narrow boat and watch a massive steam dredger in action. Peter, the shire horse, will give you a ride in his cart or you can take a short cruise from the Docks on board *Queen Boadicea I.*

The Robert Opie Collection
Museum of Advertising and Packaging
Albert Warehouse
Gloucester Docks
Gloucester GL1 2EH
Gloucestershire
0452 302309

O 2 March-31 October 10am-6pm every day.
   1 November-1 March Tuesday-Friday
   10am-5pm,Saturday and Sunday 10am-6pm
£ Adult £2.50, Child 95p, Under Five free,
   OAP £1.95, Family Ticket £5.95
P on site
BR Gloucester 15 minutes away.
   Bus stop nearby
& yes
✕ café, picnic area nearby

Robert Opie's collection may be more interesting for the adults who can indulge in a bit of nostalgia, than for children. However, if you are in Gloucester Docks, then we suggest a visit.

Robert Opie started his collection at the age of 16. He was just about to throw away the wrapper off a packet of Munchies, when he realised that that

was what everybody else was doing; hence his vast and rapidly multiplying collection of packaging and advertising of every imaginable type of article from 1880 onwards.

I used to be a friend of his sister and once went to stay for the weekend. I remember peeping into his room and wondering what my mother would say if my room looked like that. There were boxes of 'junk' from floor to ceiling. The exhibition has been described as a century of shopping basket history. The contents of our own shopping baskets wouldn't have a chance to gather as much dust as these exhibits but it all makes you think twice about our throw-away society.

Look out for brands of sweets which don't exist any more, look at how package designs for familiar products like Typhoo Tea and Bird's Custard Powder have changed over the decades, see the subtle change in shape of a Marmite jar. There are wartime biscuit tins which were used as gas mask containers afterwards, and long forgotten stuff such as Lavdust and Zog It Off paint cleaner, or knife polish and black lead. See if you can date the first fish finger. Where did the name Birds Eye come from?

Then relax in front of the huge old fashioned television to watch some commercials from bygone days.

Wildfowl and Wetlands Trust
Slimbridge
Gloucester
Gloucestershire GL2 7BT
0453 890333

O every day, summer 9.30am-5pm, winter
   9.30am-4pm. Closed 24, 25 December.
£ Adult £4.50, Child £2.25, Under Four free,
   OAP/Concessions £3.40, Family Ticket £11.25.
   Season ticket available to all sites
P on site
one bus a day from Gloucester-Dursley.
& yes. Make arrangements for loan of audio
   cassettes and players, talks and tactile exhibits
   beforehand.
✕ restaurant and picnic area

One of the eight centres in the country, established by Sir Peter Scott, for the breeding and safety of wild and domestic water fowl. All children, especially small ones, love these places. Wear boots as there is a lot of water, buy bird food in the shop, then make your way round. Children delight at getting close to the birds and feeding them. Our three year old had long

onversations with them. Good walkers
an go on nature trails to find the less
ame and more timid ones. These are
marvellous collections from all over the
world. Some fowl, faced with extinction
n their natural habitat, breed here in
afety. In a series of ponds and scrub
and, you find all variety of species,
olour and size of ducks, geese,
erons, swans, flamingoes and
pheasants.

Above, right & below: Scenes at the Wildfowl
& Wetlands Trust, Slimbridge with typically
happy and enthusiastic visitors.

HAMPSHIRE

Beaulieu
John Montagu Building
Beaulieu
Brockenhurst SO42 7ZN
Hampshire
0590 612345

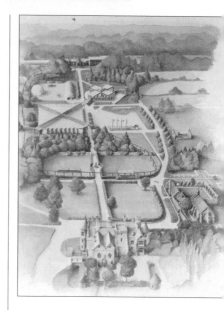

O Summer 10am-6pm every day.
Winter 10am-5pm, every day.
Closed Christmas Day.

£ Adult £6.95, Child £4.90, Under Four free,
OAP £5.40, Family Ticket,
2 adults & 4 children £21.00.
Admission ticket is to the whole site including
Motor Museum, Palace and Abbey.

P on site

♿ no

♿ to most parts

✕ restaurant and picnic area

This is a vast site centring on the main attraction, the National Motor Museum, formed from Lord Montagu's fine collection of motorcars. There is lots for children to do and see, so allow a full day for your visit.

Railway World in Miniature is a model train enthusiast's dream come true with miles of track and lots of trains. There is a bus ride on a replica 1912 London bus as well as a monorail which transports you all around the site. The marvellous museum collection, with over two hundred vehicles, shows the history and development of the motorcar from horse-drawn vehicle to the present day. The social and commercial impact of the car is also covered. The vehicles stand gleaming and proud. It is fascinating to see the changes in different parts of the

vehicle; windscreens used to open and be quite narrow. There are cars with cranking handles and running boards; car roofs became useful for storage space and boots were no longer boxes stuck on the back but integral to the overall design. Later speed and engine power became vital. Now we are totally dependent on this machine which up till one hundred years ago had barely been thought of. The evolution of the motorcar is rather like that of a highly intelligent animal who, when faced with possible extinction, smartens up his act of survival with the development of new designs, models and engine refinements. You will find many trade names, some forgotten others not— Morris, Austin, Rolls Royce, Daimler, Hillman, Rootes, Sunbeam. Take your children on the Wheels exhibit where they can tour through motoring history.

Outside again and you can have a ride on miniature veteran cars. Then peep into the exhibition of monastic life and see a Victorian garden being recreated. At the far end of the site you will find Palace House which you can go around; children especially enjoy the Victorian Kitchen.

Nearby, off the site, is Buckler's Hard, an 18th century ship-building village which is worth a visit if you have time.

Hollycombe, Steam Collection and Gardens
Hollycombe
Liphook GU30 7LP
Hampshire
0420 474740. Open Days: 0428 724900

O Sundays and Bank Holidays only, Good Friday-2nd Sunday in October, 1-6pm, rides from 2pm.
£ Adult £4.00, Child £3.00, Under Two free, OAP £3.50, Family £12.00
P on site
BR Liphook
limited
café and picnic area

We went to Hollycombe on the recommendation of a friend, whose eyes lit up so much when she described it, that we were unable to resist it. We took six children ranging from nine months to twelve years and spent one of the happiest days of the summer. The smallest hopped with childish glee from the satisfying toddler-sized buses and trains of the Orton and Spooner Steam Roundabout to the thrills of the Big Wheel, squealing with delight as we soared over the South Downs. The older ones rushed ecstatically from the Ghost House to the Steam Yacht, jostling for the best seats in the Swingboats and daring themselves for yet another ride on the Razzle-Dazzle. We all enjoyed the 'Dawn of the Century, Grand Electric Bioscope Show' with its jerky, predictable, funny silent movie. We admired the oldest surviving showman's engine, the Burrell 'Emperor' (1894) which provides steam power for the fairground rides and chatted with the friendly and dedicated steam enthusiasts; all volunteers fired by their pleasant addiction to keeping the age of steam alive. We boarded the 'Royal Scot' on the 7¼in miniature railway and sped triumphantly past the GWR-style signalling system and into the little station with its beautiful clock tower. We took the Hollycombe Traction ride through the woods to Iron Hill Farm and stroked Simon the llama and Smokey, the miniature donkey, and we laughed at Elvis and Priscilla, the Vietnamese Pot Bellied Pigs.

Hollycombe is such a small, welcoming place that we felt very relaxed; happy to let our children go from ride to ride. We could keep track of

Top left: The site at Beaulieu, with the main house and the museum complex above.
Left: Inside the exhibition hall.

all of them, from where we stood and they felt a sense of freedom and all the excitement of the fairground in a safe and friendly environment. The Hollycombe Steam Collection is run by a non-profitmaking society and therefore entrance prices are kept low; most wonderful of all is that once in you can have as many rides as you like without having to pay further. I still have the picture in my mind, of a five year old sitting at the wheel of a miniature, yellow and red, double decker bus, with an expression of pure bliss on her face. It must have been at least her twentieth ride that day.

Find out about the special Open Days such as the Festival of Working Steam, the Children's Fayre Day and Santa's Special for Christmas.

Manor Farm
Upper Hamble Country Park
Pylands Lane
Burseledon
Southampton
0489 787055

O Easter-31 October 10am-5.30pm every day.
   1 November-Easter, Sunday only 10am-dusk
£ Adult £2.50, Child £1.20, Under Four free,
   OAP £2.00, Family Ticket £7.20
   Season Ticket-Adult £10.50, Child £5.00,
   OAP £8.50
P on site
BR Botley. Blue Line bus summer Sundays.
& to some parts
X restaurant and picnic area

For a perfect family outing you need time on your hands, a long summer's day or a beautiful autumn Sunday and lots of children who want to let off steam and enjoy themselves: you may never mention the word 'museum'.

You could spend the morning roaming in the park, a stretch of ancient woodland on the banks of the Hamble River. You could get lost in Foster's or Bottom Copse, where the

woodland workers coppice the hazel, or study the animal life in the habitats and mudflats at low tide on the upper reaches of the Hamble, or watch human life around the sleek yachts that fill the marina of the lower reaches. You could follow the I-Spy Nature Trail or Woodland Discovery Walk. You could relax, play games or picnic in Barnfield or Toplands Meadow. In the summer you could take a trip on the river or have supper in the Pantry or the Manor Farm after a special evening river excursion.

In the afternoon you could explore the Manor Farm and see animals and workers going about the daily business of life on a Victorian farm. You could watch the shorthorn and Guernsey cows milked in the milking parlour with one of the earliest types of milking machines. You could scratch the backs of the Wessex saddleback pigs; climb into the rat-free granary built on saddle stones, wander round the cottage gardens, visit the privy where once the buckets were emptied round the front bushes and see Jamie the farm's shire horse in his own comfortable stable. You could finish your visit with a delicious tea of home-made cakes in the Pantry tea rooms.

On Sundays you might meet a blacksmith at work in the forge and craftsmen in the wheelwright's workshop. Events range from spinning, woodturning, cheese and butter making, rush and cane seating, toy making, scarecrow making and a Christmas Carol Service.

Mrs Sarah Earwicker is there every day, bustling from the kitchen range to the copper, blackleading the pots and pans or feeding the farmyard animals.

There are sensory trail and discovery cards round the farmyard and rick yard and interpretive panels with texts specially aimed at children. You can even have a birthday party here, go and meet all the animals and Mrs Earwicker and come back for jelly, cakes and balloons. Children with special needs are especially welcome here. Among the many activities throughout the year is a Family Fun Day for children with Down's syndrome

This is a marvellous resource for families with children of all ages and definitely worth a regular annual visit for those who are unlucky not to live nearby.

Dressing up in period costume can add to the fun at Manor Farm.

Royal Naval Submarine Museum

Haslar Jetty Road
Gosport PO12 2AS
Hampshire
0705 510354

O 1 April-31 October 10am-4.30pm (last tour).
1 November-31 March 10am-3.30pm (last tour), every day. Closed 24 Dec-1 Jan.
£ Adult £3.00, Child £2.00, Under Five free, OAP £2.00
P nearby
BR Portsmouth Harbour then ferry to Gosport
limited
café and picnic area

If you have ever wondered what it must be like in a submarine, and wanted to find out how it operates, this is the place to go. Look through a periscope and see Portsmouth across the water; find out about the first submarines; discover that life on a submarine was considered 'no occupation for a gentleman' in 1900. You can have a guided tour of HMS Alliance and watch 'The Submarine Experience' on video.

Portsmouth Naval Heritage Trust

Building 1/24
College Road
HM Naval Base
Portsmouth PO1 3LX
Information Line 0705 839766

O November-February 10am-5pm. March-June, September and October 10am-6pm
July and August 10am-7pm
£ Entrance to site is free, pay to visit the ships:
1 ship: Adult £4.00, Child £2.50, Under Five Free, OAP £3.50
2 ships: Adult £7.50, Child £4.80 Under Five Free, OAP £6.50

Family Ticket: 1 ship: £10.50; 2 ships: £20.00
All tickets are valid for one year. Entrance to Royal Naval Museum and Victory are on one ticket.
P at Historic Ships Coach and Car Park
BR Portsmouth Harbour 2 minutes walk
yes to most parts
restaurant and picnic area

Portsmouth Naval Base is a vast and fascinating area and needs plenty of time to do it justice. Decide what you want to see at the ticket office. The Mary Rose is a must, but children will have great fun exploring HMS Warrior and HMS Victory. It will all depend on time, stamina and finances!

Mary Rose Exhibition
0705 750521

O 1 March-31 October 10am-5.30pm.
1 November-28 February 10am-5pm. July and August open until 6.45pm

It is worth almost any journey to see the Mary Rose itself. Lifted from the sea bed off Portsmouth in 1982 and at present resting in No 3 Dry Dock, an 18th century ship hall, sprayed with icy cold fresh water to keep the timbers wet and prevent the growth of micro-organisms, it is indeed a staggering sight.

In the Mary Rose exhibition start by watching the film of the raising of the ship. Do you remember watching the News that day with baited breath? These were agonising moments when the lifting frame shifted with a sickening thud on the hull as it hung suspended from the great crane Tog, the weather rapidly deteriorating as a storm began to brew.

HMS Alliance, the centrepiece at the Submarine Museum.

What must Henry VIII have felt at the sight of his warship sinking on a calm July day in 1545, with seven hundred men on board?

The raising of the *Mary Rose* and the rescuing of the 'treasures' that were on board were all part of the world's longest underwater archeological operation. Among thousands of objects found on the ship you can see silk embroidered purses, woollen hose, wooden combs, leather jerkins, tallow candles; organic materials that have survived. There is the remains of the barber surgeon's cabin with its chest of surgical instruments and canisters of herbs, ointments and spices: the guns were found still mounted on their carriages on the starboard deck and whole longbows and arrows were found ready for action on the main deck.

But the story does not become complete until you walk through the airlock and into the water-laden atmosphere of the *Mary Rose* ship hall. You are given a wand to hear the commentary of archaeologist and diver Dr Margaret Rule. Over the next few years deck ladders and cabins, that were taken out of the ship underwater, will be replaced.

Above: A selection of personal objects which might have been carried in compartments of decorative pouches, possibly belonging to officers of the *Mary Rose*: bone comb, wooden seal, pocket sundial, die, thimble ring, decorative clasp, tokens, wooden whistle and rosary.

Top: Archaeologists surveying the *Mary Rose* are dwarfed by the hull towering above them to the height of a four-storey building.

Go and see the *Mary Rose* now! She is still supported on the cradle that lifted her out of the sea; she is still surrounded by the mystery of the seabed, the excitement of her discovery and the disaster of her sinking four centuries ago.

HMS *Victory*

◯ £ see above

♿ limited, ring up in advance for help with
wheelchairs

HMS *Victory*, Nelson's flagship at the
Battle of Trafalgar, involves a tour of
about forty minutes led by Royal Navy
and Royal Marine Guides. On board
you will see the Great Cabin where
Nelson planned his campaign, his
sleeping cabin and the point where he
was fatally shot on 21 October 1805. On
the Lower Gun Deck you will see where
most of the sailors ate and slept.

Royal Naval Museum

◯£see above

At the heart of the Naval Base is the
Royal Naval Museum. Its five galleries
are filled with all sorts of things relating
to maritime life during war and peace
from the rise of the Navy in 1485 to
Polaris in 1982. You can see ghosts of
past seamen, displays of ship models,
medals, silverware and porcelain, and
find out what these sailors took with
them on their long voyages.

HMS *Warrior* (1860)

◯ £ see above

♿ limited, ring up in advance for help
with wheelchairs.

HMS *Warrior* was first commissioned in
1861 as the British answer to French
threats. She was the first iron-hulled
warship, in which the guns, engine and
boiler rooms were well protected,
making her the most powerful of her
time. Later she spent a sad fifty years
as an oil jetty, floating off Milford Haven,
her upper deck being a layer of
concrete. She has been lovingly
restored and today children can wander
freely anywhere, down into the bowels
of the ship to see the stoker's
bathrooms; climb into hammocks;
examine a cat-o'-nine-tails and talk to a
quartermaster.

The imposing lines of HMS *Warrior.*

HEREFORD AND WORCESTER

Severn Valley Railway

The Railway Station
Bewdley DY12 1BG
Hereford and Worcester
0299 403816

O every day, talking timetable on 0299 401001
£ Adult £1.00, Child 50p, refundable if you travel
   on one of the steam trains.
   Return Fare for one adult and two children from
   Kidderminster to Bridgnorth is £9.50
P on site
BR Kidderminster
& yes
✕ restaurant and picnic area

Steam trains run regularly through the
Severn Valley between Kidderminster,
Bewdley and Bridgnorth on this
preserved track. This is the largest
collection of working steam locomotives,
wagons and coaches in the country as
well as engine sheds and carriage
works. Six restored stations line the
track.

   This is paradise for the railway
enthusiast, chugging along in the
steam, standing on the footplate,
stoking the fires, going through neat
bridges, all good stuff and well worth a
day's outing.

   There is a SVR Junior Club for
young enthusiasts and there is a
miniature railway in Kidderminster.

Winter on the Severn Valley Railway.

Avoncroft Museum of Buildings

Stoke Heath
Bromsgrove B60 4JR
Hereford and Worcester
0527 31886

O March&November 11am-4.30pm every day,
   closed Monday and Friday.
   April, May, September and October 11am-5pm
   closed Monday, open Bank Holidays.
   June, July and August open 11am-5.30pm
   every day.
   Closed December, January and February.
£ Adult £3.00, Child £1.50, Under Five free.
   OAP £2.10, Family Ticket £8.00
   Season ticket with membership.
P on site
BR station 1 1/2miles away. Bus 144
   Birmingham-Worcester.
& to most parts
✕ café and picnic area.

An 18th century earth closet, a windmill,
a 1946 prefab and an ice house can all
be found at this marvelous open air
museum dedicated to the preservation
of ancient buildings, many of which
would otherwise have been demolished
and lost forever. By rescuing old
buildings, painstakingly taking them to
pieces, transporting them and re-
erecting them at Avoncroft, a varied and
interesting collection has been formed.
Where many open-air museums aim to
show the social and industrial

development of a place, Avoncroft is dedicated to the history of individual buildings, ranging from the early 1500s to the 1946 prefab.

There are all sorts of buildings here for you to walk round and into. You can find out about methods of construction, building materials, types of roofs, doors, windows, chimneys as well as design and architecture and the different purposes of buildings. There is even a climbing frame built like a timber framed house.

On your tour you will find: The String of houses, a row of private houses built in Shrewsbury in 1786; the Counting House from Bromsgrove Cattle Market in 1853; a 19th century Cell Block from Ledbury; an 18th century Ice House from Tong in Shropshire (ice was used for preserving food, cooling wine and making desserts; ice houses were popular with the wealthy, built below ground at great expense). Look for the beautiful Victorian chimneys from Cardiff. Find the prefab built in Yardley, like many others throughout the country, as temporary housing for those who had lost their homes during the war.

Children will delight at the 19th century windmill from Tamworth in Arden on a site occupied by a windmill since the 13th century. Finally the privy; children are always fascinated by this

receptacle of basic human functions; this 18th century earth closet is from Leominster.

You really can spend as much time as you want here. Throughout the year there is a programme of workshops on, for example, toy making and travelling theatres and a variety of storytelling sessions.

Right: The windmill at Avoncroft is one of the site's most popular features.
Top: Enjoying a picnic with some of Avoncroft's timber-framed buildings as a backdrop.

HERTFORDSHIRE

St Albans

St Albans or Verulamium was one of the Romans' major towns in England, situated on Watling Street, the main route north from Londinium. They left behind an enormous amount of artefacts and evidence of everyday life which can be seen at the excellent Verulamium Museum. At the Museum of St Albans you can find out about later times in the city—the history of the Abbey, the medieval period and the Victorians. Both museums are worth visiting and provide excellent facilities for children. Although St Albans is a city it is not a vast urban sprawl. The cathedral stands high on the hill, but to one side you will find the town with its shops and markets and Museum of St Albans, and to the other a large open space ideal for running and picnicking. Towards the far end is a playground and then the Verulamium Museum and Hypocaust. You can easily spend a day walking around St Albans. This can make a wonderful day trip for families living in London.

Museum of St Albans
Hatfield Road
St Albans AL1 3RR
Hertfordshire
0727 819340

O Monday-Saturday 10am-5pm, Sunday 2-5pm.
£ free
P on site
bus to Hatfield Road
to ground floor and garden only
picnic area in garden

Find out about the history of the cathedral city of St Albans after the departure of the Romans to the present day. With the help of historical and ecological displays, children can see the evolution of a town, its function as gateway to a great abbey, to coaching centre, market town and now a thriving commuter city. You will also find a vast collection of trade and craft tools and objects from a Victorian schoolroom. Outside, in the urban wildlife garden, you can see pondlife through a video microscope, watch the social life of the bee in a special observation hive, and smell lots of different herbs in the herb garden. Throughout the year there are special exhibitions on natural sciences, visual arts and social history. There are exciting holiday and weekend workshops for children where they are encouraged to handle objects from the collection.

Verulamium Museum
St Michael's
St Albans AL3 4SW
0727 819341

O 1 March-31 October 10am-5.30pm Monday-Saturday, 2-5.30pm Sunday
1 November-28 February 10am-4pm Monday-Saturday, 2-4pm Sunday.
£ Adult £2.40, Child £1.40, Under Five free, OAP £1.40, Family Ticket £5.50
Friends Membership Season Ticket £5.50. Entrance also includes the Hypocaust.
P on site
bus to Bluehouse Hill
yes
picnic area nearby

This is the museum of everyday Roman life in Verulamium and there is so much here you would not be surprised to meet a Roman going about his daily chores. It is well laid out and worth the effort to get here.

Everything is well labelled, with not too many data bases to get hooked on; lots of drawers to pull out full of hair slides and combs, hinges, coins and much more in the reserve collection. There is a recreated Roman Street along which you walk and see people in their daily lives. Our five year old loved it; she was fascinated by the detail and size of the mosaics and spellbound by the skeletons. The video of the skeleton come to life describing Verulamium and his upper class life there, rendered her speechless. Even the three year old enjoyed it, especially the kitchen with the cooking utensils and vegetables. It all linked up very well with the trip we made to Hadrian's Wall later in the year.

At the beginning you will see examples of pots and other artefacts found here. There is a detailed display on Roman recreation and rites with sound effects and large pictures of the theatre, wrestling and games. You can find out about Roman merchants and wealth; look at their coins under a microscope and discover how an archaeologist can date a find from the coins left there. Then find out about work, farming and the food they ate. Do

spend time with the mosaics, you can get right up to them; look at the faces in them, the borders around and the detailed geometric patterns as well as the skill involved in finding the right colour, stonecutting and placing it. Look for the huge arch made from Purbeck stone which the Romans transported here all the way from the Isle of Purbeck in Dorset.

Along the street you will find a Roman house, a merchant writing out his accounts, decorators, a carpenter in his workshop and a kitchen. Don't forget to find the skeletons and coffins. Look for the photograph of the poor people's graves; it was only the wealthy who could afford coffins. Press the button and watch the video of the skeleton come alive.

When you have finished here make your way to the Hypocaust and learn about Roman central heating.

Left: A delightful Roman statuette at Verulamium.
Below: A section of one of the beautifully detailed mosaics at Verulamium.

HUMBERSIDE

The Museum of Army Transport
Flemingate
Beverley HU17 0NG
North Humberside
0482 860445

○ 10am-5pm every day. Closed 24,25,26 December.
£ Adult £2.50, Child £1.50, Under Five free, OAP £1.50, Family Ticket £6.50, Season Ticket £10.00
🅿 on site
🚉 BR and bus stations nearby
♿ yes
✕ restaurant

You will not miss the Blackburn Beverley transport as you enter this museum; look inside to find out about military transport planes. The Museum of Army Transport is definitely for the army enthusiast wishing to impart his or her knowledge to children. The military collections of the Royal Corps of Transport are housed here. There are vehicles from the Crimea, Boer War, the two world wars and the Gulf. There are also tank transporters and hovercraft. The extensive railway exhibition, with early 20th century locomotives and more recent railway memorabilia, shows the importance of the railways in the transport of troops and their supplies. Women at War Work, Communications and Port Operations are not forgotten. There are audio visual displays around the museum and the Astro Flight Simulator is a hit with children over three. You can even climb on vehicles in the museum's indoor playground though do keep an eye out for sharp corners and edges. Outside expend more energy on the Junior Assault Course and find out how physically resilient a soldier must be.

KENT

The Historic Dockyard
Chatham ME4 4TE
Kent
0634 812551

○ Easter-31 October: Wednesday-Sunday and Bank Holidays 10am-6pm.
1 November-March: Wednesday, Saturday and Sunday 10am-4.30pm
£ Adult £5.20, Child £2.60, Under Five free, OAP £4.50, Family Ticket £12.00
🅿 on site
🚉 BR Chatham/Gillingham Station
♿ yes
✕ restaurant and picnic area

The people of Chatham were devastated when the Naval Dockyard, which had served the Royal Navy for four hundred years, closed in the 1980s. However, within the space of a few years, that eighty acre site has been turned into a fascinating working museum and is the most complete Georgian dockyard in the world with 47 Scheduled Ancient Monuments in it.

This is a very large site, so we suggest a full day visit probably with older children who would not be exhausted by long walks and climbs. You can wander round the site at your own pace or take a guided tour.

Start at the Visitor Centre and see the audio-visual show, models, and trace the history of the dockyard. There are eight museum galleries on site and it is up to you how you pace your visit.

There are 16th century guns in the Ordnance Gallery and the ongoing restoration of *Gannet*, a Victorian sloop in the dry dock. You can see how some traditional craft methods have not changed since the time of Nelson. See ropemaking in the Ropery and flag and pennant making in the Flag Loft. In the Ordnance Mews Craft Workshops,

A 'carpenter' at work in the Wooden Walls display.

painters, sculptors and woodcarvers are all at work. You can take a cruise on the *Kingswear Castle* paddlesteamer.

The most popular gallery is the Wooden Walls where you can see the construction, at Chatham in 1758, of *Valiant*, a wooden sail-powered warship. Dockyard sounds and smells complement the experience. In the Steam Centre steam ships and locomotives are carefully restored.

Leeds Castle
Maidstone ME17 1PL
Kent
0622 765400

O 11am-5pm, every day.
   Closed 25 Dec, 26 June, 3 July, 29 Aug
£ Adult £6.50, Child £4.50, Under Five free,
   OAP £5.50, Family Ticket £18.00.
   Add £1.50 per person for entry to Castle
P on site
combined scheme operated with BR, National Express & Invictaway Buses, ring for details. Bus Maidstone, Ashford, Canterbury.
& yes, may be difficult in Castle
✕ restaurant and picnic area.

Our friends who came here were disappointed that they had not allowed more than their three hours to visit Leeds Castle. It is an extensive place with plenty of attractions. The two girls of five and eight years liked the water and money fountain, the maze, gardens, Dog Collar Museum, vineyard, fish and ducks best. Parents and children almost lost each other in the maze as they couldn't manage to find their way out.

The beautiful setting of Leeds Castle.

We suggest that you come here with older children; there is too much for toddlers and boisterous children would not be appreciated inside the castle. Pick a nice day when you have plenty of time on your hands.

Situated on two small islands on a lake, the castle is one of the oldest in the country and is named after Led, Chief Minister of Ethelbert IV, King of Kent in 857. It was a Norman stronghold and then was expanded by Henry VIII. The inside has been restored and contains collections of medieval furniture and furnishings, paintings and tapestries. Staff here are friendly and happy to answer questions.

The Dog Collar Museum, the most unusual collection we have discovered so far, is housed in the Gate Tower, and contains medieval and ornamental canine collars, from all over the world. Close by are the 14th century Barbican and fortified Mill.

In the beautiful grounds you will find woodland walks past streams, lakes and waterfalls and the Culpepper Garden with its beautiful old English fragrances. Take a look at the ancient vineyard which provides the grapes for the castle's own wine making. See rare and endangered birds in the aviary. Then find the classical maze and discover how easy it is to get lost. There is an underground grotto by the maze, which is like a fairytale with tunnels, caves and tumbling water.

LANCASHIRE

Harris Museum and Art Gallery
Market Square
Preston PR1 2PP
Lancashire
0772 58248

O 10am-5pm Monday to Saturday
   Closed Bank Holidays
£ free
P nearby
BR ten minutes walk. Bus station next door
& yes
✗ café

This lively and exciting local museum is packed with variety. You will find decorative arts, costume, painting and social history here. A strong education department enables it to work closely with children, organising exhibitions specially for them.

Visit the 'Story of Preston' and explore its history from prehistoric times to the present. There are costumes from the 18th century to the present, many with local relevance, as well as Britain's biggest collection of scent bottles. Somewhere you will find Foucault's Pendulum and illuminated manuscripts. Don't forget the paintings; the museum has a collection of Victorian and modern art. There are frequent acquisitions and a varied exhibition programme. Find out beforehand what is happening.

LEICESTERSHIRE

Snibston Discovery Park
Ashby Road
Coalville LE67 3LN
Leicestershire
0530 510851

O 10am-6pm every day.
   Closed 25, 26 December
£ Adult £3.00, Child £2.00, Under five free,
   OAP £2.00, Family Ticket £8.00
P on site
buses from Leicester St Margarets bus station
& yes, Braille labels, touch tables
✗ café and picnic area

Snibston Colliery, on the A50 Leicester to Ashby road, was operational from 1832 to 1983. George Stephenson sank the first mine shaft here and the pit was finally exhausted of coal nearly one hundred and fifty years later. Out of a potential ghost site a wonderful discovery park is evolving. The pit is still here, not working, but as a museum. The one hundred acre site has lots on offer so plan at least half a day for your visit.

The pit apart, there are woods, picnic areas, nature trails and perhaps most enterprising of all, an exhibition hall devoted to science and industry with an outdoor science play area.

The five galleries in the Exhibition Hall, have each taken an aspect of science or Leicestershire industry as their subject. There are touch tables, hands-on and interactive exhibits, so do not expect a passive visit.

Pull handles, push pedals, make a whirlwind in Science Alive where everything relates to the environment, weather and human body. In the Industry and University showcases see what local industry is doing, and the research at Leicester University on genetic fingerprinting, and much more.

How long would it have taken you to travel from Leicester to London in 1660? This, and many more questions will be asked of you; hopefully you will be able to find the answers, in the Transport Gallery where there are vintage vehicles. Computer games will give you an idea of transport in 2042.

The Extractive Industries Gallery is devoted to the underground wealth in Leicestershire - ironstone, limestone, alabaster, clay, granite, gypsum, sand and of course coal. Then you will find out about the human risk and daring involved in getting the stuff to the surface.

Move on to the age of steam engines and the development of local industry and engineering. Spend time at the collection of Imperial typewriters, look at the differences and similarities between their keyboards and those of modern word-processors. See how many different alphabets you can find too. Then have some fun looking at the lace-up corsets and couture products in the Textiles and Fashion Gallery; it was no wonder women fainted, thank goodness for Lycra! Leicester is also famous for hosiery, swimwear and footwear. Find out about a textile worker's life, the noise of machines and the long hours worked. If you have someone interested in pursuing a career in the fashion industry do take a look at the latest designs from local students.

The Outdoor Science Play area is no usual adventure playground but an imaginative way of introducing practical experiments in a play environment. There are fifteen experiments to be done, including a four way see-saw, a huge set of pan pipes and whispering to a friend one hundred metres away.

Follow the Colliery Trail — your grandfather might have worked here or somewhere similar. See where the miners worked and the harshness and dangers encountered in the 1800s through to the 1980s. Then visit the blacksmith in the Wheelwright's Workshop which was brought here, brick by brick, from Sheepy Magna where it was originally built in 1742.

The imposing pithead machinery of the former Snibston Colliery.

LONDON

We have decided to group our sites in London in subject order rather than alphabetically. For example there are three toy museums in different parts of the city and Greenwich is a place to itself. Traffic congestion is acute and parking impossible in central London so do take the Underground or bus. London Transport sell day and weekly passes for combined use on the tube and bus. Wear comfortable shoes for all the walking and plan trips before hand; the Underground map can be deceptive and make places look close together when they are miles apart.

Buckingham Palace

As this book was going to press it was announced that Buckingham Palace would be opened to the public for the first time in 1993. The Palace will be open in August and September only with charges Adult £8.00, Child £4.00, OAPS £5.50. It is sure to be popular but worth the queues and the expense.

Bank of England Museum

Bartholomew Lane
London EC2R 8AH
071 601 5545

O Monday-Friday 10am-5pm, April-September 11am-5pm Sunday. Closed Saturday.
£ free
P public car park at St Paul's
🚇 Underground Bank. DLR Waterloo and City. Bus routes through the City
♿ yes
✗ no

Money has been around for centuries; the Romans had hoards of it but banking is a recent phenomenon. This well laid out and stimulating museum is devoted to the origins and history of the Bank of England over the last three hundred years as well as being topical today. Children with an understanding of money, probably of ten years and over, should find it interesting.

Throughout the country there had been small provincial banks and in the 17th century goldsmith bankers emerged who took deposits, lent money and issued notes. Charles II borrowed heavily from them and failed to repay his debts, causing many bankruptcies. In 1688 a unified Bank of England was formed. After temporary homes it was finally decided to build the Bank on the present site in Threadneedle Street. Current banking and exchange systems in a European and worldwide context are easier to understand by examining the historical needs for unified banking, the Bank of England's relationship to

Below: The gold display at the Bank of England Museum with, *bottom*, the Bank building.

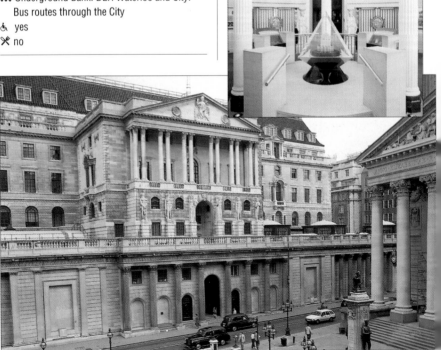

Parliament, the gold standard and exchange rates.

The original Bank of England building, on this site, was designed by Sir John Soane, the great 18th century architect, a master of the use of natural light. The high walls, still standing around the Bank, were his design and vital for security. In the museum the Bank Stock Office is a life size reconstruction of Soane's design. Light streams through windows high up in the rotunda. At the far end ledgers lie open on the counters and the cat sleeps by the fire, very different to modern computers and dealing desk.

Go into the main Rotunda and find the mound of gold bars on the dais in the middle, they represent the core of banking. The displays around the walls relate to all aspects of the history of the Bank, its origins, relationship to Parliament, role in times of war, local banks, Gilray cartoons, the Roman remains found on the site and the gold standard.

'The Bank Note Gallery', has examples of bank notes from 1699 to the present day. The watermark was introduced in 1821 in an attempt to make the forger's task harder. In 1844 the Bank Charter meant that no new bank could issue its own notes. Look at the huge printing presses.

'The Bank Today Gallery' has very impressive interactive videos which ask lots of questions. If you have wanted to know the technology behind the dealer on television, here is your chance. You can sit at the dealing desk, look at the screens, work the colour coded keyboard and telephone and receive immediate information about international exchange rates and markets.

Return to the Stock Office and you will have been from ledgers to computers in three hundred years. The technology may have changed but the principles are the same.

London Transport Museum
Covent Garden
London WC2E 7BB
071 379 6344

The bad news is that the London Transport Museum will be closed for most of 1993. The good news is that when it does open in December 1993 it will have undergone a major re-design, and no doubt will become even more popular with children and parents alike. We suggest that you telephone towards the end of the year to find out more.

Royal Air Force Museum
Grahame Park Way
Hendon
London NW9 5LL
081 205 2266
24 hour information line 081 205 9191

O 10am-6pm every day.
Closed 24,25,26 December, 1 January.

£ Adult £4.90, Child/Student £2.50, Under Five free, OAP £2.50, Family Ticket 2 adults and 2 children £12.00

P on site

Underground Colindale.
BR Mill Hill.
Bus 303 from Edgware, Mill Hill and Colindale.

& yes

✕ restaurant

Standing on the site of the old Hendon Aerodrome, this impressive collection of aircraft not only spans the history of the RAF, but exposes an intense human need to master the art of flying. Airports can be exciting, but here you can get close up to the aircraft, walk all round them and underneath and sit in the cockpit. Try out the Tornado flight simulator; when we visited it showed a film and sound tape of a 1915 dog fight, not for those with weak stomachs!

During the summer the museum runs a Flight Activities Week with model and kite flying, computer simulations, and various demonstrations. Ring for details.

The Aircraft Hall is made from two enormous World War 1 hangars and its sheer size and space is breathtaking. In here and in the Battle of Britain Hall stand the actual aircraft whose evocative names live on - the Spitfire, the Lancaster bomber, the Hawker

Experiencing an aircraft cockpit at Hendon.

An American Mustang fighter (foreground) and Flying Fortress bomber at the RAF Museum.

Hurricane, the Vulcan bomber, the Heinkel 111.

Look out for Louis Bleriot's monoplane in which he crossed the Channel in 1909. There are also displays about Amy Johnson, Tommy Sopwith and Alcock and Brown. Group Captain Douglas Bader's specially adapted Alvis car stands near a reconstructed RAF chapel from the Falklands. Standing unrestored and rather splendidly is the wreck of a plane dredged from Lake Hocklingen in Norway, years after it crashed.

By getting close you really feel the size, engineering and design of these aircraft. Some are beautiful and elegant whilst others seem menacing and ugly. Where some have huge bellies others are slender. The variety is incredible.

When your children are sitting in the cockpit of a fighter plane, ask them to imagine themselves strapped in ready to leave on a night's bombing mission, to feel the sensation of flying, hear the noise and experience the fear.

Around the hangars are displays which should not be overlooked. There is part of a World War 2 WAAF dormitory in a Nissen hut with a stern notice posted on the outside 'Out of bounds to RAF within 25 feet of this notice'. If you have ever wondered about disguise this is where to find it. There are maps of enemy territory hidden in pens and heels of boots; a reversible set of clothes for a rapid change from shot-down pilot into innocent civilian. Did you know about the airborne typewriter, the dinghy survival pack with firemaking tablets and sea water de-salting apparatus?

In the upstairs galleries there is a section on the history of flight from the Icarus legend to Leonardo da Vinci's visionary sketches and Otto Lilienthal's leather wings. One display charts the post World War 2 role of the RAF, the development of aircraft for commercial passenger use and of BEA and BOAC to become British Airways.

The Imperial War Museum
Lambeth Road
London SE1 6HZ
071 416 5000
Recorded Information 071 820 1683

O 10am-6pm every day.
  Closed 24, 25, 26 December, 1 January.
£ Adult £3.70, Child £1.85, Under Five free.
  OAP/Student £2.65, Family £9.50.
  Operation Jericho: Adult £1.30, Child £1.00,
  Under Five free, OAP/Student £1.05
P nearby
Underground Lambeth North, Elephant & Castle.
  BR Waterloo
& yes
✕ café and picnic area

Voted Museum of the Year 1990, the Imperial War Museum fully deserves it. An enormous steel barrel-vaulted shed on the back houses the new galleries, in strong contrast to the original impressive building, once Bedlam, the Old Bethlehem Royal Hospital. In the rose garden in the front are the huge barrels of two Royal Navy 15in guns and nearby a poignant reminder of the Berlin Wall, a small section covered in bullet holes and graffiti.

The museum has treated its unhappy and gory subject matter from World War

Top: The dugout section of the Trench Experience. *Above*: The museum and its gate guardians.

1 to the Gulf War with sensitivity and imagination.

In the large exhibit hall you can wander peacefully around some of the most devastating weapons of war that the world has spawned. Here is the V2 German rocket, World War 1 tanks, a Battle of Britain Spitfire, and a midget submarine. Come to rest at last in a museum they are slightly diminished and perhaps have lost their powers to terrify.

To come close to 'experiencing' the horrors of war is not something museums have ever attempted to do up till now. The Trench and Blitz Experience here take us right back into frightening times in our history; and plunge us into all the sights, sounds and smells of a World War 1 trench and the London Blitz. Look through periscopes into No Man's Land, watch the men going over the top to certain death, hear the scream of the air raid siren and the whine of the doodle bug, see the night sky light up with fire. Take a ride on 'Operation Jericho' to find out what it was like to fly with the RAF on a secret mission. Watch authentic archive film. Listen to sound recordings of people's wartime experiences. Walk through the museum's new galleries filled with hundreds of objects that vividly tell the story. Come out with a head bursting from the violence, the courage, the tragedy, the waste of it all.

A museum for children? Yes!

If you want to explore more, visit the two London outstations of the Imperial War Museum (see page 60).

HMS *Belfast*

Morgans Lane
Tooley Street
London SE1 2JH
(near Tower Bridge)
071 407 6434

○ 20 March-31 October 10am-5.20pm, every day.
  1 Nov-19 March 10am-4pm every day.
  Closed 24, 25,26 December, 1 January
£ Adult £4.00, Child £2.00, Under Five free,
  OAP/concessions £3.00, Family Ticket £10.00
🅿 no
🚇Underground London Bridge, Tower Hill
♿ Wheelchair access by lift from the gangway to
  main deck and then 50% of ship accessible
  using ramps, ring beforehand so that staff can
  assist. Loop system for hearing impaired
  visitors. Pushchairs have to be left on the
  quarterdeck.
✕ café

HMS *Belfast* is a World War 2 cruiser
moored on the Thames near Tower
Bridge. You can go all around the ship
and get a feel of what it must have been
like for the sailors living and fighting on
it. On the different decks you will find
guns and turrets, the operations room,
control tower, compass platform and
bridge wireless office.

HMS Belfast with the Tower of London and
Tower Bridge

Cabinet War Rooms

Clive Steps
King Charles Street
London SW1
071 930 6961

○ 10am-6pm, last admission 5.15pm every day.
  Closed 24, 25, 26 December, 1 January
£ Adult £3.80, Child £1.90, Under Five free,
  OAP/concessions £2.80, Family Ticket £9.50
🅿 no
🚇Underground St James's Park, Westminster
♿ yes
✕ no

Discover Churchill's secret
underground headquarters left as it
would have been at the end of the war.
You will find large maps to plot the
allied and enemy positions, old
telecommunications equipment,
scrambling devices as well as more
personal things like Churchill's
emergency bedroom. The bunker is just
behind Downing Street so within easy
access for the Prime Minister, though
apparently he hardly used it, preferring
to stay above ground. This is really a
fascinating place for older children and
especially those with an understanding
of modern history or an interest in
World War 2. We recommend you hire
one of the audio guides which give
excellent information.

nside the Cabinet War Rooms deep underground.

The Museum of London

London Wall
London EC2Y 5HM
071 600 3699

○ Tuesday-Saturday 10am-6pm. Sunday
 12 noon-6pm.
 Closed Monday except Bank Holidays.

£ Adult £3.00, Child £1.50, Under Five free,
 OAP £1.50, Family Ticket £7.50. Season
 Ticket £6.00.
 Season tickets are valid for 12 months.
 All other tickets are valid for 3 months enabling
 visitors to return as often as they wish.
 The museum is free to all visitors from 4.30
 every day.

P Aldersgate car park

Underground St Paul's, Barbican, Moorgate.
 Bus 4, 502

& yes

✗ restaurant

This is London's Museum. Everything here tells you about the story of London from the Stone Age to the Computer Age. Here you can learn two thousand years of history simply by looking at people's possessions. Some of them were rare and beautiful whilst others wore out and were thrown on the rubbish dump to be dug up hundreds of years later. You can discover London as archaeologists do, seeing how the city was built in layers of man made deposits. Here you will find objects unearthed from the very deepest layers: a Roman gymnast's leather bikini, a gladiator's trident, a medieval copper trumpet the height of a man. There's treasure too; a pile of Elizabethan jewellery dug up seventy years ago in Cheapside. You can find out about witchcraft, go through the Great Fire Experience and see the bell which was rung at dawn for the plague corpses. You can stand in a debtor's prison cell and walk through the very door of Newgate Gaol. You can stroll down a Victorian street and peer into a pub window. In the 20th century gallery you can see Selfridge's original lifts and a 1930 Woolworth's counter with nothing on sale over sixpence (2¹/₂p). You can look inside an air raid shelter and hear the sounds of London at war.

A very exciting museum. You can walk through from start to finish in one visit and even if you miss some bits you won't lose the thread. Or you can stay in one or two galleries and get to know them well. Find out about the excellent education department's holiday workshops.

Nearby you will find St Paul's Cathedral and the Barbican Centre, check to see what is on in advance, there may be an exhibition or film for children.

The Lord Mayor's coach is housed at the Museum of London and brought out every year for the Lord Mayor's Show, pulled by six horses from the Whitbread Brewery.

HM Tower of London

London EC3N 4AB
071 709 0765

○ Winter: Monday-Saturday 9.30am-5pm, Sunday 10am-5pm.
Summer: Monday-Saturday 9am-6pm, Sunday 10am-6pm. June, July, August open until 6.30pm Seasons change with clock.

£ Adult £6.70, Child £4.40, Under Five free, OAP £5.10, Family Ticket £19.00

🅿 NCP nearby

🚉 BR Fenchurch Street, Underground Tower Hill, DLR Tower Gateway, Buses 15, X15, 25, 42, 78, 100, D1, D9, D11

♿ very restricted

✖ café, picnic area on nearby wharf

Try to go to the Tower off-season, preferably in winter as in fine weather you will probably have to resign yourselves to queuing along the Outer Ward and again round the wall of the Jewel House. Summon up all your reserves because everything at the Tower is undoubtedly worth the effort (and the cost!).

We arrived one summer's day to be faced with a daunting queue. (There was no queue on a visit early, on a late autumn day.) While waiting we discussed tactics and decided what we most wanted to see. These were the children's priorities, in this order: the Crown Jewels, the instruments of torture, the shop, the Bloody Tower, the execution site, the Beefeaters, (they like to be referred to as Yeomen Warders and although their guided tours are for adults they are chatty and friendly to children), Henry VIII's armour and the ravens.

We had begun to whet appetites. Normally reluctant to be lectured at, the children began to demand information. We offered tantalising excerpts from history, like drops of water into a pool of questions. We described the forbidding portcullis over Traitor's Gate where kings, queens, villains and traitors, landing from the river, passed through on their way to imprisonment or death. We told them how ravens have clipped wings to prevent them flying away and so causing the destruction of the Tower and Kingdom. (Warning: the ravens are not tame and they do bite.) As graphically as we could we conjured up murder and intrigue; how Richard III had smothered his two young nephews in their beds in the Bloody Tower; how two hundred years later, two children's skeletons were found beneath the stairs at the bottom of the White Tower. What

child could resist that story? We embellished the facts with descriptions of the poisoning of Sir Thomas Overbury with tarts and jellies, laced with arsenic. We extemporized over clammy, rat-ridden cells, of terrible sessions of torture with racks and manacles and the infamous 'scavenger's daughter'. We told tales of the scaffold, such as Anne Boleyn's request to be executed with a sword. We regaled them further with the daring escape of John Gerard by means of invisible secret messages written with orange juice and an iron ball flung across the moat and over Cradle Tower. We told them that Henry III had once kept elephants, leopards and even a polar bear here.

By now the queue had dwindled and the children were drawn with a mixture of horror and fascination under the Byward Tower, over the drawbridge, through Traitor's Gate into the Bloody Tower. We crossed Tower Green (where the Changing of the Guard takes place every day in the summer and on alternate days in winter, usually at 11.30am) and into the White Tower.

We saw mail shirts and weapons we recognised from pictures of the Bayeux Tapestry, impressive armour for men and horses, muskets and bayonets; a massive arsenal. We climbed up narrow, twisting stone steps into St John's Chapel; tiny, beautiful and completely Norman. You must be quiet there.

The Crown Jewels are real; not copies of originals stored in secret vaults somewhere else, hence the huge alarm doors that you have to walk through into this bunker deep beneath the ground. We dutifully gasped at the Imperial State Crowns and sceptres, at the Star of Africa and the Koh-i-Noor, the largest cut diamond in the world. We spotted the tiny, almost doll-sized crown, Queen Victoria had had made especially to fit on her bun; look at drawings of her and you will see it perched there. We gaped at the splendid India Crown made for King George V to take with him on a trip to India. The crowns are not allowed to leave Britain in case the monarch pawns them, so the King had a crown specially made for his trip with diamonds, emeralds, rubies and of course gold.

As we wandered round we found the ravens and saw the Yeomen Warders resplendent in their bright red uniforms. We found the instruments of torture sed on Guy Fawkes and others. We ere amazed at the size of the Tower omplex; it is like a small town, inside ou are unaware of the hustle and ustle and noise of London.

ower Hill Pageant

Tower Hill Terrace
ower Hill
ondon EC3N 4EE
71 709 0081

1 April-31 October 9.30am-5.30pm every day.
1 November-31 March 9.30-4.30pm every day.

Adult £4.95, Child £2.95, Under Three free,
OAP £2.95, Family Ticket £12.95

NCP nearby

BR Fenchurch Street.
Underground Tower Hill.
DLR Tower Gateway.
Buses 15, X15, 25, 42, 78, 100, D1, D9, D11.

yes, a purpose built car that accommodates wheelchairs

café

Step into a time car at the Tower Hill Pageant and be transported from Roman London through the Blitz,

seeing, hearing and smelling the past.' That is exactly what we did, but however slowly the car went, the past flashed by frustratingly quickly. We were still absorbing Roman Londinium's first wooden bridge when we were 'whisked' on to the Saxon Lundenwic; the Vikings had no chance to attack before we found ourselves in a medieval lane; the fire that began in Pudding Lane in 1666 seemed to end in the fires begun by the German bombers in the Blitz of 1940. The 18th and 19th centuries seemed to have passed us by. Oh for the chance to do the dark ride all over again!

However, we do recommend it! The museum has an amazing display of archaeological finds, excavated along the waterfront over the past twenty years. There is a good reconstruction of part of a flat-bottomed sailing barge, found wrecked near Blackfriars Bridge, in spite of the coin with the head of the goddess Fortuna, which had been placed in the mast head, as a symbol of good luck.

Hard bargaining at Tower Hill.

London Toy and Model Museum

21-23 Craven Hill
London W2 3EN
071 262 9450
24 hour information line
071 262 7905

O Tuesday-Saturday 10am-5.30pm, Sunday 11am-5.30pm

£ Adult £3.00, Child £1.50, Under Four free, OAP £2.00, Family Ticket £8.00, Season Ticket £35.00

P meter parking, car park at Queensway

🚇 Undergound Paddington. Bus-12 & 94 on Bayswater Road.

♿ to some parts

✗ café

Two large terraced houses are home to this fantastic museum of toys. Their back gardens have been combined into one to make the ultimate museum playground. Spilling out into the front is the locomotive, Wytch. Inside this paradise for children, and most grown-ups, is a labyrinth of small rooms filled with cases of trains, huge German-made tin fire engines, cars, boats, aeroplanes and garages from an age when toys had a bespoke quality about them. There are early 20th century wind up toys, cooking ranges, prams piled high with dolls, armies of soldiers, parades of shops and dolls' houses. Names like Hornby, Lehmann, Meccano, are commonplace here. Sit at the old wooden school desk. Look out for the German swimming dog, slightly the worse for wear due to his exploits in the water and the child-sized working model of the Cadillac car presented to the King of Siam in 1912.

The fairground carousel at the Toy Museum.

Despite the wonders inside, children will probably want to spend their entire visit in the garden. Here train sets trundle around, through tunnels, across bridges and over ponds and paths, while peepholes and standing platforms enable even the smallest child to have a look. A large hand-operated 1920 fairground carousel gives rides and plays evocative music. A sit-on-train transports children around the garden, through tunnels and across the pond. Parents can watch from the terrace café. Be warned! It is almost impossible to drag children away from here.

Bethnal Green Museum of Childhood

Cambridge Heath Road
London E2 9PA
081 980 4315
Information line 081 980 2415

O Monday-Thursday and Saturday 10am-5.50pm Sunday 2.30-5.50pm. Closed on Friday.

£ free

P on site

🚇 Underground/BR Bethnal Green. Bus 8, D6, 106.

♿ limited

✗ café

Situated in the East End this branch museum of the Victoria and Albert Museum is devoted to the history of childhood. There is an ambitious children's programme every Saturday and special exhibitions throughout the year where children can make anything from Goblins and Trolls, to pop-up Christmas cards and bathroom tiles. (For three years and upwards.)

At Bethnal Green you will find puzzles and games, puppets and dolls, dolls' houses and shops, cars and train sets, Noah's Arks, rattles and nursery toys, soft toys, dolls' clothes, children's furniture, money boxes, educational toys, children's books. There is a new exhibition on the history of Birth and Infancy from the 17th century to the present day. There are large collections of children's dress and nursery furniture. At times it seems daunting as there is so much. Whilst children are indeed impressed by Bethnal Green it is important to explain to them beforehand that they will be unable to play with or touch the toys, mouthwatering and enticing as they are. However if you need to date or find out about a toy, then this is the place to come and ask.

Pollocks Toy Museum
1 Scala Street
London W1P 1LT
071 636 3452

O Monday-Saturday 10am-5pm.
   Closed Sunday and Bank Holidays
£ Adult £2.00. Child 75p
P no
🚇Underground Goodge Street. Buses 14, 24, 29,
   73 to Goodge Street.
♿ no
✕ no

Pollocks Toy Museum, in the midst of
the noisy West End, is loved by
hundreds of adults and children alike.
Many a lunch hour is spent here away
from the office and some grown-ups
have been known to play hopscotch on
the pavement outside! Children from
four upwards find it quite magical. There
are lots of stairs, so buggies and
toddlers are not really compatible. Two
tiny houses have been knocked
together to make the museum. You
walk in, buy your ticket and start the
tour. The building is tiny and ceilings
low, rooms and staircases are crammed
with toys. It is like being on a treasure
hunt in a life-size dolls' house in 'Alice in
Wonderland'.

The museum has collections of
optical, mechanical, construction and tin
toys; board games, dolls and teddy
bears, puppets, lead miniatures, dolls'
houses as well as folk toys from the
Alps, Russia, Poland, the Balkans,
India, Africa, China and Japan. There is

Top: Some of Bethnal Green's extensive family
of teddy bears.
Above: A charming Victorian dolls' house at
Pollocks Toy Museum.

a collection of 19th century toy theatres,
some by the famous Benjamin Pollock
from whom the establishment takes its
name.

Finally, you land in the most
wonderful toy shop from another era.
There are things of all prices here from
all over the world. Staff are enthusiastic
and you really do feel they enjoy their
work and understand children as well as
the child lurking within the adult.

The British Museum
Great Russell Street
London WC1B 3DG
071 636 1555
Recorded information 071 580 1788.
Recorded information for visitors
with disabilities 071 637 7384

O Monday-Saturday 10am-5pm, Sunday
2.30-6pm.
Closed during Christmas period, 1 January,
Good Friday and first Monday in May.

£ free

P no

🚇 Underground Tottenham Court Road, Holborn,
Russell Square.
Buses to Tottenham Court Road, Gower Street
and Southampton Row.

♿ yes, there is a leaflet for disabled visitors. A
booklet/tape tour is available from the
information desk. Blind and partially sighted
visitors are invited to use the touch tour of
Roman sculpture starting in room 85. The First
Aid Room, off room 25, may be used by
parents with babies.

✕ café

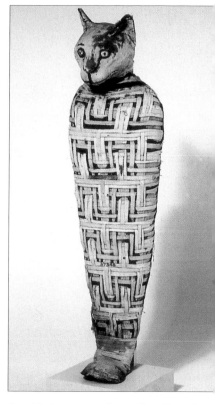

An intricate mummy of a cat, from Egypt in
the first century BC.

When I was a child we made frequent
visits to London. I distinctly remember
being told, on numerous occasions, that
on our next visit we would go to the
British Museum; but we never did.
There were various excuses, the most
common was that because it was so big
we would never be able to see
everything. My mother has still never
been and I do believe, like many
parents, she was and still is, daunted by
its size, stature and the fear of getting
lost or losing me. I was a twenty year
old student when I first went; I did get
lost and still do each time I visit, but
nobody minds, the attendants seem to
assume most people are and happily
advise you where to go. My six year old
daughter suddenly remarked on our last
visit, as we asked the way again
'People [the attendants] are very kind to
tell us where things are'. The BM, is
there for all of us, it is huge and would
take weeks to go round it all, but it is a
marvellous treasure palace and well
worth visiting many times. Whatever
you may feel, the museum welcomes
children; nobody minded when my
daughter sat on the floor to draw
skeletons and mummies. A children's
shop has been opened specially for
pocket money spending power (room 26
ground floor). Parts of the museum hum
with the noise of children excited at
seeing objects they have read about
and seen pictures of; the sight of the
real thing is so much better.

Walk across the forecourt, up the
great flight of steps (there is wheelchair
and pushchair access), between the
great Ionic style Greek columns and into
the foyer. Go upstairs and straight to the
Egyptian Galleries in rooms 60-64. On
your way you may pass the Lindow Man
at the top of the stairs by room 35. He
was discovered in 1984 and was
probably killed by Druids, two thousand
years ago, who placed his body in a
peat bog which preserved him until his
later discovery. At last you will arrive at
the Egyptian Galleries and your children
will be enthralled; there are so many
artefacts arranged in four rooms. Have
lots of paper

bronze of a warrior on horseback, beautifully finished and over 2500 years old.

Terracotta figures of actors performing in a mime, first century AD.

and coloured pencils at hand, your children will want to draw what they see. Rooms 60, 61 and 62 are devoted to the Egyptian way of death with coffins beautifully decorated inside and out, mummies of humans and animals including, cats, fish, gazelles, and falcons. There are canopic jars in which organs were stored. The Egyptians discovered that if the organs were removed immediately after death the decomposition process would be halted. The organs were preserved and put in the canopic jar which was placed beside the mummy in the coffin. Do look closely at the variety of mummy bindings, some use leaves and others cloth. Room 62 contains a host of funerary equipment including a book of the dead written in hieroglyphics on papyrus. Everyday life is covered in room 63. There are combs, wigs, perfume bottles, sandals made of palm leaves, musical instruments, hunting weapons, models of boats

and a display on the role of magic in daily life.

The Ancient Greeks and Romans in 68-70 are also well displayed, with easy to read information panels describing the life and culture of these two great civilizations. Reading and writing, cooking, games and toys, music, dance and drama, marriage, parties and death are all examined. The Greeks and Romans were great warriors and there are lots of helmets and suits of armour on display. Look at the details of the design and evolution of the Greek Corinthian helmet in room

Above: The gruesome but fascinating Lindow Man, preserved in a peat bog.

68; then find out about Roman gladiators and chariot racing. There are also wonderful displays of more delicate and refined artefacts like jewellery, glassware and ceramics.

Room 70 has two marvellous pieces of mosaic pavement, made at Populonia in AD100. The designs incorporate edible fish, lobster, eel and octopus all made out of tiny, 5mm square pieces of stone. We were intrigued at the Ancient Egyptian parade armour suit and wig made out of crocodile skin, also in this room. Do go and see the Mildenhall Treasures in room 40. This set of silverware, all engraved with different images, is from 4th century Roman Britain, and was found in Mildenhall in Suffolk. You will find the Sutton Hoo Ship in room 41.

All this may have taken you two hours.

If you want to see more do, but don't force your children, they can always come again on another visit and it may be best to keep the visit comparatively short.

If you do want to venture further then take a look at the newly refurbished Chinese Galleries. Find out about special exhibitions. My daughter was overwhelmed by the delicacy and skill of the illuminated manuscripts, Bibles and bindings in the British Library in room 30a. We passed the Magna Carta, in room 30, on our way to the Hebrew and Arabic illuminated manuscripts in the

Above: A stag figurine found among the treasure at the Sutton Hoo ship burial.

King's Library. The Japanese drawings and woodcuts, in rooms 92-94, are an inspiration.

In room 25, near the shop on the ground floor, is a vast collection of sculptures from Ancient Egypt and here you will find the Rosetta Stone, discovered in 1799 but dating back to 196BC Memphis. We were spellbound by the huge heads, arms and fists of these works. Find room 7 and the breathtaking Nereid Monument from Xanthos in Greece.

Each time you come to the BM you will find something you have never seen before, it is so full of surprises. Take your children, they will never forget it.

The Horniman Museum and Gardens

100 London Road
Forest Hill
London SE23 3PQ
081 699 2339/1872

O Monday-Saturday 10.30am-5.30pm. Sunday
  2pm-5.30pm, Closed 24-26 December
£ free
P in Sydenham Rise
BR Forest Hill. Bus 176,185,94,63,122,115
& most parts
✗ café and picnic area.

If you don't live nearby it is well worth
the journey to the Horniman Museum
which is full of treasures from all over
the world. Even young children of three
and four love this place whilst older
ones will find it an invaluable source for
study.

Its founder, Frederick Horniman,
made a fortune as the first man to sell
tea in packets. His own collection,
resulting from his travels, is in the
museum. Read his heartwarming
inscription on the front of the building
'..dedicated to the public forever as a
free museum'. A pioneer in museum
education, the museum runs an
excellent series of weekend and holiday
workshops for children on anything from
pottery making to recorder playing.
These are all very popular so it is no
surprise that it is essential to book in
advance.

When you enter do not be put off by
the formal layout. Children can wander
and look, the objects will soon work
their own magic. Start with the Masks
which take up most of the ground floor.
This must be one of the most extensive
collections in the country; there are ugly
and grotesque masks, of demons and
wild animals, of spirits and deceased
ancestors; masks for dancing in, festival
time as well as for hunting and warfare.
Look out for the South American mask
with light bulbs for eyes, and others with
painted eyes and tiny slits beneath the
eyebrow for the wearer to see through.
Find the wonderful collection from Africa
where leather, straw and shells are
used; some cover the head whilst
others cover the whole body and some
incorporate a hat. There are different
kinds of magic in the African carvings of
the mother ancestor, in the benign
Buddhas, and in the Hindu gods and
goddesses with elephant heads,
multiple arms and weapons and
tongues dripping with blood.

Go upstairs to see the Javanese

One of the many spectacular figures from the
Horniman Museum's ethnography collections.
This is Sirat Maharaja, father of Semi Rama,
from Kelantan in Malaysia.

shadow puppets and Punch and Judy
figures with a range of expressions. In
the musical instrument galleries there
are over six thousand examples of
musical serpents, glasses, nose flutes,
whistles and rattles as well as a
handsome selection of many more
conventional items.

As if this were not all, the museum
has a huge collection of natural history.
There are massive elephants skulls,
stuffed eagles, vultures and ostriches,
huge scale models of insects and even
a spectacular ancient mummified
crocodile.

It seems that the museum goes
underwater in the Aquarium with its
elephant-nosed fish, giant anemones
with voracious stinging tentacles, tiny
water dragons and ominously beautiful
striped lion fish with lethally poisonous
spines.

Continue outside in the Horniman
Gardens where, by way of peaceful
contrast, there are nature trails, water
gardens, Dutch barn, animal enclosure
and picnic places.

National Gallery
Trafalgar Square
London WC2N 5DN
071 839 3321

○ Monday-Saturday 10am-6pm, Sunday 2-6pm.
Special exhibitions 10am-6pm every day.
Some late evening openings in the summer.

£ free. Admission charge for special exhibitions.

P Whitcomb Street car park. Recommend using
public transport.

🚇 Underground Charing Cross, Embankment,
Piccadilly Circus, Leicester Square.
BR Charing Cross.
Any bus to Trafalgar Square.

♿ wheelchair users should take the Orange Street
or Sainsbury Wing entrances.

✗ restaurant

Bring everybody to the National Gallery.
Show your three year old Rousseau's
'Tropical Storm with a Tiger', your five
year old Uccello's 'George and the
Dragon', both of them the early Italian
paintings of the Madonna and Child.
Take your six year old to Seurat's
'Bathers at Asnieres' and your ten year
old to Holbein's 'Ambassadors' or Jan
van Eyck's 'Arnolfini Marriage' and
yourself to the Leonardo cartoon. Send
someone to the Micro Gallery. Touch
the colour computer screens to browse
and explore, put together your own
gallery tour and get a print-out showing
exactly where the paintings are.
Irresistible to the most reluctant
museum visitor!

The National Gallery houses a
collection of over two thousand
European paintings from about 1250 to
1900. The earlier pictures are in the
exciting new Sainsbury Wing, the others
in the main galleries.

In spite of its imposing building and
grand rooms the National Gallery is
extremely welcoming to the very young
and the very old. It is not a stuffy art
gallery but a busy, dynamic and
enthralling place. Don't hesitate to sit on
the carpet and sketch a picture (with
pencils or felt tips). Nobody will worry
about your children's questions and
exclamations. Join one of the guided
tours or buy the booklet on 'Twenty
Great Paintings' or the excellent
'National Gallery Children's Book'. Ring
in advance to book a children's quiz.
They are fun and jokey and get children
to look clearly at paintings.

Don't try and thrust the paintings at
your children; just let them roam
around. We often go to the National
Gallery and even our three year old has
to go searching for the paintings she
saw last time, so powerful are the
images. You can even play I-Spy with
some of them , looking for different
objects, shapes or colours within the
paintings. Take them home whilst they
are still enjoying it. Don't drag them

Right: Leonardo's *The Virgin of the Rocks* in
the Sainsbury Wing of the National Gallery.
Below: Room 66 has Piero della Francesca's
The Baptism of Christ and *The Nativity.*

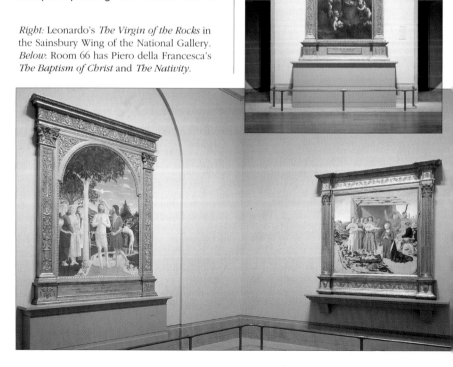

round saying 'just one more painting'. If need be, look at no more than three, go home and if you can, come back another time. When you get home why not get out the paintbrushes and the yellow and black paint and paint a tiger. In other words be inspired by one of the greatest art collections in the world.

National Portrait Gallery
St Martin's Place
London WC2H OHE
071 306 0055

O Monday-Friday 10am-5pm, Saturday 10am-6pm, Sunday 2-6pm.
  Closed 24,25,26 December, 1 January
£ free. Occasional charges to special exhibitions
P Whitcomb Street car park. Recommend using public transport.
🚇Underground Charing Cross, Leicester Square. BR Charing Cross.
  Buses to Trafalgar Square
♿ restricted
✕ no, restaurant next door in National Gallery

I took my serious-minded ten year old to the National Portrait Gallery as, needless to say, the Tudors and Stuarts are featuring highly in her school year. I was intrigued by her reaction to our surroundings: she roundly scolded me for talking too 'loudly' and for being over enthusiastic. 'Be quiet, you're embarrassing me.' I was made to behave myself and whisper otherwise she would disown me. Occasionally, however, her own enthusiasm got the better of her, as she instructed me on the identities and destinies of the Tudor

and Stuart kings and queens. At times I tactfully feigned ignorance. To see pictures which she was familiar with in reproductions was very satisfying.

We lingered over the Holbein Cartoon with its massive figure of Henry VIII; over Marcus Gheeraerts the Younger's 'Ditchley Portrait' of Queen Elizabeth I and discussed red wigs and false teeth. We liked Gerrit van Honthorst's portrait of a young and optimistic Charles I and a debauched, defiant painting of Charles II attributed to Thomas Hawker. We wondered over the 'Chandos Portrait' of Shakespeare with his black hair and gold earring. I was allowed, though quietly, to read out

Right: Marcus Gheeraerts' portrait of Elizabeth I, the floor under the queen decorated with a map of England.
Below: The Portrait Gallery's 1914-45 section.

the caption of Hayls's portrait of Samuel Pepys; how he had hired an Indian gown and endured the discomfort of six sittings ('I....do almost break my back looking over my shoulders to make the posture for him to work by') and how he paid fourteen pounds for the picture and nearly five shillings for the frame. We both loved the miniatures and compared the finery of the Elizabethans in Nicholas Hilliard and Isaac Oliver's work with Samuel Cooper's Oliver Cromwell with untidy hair and severe black chin-high armour. We stopped in front of Bramwell Brontë's pictures of his sisters. My daughter wanted to know why the picture was so badly marked and what was the meaning of the shadow behind? She was surprised to learn that the reason their lips were tightly sealed was because they had no teeth.

Perhaps the paintings of the present royal family (House of Windsor) caught our imagination most; Annigoni's formal and remote royal sovereign, hanging nearby Michael Leonard's Queen with yellow suit, pearls and royal corgi; we tried to read behind the lines of the ever smiling face of the Princess of Wales.

I would have liked to spend much longer in the 20th century gallery reliving the pleasure I had coming here as a student. I pointed out the marvellous portraits of Virginia Woolf, Lawrence of Arabia, T. S. Eliot, Lady Ottoline Morrell, Lytton Strachey and all the others I remembered so well, and also some new ones such as Maggi Hambling's portrait of the scientist Dorothy Hodgkin, with four hands expressing her vigour and energy, but Martha had had enough. I hope that these will be pleasures in store for her and that the loud enthusiasm of an embarrassing mother might only be a temporary hindrance.

Perhaps not for small children, the National Portrait Gallery, with its vast collection of paintings, watercolours, drawings, miniatures, sculpture and photographs, is a marvellous place to inspire and encourage children who are struggling with the rigours of the National Curriculum, GCSE or further studies. The Education Department here is well known and actively helps both groups and individual children enjoy the Gallery and its temporary exhibitions. There are practical portraiture workshops and plenty of holiday activities. Make sure you also have time to browse in the shop; the book selection is brilliant.

The Tate Gallery
Millbank
London SW1P 4RG
071 821 1313

O Monday-Saturday 10am-5.50pm, Sunday 2-5.50pm.
Closed 24, 25,26 December, 1 January, Good Friday, May Day Bank Holiday.

£ free. Entrance fee to special exhibitions.

P meters in Atterbury Street

Underground Pimlico
BR Vauxhall
Buses 88, 77A, C10, 2, 3, 24, 36, 159, 185, 507

& wheelchair entrance in Atterbury Street

✖ restaurant

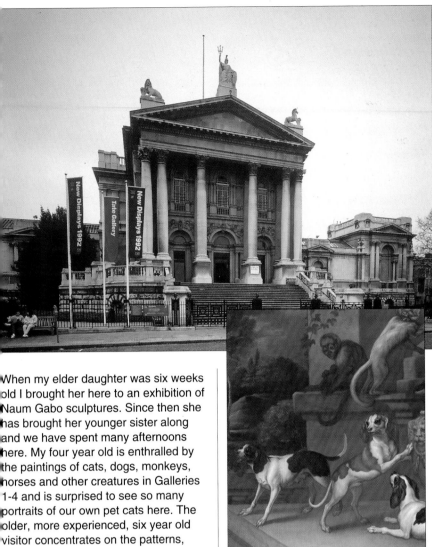

When my elder daughter was six weeks old I brought her here to an exhibition of Naum Gabo sculptures. Since then she has brought her younger sister along and we have spent many afternoons here. My four year old is enthralled by the paintings of cats, dogs, monkeys, horses and other creatures in Galleries 1-4 and is surprised to see so many portraits of our own pet cats here. The older, more experienced, six year old visitor concentrates on the patterns, illusions and colours of the geometric works by Mondrian and Bridget Riley. Both enjoy the huge comic-strip inspired paintings by Roy Lichtenstein. Then we try and find the faces, musical instruments and other objects in the Cubist paintings of Braque and Picasso. Machine-like shapes are discovered in paintings by Fernand Leger and Max Ernst. Miro's work reminds us of dreams with odd floating images in his paintings and witty sculptures. Two years ago they spent ages climbing up and down a tower built by Anthony Caro, and on temporary display. As budding ballet dancers they enjoy the poise and grace of Edgar Degas' 'Little Dancer'. They have fun peering through the spaces in Henry Moore's great reclining figures.

There are conceptual works of the last twenty years. My six year old loves to find out how many paces there are around Richard Long's stone sculptures which spread across the floor.

Children do respond to the works of

Above: Monkeys and Spaniels Playing by Francis Barlow, from the Tate Gallery.
Top: The traditional facade of the Tate contrasts with the modernity of many of its treasures.

art here; they share a creative bond with the modern artist, both understand how to make something immediately, without inhibition. Do come and watch your children's reactions. The gallery has a lively education department and there are often school groups walking around.

Recent policy at the Tate means that galleries are regularly re-hung with paintings from the collection not normally on show. I have watched teenagers look in detail at Stanley Spencer's work full of symbolism, resurrections, colours and textures. Others will look carefully at the good collection of paintings by William Blake, which I too enjoyed when in my Zen phase at college. There are all the Turner paintings to discover in the Clore Gallery.

Left: A Degas figure, *Little Dancer Aged 14.*

The Victoria and Albert Museum

Cromwell Road
South Kensington
London SW7 2RL
071 938 8550, Recorded Information 071 938 8441, Exhibitions 071 938 8349, Courses and Events 071 938 8638, Information for Disabled Visitors 071 938 8638

○ Monday 12 noon-5.50pm, Tuesday-Sunday 10am-5.50pm

£ donations expected, charge for special exhibitions

🅿 few meters in Exhibition Road.

🚇Underground South Kensington. Bus 9, 10, 14, 30, 33, 45, 49, 52, 52A, 74, 503, C1

♿ wheelchairs available at both entrances. Lifts to upper floors but some steps between galleries. Contact Chief Warder 071 938 8540 or Information Line.

✕ restaurant and picnic area.

Young visitors deeply engrossed in the sculpture gallery at the V&A.

Prince Albert founded The Victoria and Albert Museum, a sister to the Science Museum across the road, primarily as a museum of decorative arts and design. It still collects and shows things which have been made for their beauty, aesthetic qualities and function. You might well disagree and consider some of them ugly or dull, but this is all part of the fun. This really is a vast place; seven miles of galleries across a thirteen acre site so you do need to know where you are going and what you plan to see. The shop sells a 'Young Visitors Guide' which has suggestions for a Treasure Trail and a 'Zoom In ' on nine special things. We suggest the jewellery in rooms 91-93, where gold and precious stones glitter like an Aladdin's Cave; the Bed of Ware in room 52, the longest and most famous four-poster bed in England; the Cabinet of Mirrors, room 7, an oval room with a star-patterned floor and mirrored walls; the Musical Instrument Gallery, room 40, and the miniatures in room 55. Look out specially for Nicholas Hilliard's unknown courtier with his shapely legs, black and white striped jacket, black cloak hung nonchalantly from his shoulder and his hand on his heart, perhaps desperately in love with the unfeeling Elizabeth I. The Emperor's Robes in room 44 are rich and rare; here too are the Chinese tomb horses, once buried as tokens of their owner's most valued possessions on earth. In room 42 is a carved wooden pulpit, the gift of a Sultan to his Cairo mosque. The Indian miniatures, in room 47a and b,

are delightful, each one tells its own story. The one thing that you must not miss in the whole of this huge collection is Tipu's Tiger, a painted wooden figure of a tiger mauling a British soldier. Inside is a pipe organ and bellows that produce roars and groans as the tiger attacks the man. It is now placed conveniently just outside the smart new restaurant. This is just the tip of the iceberg of all the marvellous things to see here. Like all big museums you need to pace it carefully and, as the guide says 'sit down before you feel tired out'!

The Science Museum

Exhibition Road
London SW7 2DD
071 938 8000

○ Monday-Saturday 10am-6pm, Sunday 11am-6pm.

£ Adult £3.75, Child £1.90, Under Five free, OAP £2.00, Season Ticket £16.50

🅿 few meters in Exhibition Road.

🚇Underground South Kensington. Buses 9, 10, 14, 30, 33, 45, 49, 52, 52A, 74, 503, C1

♿ yes

✕ restaurant and picnic area

The mother of all museums and sprung, with the Victoria and Albert Museum and Natural History Museum, from the Great Exhibition of 1851. The Science Museum was founded on solid Victorian principles of didacticism and hard work. The nation's pride, it stood as a monument to human scientific achievement. Now it has exploded into a building packed with light, colour, noise, invention, experiment, change and ideas; intense activity (of men and women) to do with all things scientific, technological and medical.

I went there regularly as a child when we used to call it the 'push button' museum, and now take my children, not as the dreary, rainy afternoon excursion it used to be, but as an adventure. We have been to the Launch Pad five times since it opened in 1986, sometimes spending half an hour at an old favourite such as the Grain Pit or the Robot's Mechanical Arm, or other times sampling at random, rushing from the Tiptoe Tester to the Sound Dishes, from Human Battery to the Magnetic River.

We have been to the Food for Thought exhibition twice and enjoyed its interactive, computer and audio-visual exhibits. Grandparents might enjoy the 1920s Sainsbury's store while smaller children will want to load up mini trolleys with boxes and packages and ring up their shopping on the check out.

The Apollo 11 command module, in the Exploration of Space, looks worryingly tinny and Dr Who'ish. It also looks battered enough to have survived many a star war and it is extraordinary to think it really took three astronauts to the Moon in 1969. A V2 rocket along with satellites, spacecraft and other hardware hang menacingly about and there are always the intriguing practical and personal details of coping with daily life in space.

There have been times when we needed to find out about topics such as optics, early photography and film, electricity and telecommunications and the history of medicine. We have successfully ventured upstairs to the top floor where it is usually restful, except when the Japanese robots took over, and always helpful. We have also met Alexander Graham Bell, Joseph Crapper and Marie Curie in person!

The 'Guide to the Science Museum' helps you plan your visit, suggests what to do if time is short, what is good for children, what demonstrations and events are happening and where to find a live character from the past. On busy days you may need special tickets to reserve places in the Launch Pad. Go up the see-through lifts and check at the first floor gallery entrance before you look round the other parts of the museum. You will need plenty of time and stamina.

Below & bottom: The Launch Pad section of the Science Museum.

The Natural History Museum
Cromwell Road
South Kensington
London SW7 5BD
071 938 9123

○ Monday-Saturday 10am-6pm. Sunday 11am-6pm.

£ Adult £4.50, Child £2.20, Under Five free, OAP 2.20, Family Ticket £12.00, Family Season Ticket £21.00

🅿 few meters in Exhibition Road.

🚇 Underground South Kensington.
Bus 9, 10, 14, 30, 33, 45, 49, 52, 52A, 74, 503, C1.

♿ yes

✗ restaurant and picnic area.

How many generations of children have gaped at the skeleton of Diplodocus standing like a giant sentinel in the cathedral-like central hall of the Natural History Museum? How many of us have childhood memories of long afternoons spent with the dinosaurs and the blue whale, browsing amongst the serried ranks of long dead animals, dusty fish, endless bones, rocks and fossils? Bringing my children back here, thirty years later, is like a revelation. The place is alive and blooming. Diplodocus is still there but she now has the company of fifty or so other dinosaurs in the most extraordinary and thrilling dinosaur exhibition that any museum has ever produced. Stroll along a walkway, high up in the ribs of the building to meet Camarasaurus and Triceratops eyeball to eyeball. Head for the screams and flesh-tearing sounds of a carnivorous dinosaur devouring its prey. Dinosaur mad or not, no child could resist it. Drag them, bribe them but make sure they get here.

In the ecology exhibition a huge green man extends his arms with a message to all of us. He stands in the world's first permanent exhibition on global ecology. Very direct, very simple and addressed to children, this exhibition lays bare the impact of human interference in the world; the disappearance of the rain forests, the extent of global warming, the fragile state of the ozone layer, the horrors of pollution. Set in a green forest of mirrors, is the largest video wall in the world. A myriad of colours burst as vapour rises from the oceans, clouds swell, rain falls, plants open, animals move and rivers flow down to the seas.

A giant squid stands guard over the marine invertebrates while the blue whale surveys a kingdom of mammals and fossil ancestors. In 'Discovering Mammals' stare into the cavernous mouth of a hippopotamus, listen to the song of the whale and come face to face with camels, elephants, porpoises and dolphins.

'Creepy Crawlies' is not for those who are scared of spiders. The room seethes with centipedes, crabs, spiders and insects all known as arthropods. Watch out for the claws and poisonous sting of the scorpion, investigate the metamorphosis of the caterpillar and gaze up at the life-sized towering termite mound. Nerve yourself to enter No 1 Crawley House to meet the Arthropods that share your own home.

Find out about human biology, (there is a model of a seven month unborn baby looking very worried) about evolution, the origin of the species, minerals, rocks, meteorites, gemstones and fossils.

You cannot possibly cope with all this in one visit but make sure you have time for the museum's brilliant hands-on 'Discovery Centre'. It is geared for seven to eleven year olds, though our four year old was intrigued. Touch the specimens and talk to the helpful museum staff about the python's skin, a penguin's wing, the sword of a swordfish. Reach into the 'feely box' to identify the mysterious objects within. Elephant's tooth? Ammonite? Coral? Make and launch a winged paper seed and see how far it travels. Collect data all about yourself: what sort of earlobes do you have? Which leg do you hop on? Can you twist your tongue? What are your fingerprints like? Our eleven year old managed to pick up ninety eight beans in one hand. Beat that!

The Natural History Museum.

MOMI, The Museum of the Moving Image
South Bank
Waterloo
London SE1 8XT
071 401 2636.
Group Bookings 071 928 3535

○ 10am-6pm every day, last admission 5pm.
  Closed 24, 25, 26 December.

£ Adult £5.50, Child £4.00, Under Five free,
  OAP/Student £4.70, Family Ticket £16.00

P Beneath Royal National Theatre, Hayward
  Gallery & Jubilee Gardens

🚇 Underground Embankment, Waterloo.
  BR Waterloo.
  Buses 1,5,68,70,N96,171,171,177,188.

♿ wheelchair users are advised to book in
  advance for assistance. Pushchair access
  difficult.

✗ restaurant and nearby picnic area

Top: Making zoetrope strips at MOMI.
Above: MOMI has actor-guides like this
'usherette' to help young visitors.

The Museum of the Moving Image, the 'world's most exciting cinema and television museum', is vibrant and exciting. It is also overwhelming. You and your children might feel bombarded. How to make sense of it all? We suggest you follow the yellow brick arrows and keep a weather eye open for the 'Pacing the Museum' signs. Spend some time on the early part of the museum, resisting the temptation to rush blindly onwards, where there is much to find out about the development of the moving image.

Here is the terrifyingly realistic Phantasmagoria, a magic lantern show with bloodthirsty images projected into clouds of smoke. There are thaumatrope discs to spin, zoetropes to rotate, peepshow what-the-butler-saw mutascopes to run. You might even catch one of MOMI's regular magic lantern shows.

En route you can talk to MOMI's actor guides: a magic lanternist, a guard on a Russian agit-prop train or a uniformed commissionaire. The Film director in the Art Deco Odeon might lure you into having a film test on his Hollywood studio set. Watch MOMI's animator in residence in a small studio workshop making cartoons or models for a future film.

Look at the video of 'precious moments in cinema' where images from kisses to slaps to car crashes are rapidly superimposed. Find out about early television, try your hand at reading the News at Ten on the Autocue, have a screen interview with Barry Norman and soar over London like Superman. Meet Storm Troopers and C3PO from Star Wars, Daleks from Doctor Who, an early 'silent' robot called False Maria, and King Kong himself, a 45cm model made of steel, rubber and rabbit fur.

Try out the Youth Culture Juke Box. Pick a topic, such as 'make up' or 'rebels', push a button and let the video play.

Gunnersbury Park Museum
Gunnersbury Park
London W3 8LQ
081 992 1612

○ 1 April-31 October, Monday-Friday 1-5pm,
Saturday and Sunday 1-6pm.
1 November-31 March 1-4pm.
Victorian Kitchens open April-October,
weekends only.
Groups can book.

£ free

P on site

⊞ Underground Acton Town
Bus E3, 7 on Sunday

♿ yes, small step at front door.

✗ café and picnic area

A small local history museum with little to offer on a first impression, but delving further in, you will find many unexpected delights. Once a Rothschild home, it still has their impressive staircase, continental and town carriages rather incongruously displayed in the Rothschild drawing room, and a large elegant room looking out over the park, with a painted ceiling and dark red and gold scagliola pillars.

The library, in spite of unfortunate council 'alterations' in the past, has now been transformed into an exciting costume gallery with displays varying from Victorian bustles to thirties gowns. Some of the museum's costumes are stored in Baroness Rothschild's extensive wardrobes upstairs.

Compare the grandeur of the family's part of the house with the cold, dim corridors in the servants' quarters. In the kitchens you can see the original open and closed ranges installed in the 1840s and 70s. Coming from the Continent and unlike most of their English counterparts, the Rothschilds were obviously keen on the latest, most modern kitchen conveniences. There is a very early gas range, a 'hot' table for keeping dishes warm, a fridge in the shape of a huge oak and zinc-lined cupboard with a compartment on the top for blocks of ice and, a great luxury, a 'retiring room' for the housekeeper. In the 1880s two young French chefs were working in these kitchens. Their employers obviously had little regard fo English cooking. The room once used for rolling out pastry, now has a box mangle and rows of irons.

The museum is making great efforts to be more friendly to children. There is now a policy for specially written and designed captions for children to read and an interactive or hands-on element in the exhibitions. Pinafores, sailor jackets, hats and other costumes can be tried on, hopscotch and Victorian games played with, penny-plain Victorian pictures coloured in, board school desks sat at, work copied on slates and a replica chimney can be climbed and 'swept'.

Outside is a wonderful park with a boating pond, pitch and putt course, a lake, an 18th century temple, playgrounds, a rockery, the Orangery built by Sydney Smirke and mock ruins, put up by the neighbours in next door's mansion, to hide the Rothschild's impressive stables, now sadly neglected.

Victorian games and costumes at Gunnersbury

Model of Captain Cook's *Endeavour*.

Greenwich

Greenwich is known around the world as the setter of GMT. Henry VIII, Elizabeth I and Mary I were born here, a favourite Royal Palace stood here in Tudor times but was destroyed by Cromwell. It is still an elegant and fascinating part of London.

We can thoroughly recommend spending a day in Greenwich as there are so many things to do and see. The Royal Park is a place for families to walk, picnic, watch puppet shows in summer and play in the playground. Then there is the National Maritime Museum, the *Cutty Sark* and the Old Royal Observatory, as well as a walk through the old village of Greenwich itself.

Parking can be difficult but getting here by public transport is fun. Take the Docklands Light Railway to Island Garden, then walk through Brunel's pedestrian tunnel beneath the Thames, using the huge round lifts at either end. Travel by River Bus or Cruise along the river from Charing Cross and Tower Piers. BR trains run from Charing Cross, Waterloo East and London Bridge to Maze Hill. If you are on the 188 bus route you will get here too. How you go about Greenwich is up to you; one warning, the hill up to the Observatory is steep.

National Maritime Museum
Romney Road
Greenwich
London SE10 9NF
081 858 4422

○ 1 April-30 September, Monday-Saturday 10am-6pm, Sunday 12-6pm.
1 October-31 March, Monday-Saturday 10am-5pm, Sunday 2-5pm.
Closed 24, 25, 26 December
£ Adult £3.75, Child £2.75, Under Seven free, OAP/Concessions £2.75
Passport Ticket to all sites: Adult £7.45, Child £5.45, OAP/Concessions £5.45
🅿 nearby
🚇 see above
♿ wheelchair access to 70% of site. Special tours, by arrangement, for visitors with visual or hearing impairments.
✕ restaurant and picnic area.

This is a maritime museum to visit in all weathers as everything is under cover. Situated by the Queen's House it contains a large collection of maritime artefacts, boats and craft from all over the world, dramatic paintings of the sea and ship models. During the summer months the museum puts on a large, specialist exhibition aimed at children. In recent years these have included blockbusters like 'The Armada' and 'Pirates'. They are well worth coming to, but do attract hordes of children, so beware of crowds.

My children of four and six years were enthralled by Neptune Hall where we walked through the engine room of the *Reliant* steam tug, looked into the cabins and then climbed up steep ladders onto the deck. They paced around the huge black funnel and rang the big, shiny bell of the *Mauretania*. From here they saw the lighthouse flashing across the hall and peered over the side into the luxurious, private steam yacht built, in 1893, for Alfred Palmer, of biscuit fame. We were all surprised to see the cabin table set for tea with china teacups and Huntley and Palmer Bourbon biscuits. How different this lifestyle was, cruising along the upper reaches of the Thames, compared to the drudgery and muck of hard work on the *Reliant*.

We climbed down to ground level and looked at the variety of small sailing craft from all over the world, at the models of North Sea oil drilling rigs and then at the array of ship figureheads. From the brightness and noise of Neptune Hall we were surprised by the darkness of the Barge House. Do not expect to find the craft we see on the Inland Waterways of Britain but the most elegant, almost fairy like barges belonging to Queen Mary. Look for Neptune, seahorses, fish and other sea creatures in the intricate carvings, encrusted with gold. Look at the richness of the interiors with their red and deep pink upholstery. My children thought they were in another world.

We came back to earth and looked at the archaeology of boats and found some very old ones. The work of the archaeologist and restorer was described and shown. Older children, eager to find out about 20th century sea power, are fascinated by the operations room, submarine, radar and videos.

I was fascinated by the drama of the huge paintings of rough seas, battles and bravery in the maritime works of Turner, Reynolds, Canaletto and others. Paintings such as these are an important historical record of life at sea and should be regarded, like modern photography and film, as documentary evidence of what actually took place.

Outside the museum there is a boat-shaped climbing frame which was covered with children; no one seemed to mind two more joining the voyage.

The Queens House
Romney Road
Greenwich
London SE10 9NF
081 858 4422

○ 1 April-30 September, Monday-Saturday, 10am-6pm, Sunday 12-6pm.
1 October-31 March, Monday-Saturday 10am-5pm, Sunday 2-5pm.
Closed 24, 25, 26 December.

£ Adult £3.75, Child £2.75, Under Seven free, OAP/Concessions £2.75
Passport Ticket to all sites: Adult £7.45, Child £5.45, OAP/Concessions £5.45

🅿 nearby

🚻 see above

♿ wheelchair access to 40% of the site. Special tours, by arrangement, for visitors with hearing or visual impairments.

✗ restaurant and picnic area.

We recommend a visit to the Queens House for older children interested in history and architecture. This beautiful building was designed by Inigo Jones and completed in 1635 for the lavish tastes of Charles I's wife, Henrietta Maria. It has recently been restored to its original splendour and you can see how royalty lived. There are silk tapestries, a renowned collection of 17th century paintings and beautiful furniture. Look into the brick vaults and see the Treasury.

The *Cutty Sark*
King William Walk
Greenwich
London SE10 9HT
081 858 3445, recorded information
081 853 3589

○ 1 April-30 September, Monday-Saturday 10am-6pm, Sunday 12-6pm.
1 October-31 March, Monday-Saturday, 10am-5pm, Sunday 12-5pm.
Closed 24, 25, 26 December.

£ Adult £3.25, Child £2.25, Under Seven free, OAP/Concessions £2.25
Passport to all sites: Adult £7.45, Child £5.45, OAP/Concessions £5.45

🅿 no

🚻 see above

♿ limited

✗ no

In the centre of Greenwich, in what would have been the quay, stands the *Cutty Sark*; you cannot miss it. This clipper, with its 152 foot mainmast, was launched on the Clyde in 1869. She was originally designed to transport tea from China but her main voyages were

ringing cargoes of wool from Sydney to
London. Climb aboard and walk round
the decks, go into the dry-dock to see
beneath the water line, then go below
deck and find the cabins and an audio-
visual presentation on the life of the
Cutty Sark.

The Old Royal Observatory
Greenwich Park
London SE10 9NF
081 858 4422

○ 1 April-30 September, Monday-Saturday 10am-
6pm, Sunday 12-6pm.
1 October-31 March, Monday-Saturday 10am-
5pm, Sunday 2-5pm
£ Adult £3.75, Child £2.75, Under Seven free,
OAP/Concessions £2.75
Passport Ticket to all sites: Adult £7.45, Child
£5.45, OAP/Concessions £5.45
🅿 on site
🚌 see above
♿ about 20% accessible to wheelchairs. Special
tours, by prior arrangement, for visitors with
visual and hearing impairments.
✗ restaurant and picnic area.

We have spent many lazy summer
afternoons sitting at the top of the hill in
Greenwich Park, outside the Old Royal
Observatory, looking down on some of
the finest architecture in Britain. At the
foot of the hill is the Queen's House,
built by Inigo Jones in 1635. The
delicate, colonnaded walkways, on
either side, emphasise the proportions
and elegance of this building. Beyond it,
providing a gateway to the river are the
two arms of the Royal Hospital built in
1663 by John Webb, a pupil of Inigo
Jones. I am always astounded at the
symmetry of the architecture and try to
find a spot where I can look 'straight
down the middle' and into the Thames
and across to the Isle of Dogs. The
National Maritime Museum is now
housed in this complex and the Royal
Hospital is still partly used as such by
the Royal Navy. Across the river is the
Isle of Dogs and the contrast between
elegant, maritime Greenwich and the
old docks of the Port of London, now
being revamped by property developers
into Docklands, is great. We often
imagine what it must have been like
when cargo ships and steamers
chugged up and down this river, to and
from all parts of the globe.

The Old Royal Observatory was built
by Sir Christopher Wren for Charles II.
On our last visit we played games as we
stood on either side of Longitude 0,
outside the Meridian Building. This is

The *Cutty Sark's* masts and rigging tower over
the visitor.

the base point of world time, known as
Greenwich Mean Time, GMT. In
Flamsteed House we learnt about time
keeping, ways in which people have told
the time in the past and the latest
atomic and quartz clocks. Then we
looked at the old telescopes and the
rooms in which the Astronomer Royal
once lived. Inside the Meridian Building,
we looked at the ways movements of
stars are charted and used for
navigation. Finally, we climbed up to the
giant telescope in the Equatorial
Building and felt we had been privy to
the romantic, exciting and dangerous
world of the seaman.

GREATER MANCHESTER

Museum of Science and Industry in Manchester
Liverpool Road
Castlefield
Manchester M3 4JP
061 832 2244

O 10am-5pm every day.
Closed 23, 24,25 December
£ Adult £3.50, Child £1.50, Under Five free,
OAP/Students £1.50
P on site
🚌 bus 33 from Piccadilly bus station
♿ to most parts
✕ café. Picnic area nearby

Go from Roman sewers to outer space in seven acres here at this marvellous, non-stop, interactive museum. Children of all ages, and adults are introduced to the fascinating world of experimental science and the development of industry. In fourteen galleries you can find out about the history of Manchester even how it smelt. Follow the development of energy sources to power homes and industry, steam engines and textile machines.

As there is so much to see, we suggest that you allow at least three hours for your visit. It is not uncommon for children to spend an hour in 'Xperiment' on the second floor. This is a permanent hands-on interactive science gallery, where different work stations focus on various themes like light, energy and magnetism. You can try to create your own laser patterns, conduct electricity, find out how solar power works, take a picture of your own

The world's 'oldest' railway booking hall!

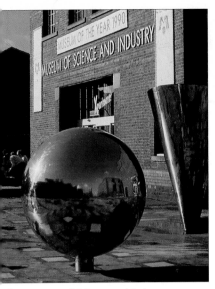

The Museum of Science and Industry.

the Future Exhibition' where you can learn all about nuclear power and use the visual data base terminal to find out how much radiation you might be subjected to at home and at work.

The museum itself is located in the buildings of Liverpool Road Station, the oldest passenger railway station in the world. It was from here that Stephenson's *Rocket* steamed down the line to Liverpool.

Go beneath the streets in 'Underground Manchester' and trace the history of this city from Roman times to the present. There are Roman water supply systems and a reconstructed Victorian sewer with sounds and smells! Then on to the 'Booking Hall' of the world's oldest (1830) passenger railway.

The 'Air and Space Gallery' is a museum on its own but is included in the overall admission price. On the ground floor there are aeroplanes, some with cut-out sections to show engines and plane interiors. Information panels explain about the history of flight and have features on specialised aircraft. Upstairs in the 'Out of This World' space gallery, you can play inter-active video games with facts about the planets and Voyager space flight visuals. Visit the galactic travel agency and organise day trips and scenic routes to different planets. Find out about gravity and space travel. Relax, watching videos of old sci-fi films in a 1950s sitting room. Have fun looking at our ideas of extra-terrestrials.

The museum runs children's workshops in the summer holidays; these are very popular so book in advance.

shadow, shake hands with yourself and play optical snooker. There are helpers to answer questions and introduce you to new concepts. Under fives can play in the special play area and parents can sit and relax whilst their children enjoy themselves.

In the same building are the 'Textile, Machine Tools and Printing Galleries', all part of Manchester's industrial history. Here and in the 'Power Hall', with the largest collection of working mill steam engines in the world, demonstrators show how the machines work. Find the 1930s and 1950s kitchens and living rooms in the 'Gas and Electricity Galleries'.

The large 'Computer Gallery' has some enormous, early computers as well as more streamlined up-to-date models. Try your hand at some word processing at the two terminal work stations. Go upstairs to the 'Energy for

Former Pakistan Railways steam locomotive.

MERSEYSIDE

Liverpool, easily accessible by road (M62 and M57) and rail from all parts of the North West, has three of the most exciting museums in the country, all close together. So a day here will be well spent.

Merseyside Maritime Museum and the Tate Gallery Liverpool are both situated in the restored Albert Dock, part of the largest collection of Grade 1 listed buildings in the country. Liverpool Museum with its large and fascinating collections is nearby in William Brown Street. Do be careful with children along the Dock; quaysides and machinery can be dangerous, so make sure they are accompanied at all times.

Liverpool Museum
William Brown Street
Liverpool L3 8EN
051 207 0001

O Monday-Saturday 10am-5pm. Sunday 12 noon-5pm.
Natural History Centre open every afternoon except Monday.

£ free, small fee for Planetarium

P in front of museum

🚆BR Lime Street

♿ yes

✗ restaurant

All ages love Liverpool Museum. The collections are well presented with both children and adults in mind. There is a lively programme of family events which includes storytelling and dancing, crafts and environmental issues. If you live locally you can just pop in for a few minutes and see your favourite thing or come for longer - a whole day if you are really smitten. If you want to visit the planetarium you must buy a ticket from the museum shop on the ground floor. During the holidays the museum staff run a Discovery Centre with lots of workshops for children to handle objects, make pots, try out musical instruments. (Ring for details.)

The collections range from the Aquarium and Vivarium, to dinosaurs, ceramics, transport, space, ethnography and ancient history. The museum has an excellent collection of masks.

Start your tour on the ground floor, check the Temporary Exhibition Area. Then go into the Ceramics Department where you can see decorative ceramics from medieval times to the present. Computer terminal data bases give detailed information about the craftspeople, style and materials. Go through the King's Regiment display and look at the view from the World War 1 trench.

Into the basement and the Aquarium and Vivarium which is always popular with children and see the large collection of cold water and tropical fish and animals. Look at Liverpool's transport facilities from the 19th century onwards in the Transport Gallery.

Take the lift to the third floor, have a drink if you need to in the coffee bar. In the Space Gallery find out about satellites and space technology and then sit back in a comfortable chair in the Planetarium and watch the heavens open above you. There are marvellous shows on star patterns, planets, eclipses and the search to find life on other planets.

Come back to earth and walk down to the natural history section which takes up the whole of the second floor. As you enter look out for the footprint of Merseyside's own dinosaur found on the Wirral. The Natural History Centre is open every afternoon, except Monday,

The Planetarium is one of the top attractions at the Liverpool Museum.

and is a marvellous place for the whole family to explore the natural world. Specimens of rocks and minerals can be handled and insects examined under a microscope linked to a video camera. There are computer data bases to provide more information as well as a highly sophisticated one to enable you to analyse different geographical features. Demonstrators are on hand to help and answer questions.

Also on this floor are excellent displays on evolution, human history and dinosaurs.

Go downstairs to the first floor and the wonderful collection of Antiquities and Ethnography. Here you will find the Egyptian mummy of Peduamum, Benin bronzes, a North American Indian totem pole, masks from Africa and Papua New Guinea, Anglo Saxon tools and artefacts and evidence of life in early Britain.

Return to the ground floor and you will have had a most stimulating and exciting tour round the museum and will no doubt want to return for more at a later stage.

Merseyside Maritime Museum
Albert Dock
Liverpool L3 4AA
051 207 0001

○ 10.30am-5.30pm last ticket sold at 4.30pm
£ Adult £2.50, Child £1.25, Under Five free, OAP £1.25, Family Ticket £7.00. Reductions for local residents. Passport Ticket available, valid for one year.
🅿 on site
🚌 bus every 20 minutes from city centre to Albert Dock complex.
♿ yes
✗ restaurant. Picnic areas along the Dock.

The Albert Docks and River Mersey are perfect locations for this museum which occupies several buildings and vessels, devoted to the history of the port of Liverpool. The museum is large; we suggest a half day for your visit. Because of the proximity to the quay, parents are strongly warned to keep a close eye on children, especially under fives.

The splendid dockside setting of the Merseyside Maritime Museum.

There are many outdoor events on the water including real and model sailing boat races, divers identifying items from the depths of the sea and sea shanty singing sessions. In the summer there are lots of hands-on activities for the whole family with microscopes, computers and videos.

During the last century and for much of this, Liverpool was the last place in Europe for many thousands of desperate refugees and others wanting a new and better life in America. Some of them had trekked so far across Europe, many from Russia, that by the time they reached Liverpool they thought they were in America. Here, in the 'Emigrants to a New World Exhibition' (Main Building) you can see and experience, with actors, the gruelling time they had in Liverpool, during their voyage and on their landing at Ellis Island in 1850. You can feel the swell of the ocean beneath your feet, and imagine the anxiety and anticipation of the emigrants.

Look at the fully furnished Piermaster's House next door and then the display of barrel making in the Cooperage (not suitable for wheelchairs). Across the dock is the Pilotage Building and Boat Hall. Outside, wander around the Maritime Park to see boats like the *Edmund Gardner* pilot cutter which you can climb aboard and really explore, as well as many other sailing craft. Find the anchors in the heavy metal area on the corner of Canning Dock.

During your visit spare some time to look at the docks. Imagine the noise and bustle when they were really booming, unloading their cargoes of bananas and cotton as well as the numerous emigrants searching for a better life across the ocean.

Tate Gallery Liverpool
Albert Dock
Liverpool L3 4BB
051 709 3223
Information line 051 709 0507

○ Tuesday-Sunday 10am-6pm.
   Closed Monday except Bank Holiday Monday.
£ Free. Charges to special exhibitions.
P Albert Dock
🚌 bus every 20 minutes from city centre to Albert Dock
♿ yes
✕ café

The Tate Gallery Liverpool houses the National Collection of Modern Art in the North of England and is situated next door to the Merseyside Maritime Museum. If you have never thought about introducing your children to modern art, now is the time to do it, for they may be introducing you to it! Many children find it easy to relate to modern art; to them it can be stimulating and refreshing. Perhaps their outlook is less jaded than ours? They have the playful minds that many artists try to rediscover and both want to convey their feelings by painting and drawing. So let your children take you on a tour of this marvellous place and be prepared to have your eyes opened.

There are six large galleries at the Tate with changing exhibits. Many are brought from the Tate in London, so it is worth finding out in advance what is on.

The Tate has an excellent education department which runs workshops for children; even three year olds are welcome. They range from plaster casting, sculpture with natural materials, and looking at works of art. Ring to book workshops in advance as they are very popular and allow 3-4 hours for your visit if it includes a workshop.

Liverpool's Tate Gallery successfully blends a modern conversion into a traditional setting.

MIDDLESEX

Kew Bridge Steam Museum
Green Dragon Lane
Brentford TW8 0EN
Middlesex
081 568 4757

O 11am-5pm every day.
  Engines 'in steam' weekends 11am-5pm.
  Closed Christmas week & Good Friday
£ Weekdays: Adult £1.70, Child 90p, Under Five
  free, OAP 90p, Family Ticket £4.75.
  Weekends: Adult £2.50, Child £1.40, Under Five
  free, OAP £1.40, Family Ticket £7.25
P on site
Underground Gunnersbury then bus 237, 267,
  65, 391. 7 on Sunday.
ground floor only
café

The Victorian brick standpipe tower of
Kew Bridge Pumping Station is a local
landmark and holds its own against the
modern tower blocks nearby. Once
inside the former Grand Junction
Waterworks Company's Pumping
Station, you enter a different world: the
successful and celebrated world of 19th
century industry. Near the Thames, this
was an excellent site for the giant
Cornish pumping engines to draw the
water supply for London.

These massive beam pumping
engines tower impressively over the
visitor. You can walk in amongst them,
climb up a steep stairway to the dizzy
heights of the beam floor of the Grand
Junction 90in Engine, right up in the
roof of the building. Here you get a
close view of the crank wheels and
beams of the world's largest working
beam engine. Every weekend,
throughout the year, you can watch
these giant engines judder into action,
revealing the astonishing power of
steam, pumping one hundred and thirty
gallons of water at a stroke. You can
see the waterwork's railway, a working
forge and a 19th century machine shop.

The engines are elegantly designed
and beautifully painted. The most
recently acquired was working until
1940. Underneath its flaking, battleship-
grey paint, was revealed the original
gold and brown. Now restored, it is run
and maintained by the museum's band
of steam enthusiasts: you can recognise
them immediately. I know the type well
because my brother is one of them.
They are usually wearing filthy trousers
and clutch an old rag with which they
polish their engine and then their hands
and faces which are permanently black
from oil. But inwardly they glow. They
tend their engines with loving care,
coaxing them into life, polishing them so
they shine, proudly extolling their virtues
to anybody who has time and patience
to listen. If your children show signs of
similar enthusiasm then they are a lost
cause. The steam buff likes to catch
them at an early age.

Escape while you can, and walk a
few yards down the road to the Musical
Museum.

Musical Museum
368 High Street
Brentford
Middlesex TW8 0BD
081 560 8108

O July and August Wednesday-Sunday 2-5pm.
  April-October, Saturday and Sunday 2-5pm.
£ Adult £2.80, Child £2.00, Under Five free,
  OAP/concessions £2.00, Family Ticket £8.00
P in North Road
Underground Gunnersbury. BR Kew Bridge.
  Bus 237, 267, 65
Disabled visitors should ring in advance. No
  toilets for disabled
No

Find the automatic musical instruments,
including a giant Wurlitzer pipe organ in
this deserted church. There are one and
a half hour demonstration tours and
fortnightly evening concerts. Send a
SAE for details and booking.

Within sight you will find Watermans
Arts Centre, where you can eat and
drink, listen to the music, join
workshops or enjoy the theatre or
cinema. Children very welcome.

Watermans Arts Centre
40 High Street
Brentford
Middlesex TW8 0DS
081 568 1176 Box Office

O Tuesday-Sunday 12.30-6.30pm
£ Free except to theatre, cinema etc. Discounts
  Tuesday-Thursday available to OAP,
  concessions and children
P on site
BR Kew Bridge. Underground South Ealing,
  Gunnersbury. Bus 65, 237, 267, N97
yes
Bar and café.

WEST MIDLANDS

Birmingham Museum and Art Gallery
Chamberlain Square
Birmingham B3 3DH
021 235 2834

○ Monday-Saturday 11am-5pm, Sunday 11am-5.30pm
£ free
🅿 nearby
🚍 BR Birmingham New Street, city centre bus routes
♿ yes, from Edmund Street entrance
✕ restaurant

Do not be daunted by the immensity of this museum. It is a fascinating place, well endowed by Birmingham's wealthy Victorian patriarchs and packed full of objects relating to the city's social and industrial past. It was the city's first purpose-built museum and opened in 1885. Staff are very friendly and helpful. There is lots to interest children as well as a programme of workshops. This museum is vast, forty-three galleries altogether.

We recommend these galleries:- natural history; archaeology; the Pinto Collection of wooden bygones - pipes, matches, farm implements and furniture; pre-Raphaelite paintings; stained glass; ceramic tiles; metalwork and jewellery; fashion; ethnography and ancient people; local history.

Perhaps the most memorable aspect of our visit here was the excellent way in which the museum has looked at Birmingham's multicultural population in the 1990s. There was an exhibition of photographs from India and a most stimulating gallery, number 33, devoted to the major religions of the world. Here you can find out about the similarities and differences between different groups. Find out how Hindus, Muslims, Buddhists, Jews and Christians make music, dance, cook food, dress, celebrate festivals, cope with death. Display cases are full of relevant artefacts and the gallery hums with global music. Databases provide information and you can even trace your ancestors. This was a very enriching and positive place to be.

When you leave the Museum and Art Gallery do find time to visit the Museum of Science and Industry a short walk away.

Museum of Science and Industry
Newhall Street
Birmingham B3 1RZ
021 235 1661

○ Monday-Saturday 11am-5pm, Sunday 11am-5.30pm
£ free
🚍 West Midlands 101 Bus Service stops at the entrance
♿ good access for wheelchairs though a little help will be needed from staff. Pushchairs must be left at reception.
✕ picnic area next door in Canning Walk overlooking the canal.

Walk into this museum and you are immediately surrounded by the might, splendour and noise of machines. The 'Light on Science' gallery is full of hands-on exhibits for children to explore with helpful staff to answer questions.

Throughout the year there are steam days, traction engine rallies and other events relating to the exhibits. Children are delighted at the locomotive in the Locomotive Hall which actually moves on the hour, every hour; the tramcar and the cars and motorcycles which are all part of Birmingham's industrial history. Upstairs, in the Science Section, see the first light bulbs, early X-ray machines, telegraph and telephone systems and find out how a loud-speaker works. From here you can pass into a small gallery of pens and grandfather clocks and then wander round the RAF Spitfire and Hawker Hurricane in the Aircraft Section. Don't miss the Replica Workshops to see the dirty, cramped conditions in which these fine pieces of engineering and craft were made. By now you will

A young lad about to learn about gyroscopes at Birmingham Museum of Science.

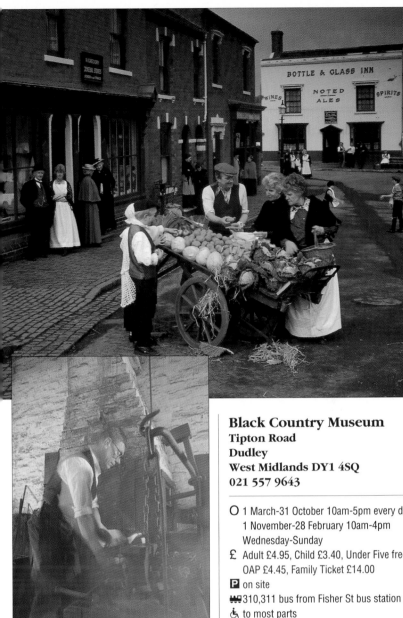

Above & top: The Village at the Black Country Museum is a hive of activity.

Black Country Museum
Tipton Road
Dudley
West Midlands DY1 4SQ
021 557 9643

○ 1 March-31 October 10am-5pm every day
   1 November-28 February 10am-4pm
   Wednesday-Sunday
£ Adult £4.95, Child £3.40, Under Five free,
   OAP £4.45, Family Ticket £14.00
🅿 on site
🚌310,311 bus from Fisher St bus station
♿ to most parts
✗ restaurant and picnic area

The Black Country Museum is an open-air museum of the social and industrial history of Dudley and surrounding towns. Established in 1975, it is situated on a twenty six acre site in Dudley itself. As most of the museum is outdoors it is best to visit on a fine day.

This is a large and fascinating place for children, parents and grandparents and it is definitely worth planning to spend a day here. There are lots of rest places - pubs, restaurants and picnic areas as well as a tram and bus system to get around the site. For the really ambitious there is a guided canal trip through the caves. Our two under fives thoroughly enjoyed themselves and talked about Dudley for weeks afterwards.

Walk through the entrance building to

have walked through an unusual building, part of which used to be Elkington's Electro Plating factory, with its odd ceilings, narrow corridors and passageways. Make your way back to the Locomotive Hall and see the engine move. Then, go up to Level 1, and the Smethwick Engine which is the oldest working steam engine in the world.

This is a marvellous collection showing the history of science and industry as well as the breadth of the craftsmanship in Birmingham, from huge, powerful engines to the fine work of pens and jewellery.

Above & top: A miner and a chemist at work in the museum.

the Depot where you will be transported on one of the many trolley buses and trams to various destinations on the site. If there is a wait, look around the garage at all the vehicles being renovated; they are like mechanical skeletons at various stages of revitalisation. Your bus or tram conductor, maybe the inspector if you are lucky, will give you a ticket from his ticket machine, press the bell and you are off. Note how low the bus ceilings are, the 'No Spitting' signs, the conductor's uniform, all very different from today's driver-operated vehicles. There is a driving post at each end of the tram.

The first stop is the Village. Seen from the bus stop on the hill above it looks like a well established, bustling, industrial community. However, all the buildings have been transported here and the Village reconstructed for the museum. On fine days girls, in long black skirts and crocheted shawls, sit on the pavement to welcome the visitors. They sell sweets — humbugs and milk bottles — from their large baskets and demonstrate old fashioned toys and games. Our family spent ages with the cup and ball, diabolo, hoops, skittles and trying to skip with rope threaded

into old shuttles for handles. There were heated discussions between others about the regional variations of hopscotch — how did we do it in London? in Lancashire? in Glasgow? Such simple toys but so time consuming and a wonderful introduction to this lively museum.

You can walk around the shops and houses in the village. Huge dressers and chairs fill tiny front parlours painted eau-de-nil green. Through the scullery and out into the yard there is the privy with its wooden seat and torn up newsprint for toilet paper. In the workshop beyond, the glass cutter showed us how to cut glass, a traditional Black Country craft.

In the Bakery you can buy jam and Bakewell tarts. The Hardware Store is hidden beneath an array of tin baths tied to its front (there were no bathrooms, just a tin bath, in front of the kitchen fire). Look at all the corsets, suspenders and trimmings in the Haberdashery and the pills and potions at the Chemist. Go into the cold stark Methodist Chapel for a feel of how Sundays were spent on hard pews after a gruelling, dirty week toiling at work. No wonder the Bottle and Glass Inn, opposite, was such an important place of refuge with its pints of beer and stench of raw and pickled onions.

Go behind the main village street to the canal, which was a vital part of the transport system in this area. You may want to take a guided trip along the canal and through the hill which was originally excavated for its limestone before becoming a complex canal system. This is a damp and dark ride; young children may be rather frightened whilst older ones will find it exciting. Inside the canal chamber look out for fossils and stalactites. Watch the audio-visual show, on the side of the rock, for the geological history of Dudley and see the short drama about the Victorian Earl of Dudley and the gas-lit parties he held here, on the canal inside the hill. Imagine too, the hard graft of those men who dug out the tunnels, for long hours, on their knees without power tools, electricity or safety procedures.

Back in the Village, find the blacksmith with his great fiery furnace, anvil, heat, dirt and sparks.

Children will have great fun at the fairground with its hall of mirrors and what-the-butler-saw. The boat swings need good co-ordination to make them work.

Catch a tram or bus to the Colliery. Coal, limestone, fireclay and ironstone all used to be mined beneath the site and Racecourse Colliery has been built as an example of a small, 1910, local pit. In this drift mine you can wander around the underground roads and safely see the hard conditions in which men and ponies worked for long hours bringing the special Staffordshire Thick Coal to the surface.

It is fascinating to see the life-size reconstruction of one of the first steam engines in the world, originally built on Lord Dudley's estate by Thomas Newcomen in 1712. Who would have thought that this would have brought so much industrial and social change, revolutionising everybody's life?

This is a marvellous museum, well worth a detour and a day's visit and although very young children will not understand the full implications of what they see they will certainly enjoy themselves. Older ones may find some thread of their own family history here as well as being able to see the harshness of industrialisation and the complex way in which a small village knits together to become a unit.

The National Motorcycle Museum
Coventry Road
Bickenhill
Solihull
West Midlands B92 OEJ
0675 443311

○ 10am-6pm every day.
   Closed 24, 25, 26 December
£ Adult £3.75, Child £2.50, Under Five free, OAP £2.50
🅿 on site
🚃 BR Birmingham International.
   Bus Birmingham-Coventry
♿ yes
✕ restaurant

This is definitely a museum for the motorcycle enthusiast. There are over six hundred machines here with examples of every different period, design and purpose from the first beginnings of motorised bicycles in 1898. Many were made in and around Birmingham and famous names abound - Norton, BSA, Wilkinson and Honda. At times the demarcation between a motorcycle and a car seems very narrow, whilst others are more like bicycles. There are wonderful gleaming motorcycles and sidecars, motorcycles used as delivery vehicles, speed bikes as well as various collapsible bikes used by the army.

The role of the motorcycle in the early days of the AA and RAC and in modern police work is not forgotten. Filling five large halls this museum is really for older children with a passion for motorcyles, others may well be disappointed.

Below: A 1912 Wilkinson motorcycle. Manufactured by Wilkinson Sword, makers of razor blades.

Walsall Leather Centre Museum
Wisemore
Walsall WS2 8EQ
West Midlands
0922 721153

O Tuesday-Saturday 10am-5pm, Sunday
  12 noon-5pm
  November-March closes at 4pm
£ free
P in Day Street, opposite
BR Walsall station ½mile
  bus station ½mile.
& Yes
✗ restaurant & picnic area

Walsall has been the centre of saddlery and harness-making in Britain for centuries. However with the advent of the motorcar the craft could have disappeared; it is a tribute to the craftsmen here that they have found a new market, in the production of fine leather goods - belts, handbags, cases, boxes and gloves. This small museum is housed in a Victorian leather goods factory built in 1891. There is a lively programme of practical events in leather craftsmanship throughout the year, many specifically for children.

On the ground floor you can watch and listen to men and women, who have spent all their working lives in the industry, handle and talk about leather. By their descriptions of its various qualities, ways of cutting, sewing and glueing you will see what fine work this

Above: Saddle making at the museum.

is. Around you hang different types of tanned skin; the smell is quite special. Even five year olds are intrigued at this. Upstairs there is a display of the various products, old and new, made by the leather companies of Walsall.

Below: Leatherworkers at Winer and Plant, Walsall 1906

NORFOLK

Cromer Museum

East Cottages
Tucker Street
Cromer NR27 9HB
Norfolk
0263 513543

Monday-Saturday 10am-5pm, Sunday 2-5pm.
Monday closed 1-2pm Closed Christmas week.
Adult £1.00, Child 50p, Under Five free,
OAP/concessions 60p
Season Ticket to all Norfolk Museum Service
Sites-Adult £7.00, Child £1.50,
OAP/Concessions £3.50, Family £14.00
nearby
bus to town centre
no
no

A small, local museum, but we think it is worth dropping in if you are in the area and want a change from the beach. It occupies what was once a row of Victorian fishermen's cottages. There are displays on natural history, fossils and Cromer's fishing and tourist trade. Explore the furnished 1890s home of a local fishing couple. Find out about the famous Cromer Crabs, Henry Bloggs's lifeboat rescues and genteel holidays in Victorian 'Poppyland' with bathing machines and costumes from neck to knee by law.

Local children can come here, dress up in period costume and turn their hands to many things from dolly-pegging, and ironing with flat irons to Victorian cooking. One of them told us that it was 'a nice place full of surprises'.

A fisherman in his cottage at Cromer Museum seems to be having a well-earned rest after a hard day at sea.

Why don't you go and find out what they might be?

When you have been to the museum walk along the promenade and find the Lifeboat, if the large doors at the top of the ramp are open take a look at it; you may be able to go round it. Take the opportunity to see this amazing, tiny boat.

Below: Dolly-pegs and pinnies at Cromer Museum.

Norfolk Rural Life Museum
Beech House
Gressenhall
Dereham
Norfolk NR20 4DR
0362 860563

○ 4 April-31 October, Tuesday-Saturday and Bank Holiday Monday 10am-5pm, Sunday 12 noon-5.30pm

£ Adult £3.00, Child £1.00, Under Five free, OAP/Concessions £2.00

P on site

🚌 bus from Norwich

♿ yes

✗ café and picnic area

A large, welcoming museum for roaming and exploring; outdoors with a picnic if it is fine, indoors down corridors and passages if it is raining.

Housed in a former workhouse, the Norfolk Rural Life Museum is crammed with displays from steam engines to cheese presses, chimney pots to sunbonnets, witches' bottles to pig troughs. There is a wide selection of tools for farming, plumbing, bricklaying, thatching, plastering, glazing and carpentry to name but a few. Walk down Craftsmen's Row where you will find a linen weaver's workshop, a wheelwright, a saddler, a basketmaker and a bakery. Stop at the village shop, which overflows with everything under the sun: pure silk Wolsey stockings to Carter's Little Liver Pills, bottled beer to garden seeds, chocolate to distemper, children's clothes to veterinary products, senna pods to Bluebell metal polish. On the counter are weighing scales, cheese and bacon slicers and a coffee grinder. There is even a cast-iron machine for cleaning currants.

When you finally tear yourself away from the delights of the village shop, go into Cherry Tree Cottage, undoubtedly the best part of the museum. This is not just another museum display of period room settings but an entire cottage and garden typical of the early part of this century. There are no museum attendants hovering in the background so you can really step out of the role of museum visitor and imagine that you are being received as an important guest in the parlour, admiring the best china and making polite conversation. Perhaps you are sitting over a cup of tea at the kitchen table warming yourself at the coal-fired kitchen range. Nearby a pair of boots is drying out, the clock ticks on the shelf, the flat irons heat up on top of the stove, there is homemade jam in the corner cupboard. In the bedroom one of the children has left an iron hoop leaning against the wall. A reed rattle and a tiny comb and hairbrush have been left lying in the baby's cot.

Wander out of the kitchen door and into the garden, abundant with rambler roses, lavender and sweet peas. All the fruit and vegetables grown here are of varieties developed before 1912. Garden rubbish is composted and mixed with manure to make a heap to grow pumpkins and marrows. Chickens, a rare breed called Norfolk Greys, scratch in a run and the Cherry Tree Cottage rabbit is an Old English White.

Finally, make sure your children find the activities room which is in a separate building with its own little garden. A welcoming sign on the door draws you in. There is a dressing up box, filled with bakers' hats and farmers' smocks. There are puzzles, crayons, drawing paper, quiz sheets and even a computer.

A museum to spend a lot of time in with beautiful grounds, a welcoming atmosphere and much to enjoy for all ages.

The 'Wildlife Garden' at Norfolk Rural Life museum.

Bressingham Steam Museum
Bressingham
Diss IP22 2AB
Norfolk
37 988 382/386

○ Easter-31 October 10am-5.30pm every day
  Adult £3.50, Child £2.50, Under Four free,
  OAP £2.50
  Season Ticket Adult £12.50, Child £8.50
☐ on site
⊟ BR Diss 3 miles
⚲ yes
⚲ restaurant picnic area nearby

Here is a museum both for train buffs, eager to do some serious 'train spotting' and young children who want to climb into the cab of a locomotive, have a train ride with a footplate demonstration up beside the driver of a standard gauge engine or ride the famous Victorian Gallopers roundabout.

One of the most renowned locomotives in the world, the *Royal Scot*, is on display among at least fifteen others in the locomotive sheds. The Norwegian State Railway's *King Haakon 7* steams regularly along a half mile track; the Royal Coach No 396, built at York in 1908 for King Edward VII and Queen Alexandra, is here. Visitors can climb up alongside the saloon and look in at the plush sofas, elegant writing table and chairs.

There are also traction engines, (two named *Bertha* and *Brenda*) steam wagons (*Brutus* and *Boadicea*) and fire engines. Paradise for those fascinated by steam, especially those who might want to relive their childhood ambitions of being engine drivers. For those not so keen, there are six acres of Alan Bloom's beautiful dell garden to enjoy.

One word of warning: each ride has to be paid for on top of the entrance fee so it can get expensive.

Below: Traction engines at Bressingham.
Bottom: Steam trains and steam gallopers, not to be missed at Bressingham.

The Thursford Collection
Thursford
Fakenham NR21 0AS
Norfolk
0328 878477

O April & May - ring to check opening times, June-August 11am-5pm, September & October 1-5pm. Closed winter.

£ Adult £4.20, Child £1.80, Under Four free, OAP £3.80

P on site

& yes

✕ café and picnic area

A Gondola switchback ride, a children's Gallopers Ride, a Wurlitzer organ and a children's adventure play area surround the traction engines at the Thursford Collection. Lots to do and lots to eat at the pantry and ice cream parlour.

The Muckleburgh Collection
Weybourne
Near Sheringham
Holt NR25 7EG
Norfolk
026 370210/608

O 22 March-1 November, 10am-5pm every day

£ Adult £3.00, Child £1.60, Under Five free, OAP £2.50, Family Ticket £7.80

P on site

🚌 bus Sheringham-Holt

& yes

✕ restaurant and picnic area

Here is the ultimate collection of 'living military history'; two thousand exhibits from working World War 2 tanks to Iraqi AA guns captured in Kuwait, all displayed in the Weybourne Military Camp, one of the main live firing training camps for 'Ack Ack' Command in World War 2. The old camp NAAFI building was restored in 1987 and converted into a military museum. Here are vehicles, tanks, heavy artillery and armour from all over the world, even from Goose Green in the Falkland Islands. The Museum is understandably proud of the collection of early uniforms, helmets, regimental banners and rifles from the Suffolk and Norfolk Yeomanry, founded in 1782. Look out for the elegant dress uniforms, cocked hats and the World War 2 horse's gas mask. Children can touch the tanks, man the guns (within limits), see the new working M47 General Patton battle tank and climb aboard a Gama Goat, an articulated US Army Truck, for an exciting coastal reconnaissance ride

down to the sea.

Events include commemorations, parades, bands, demonstrations and 'battles' with 'enemy troops' being deployed. If there is a veteran in your family then this must be the place for him to relive some memories with grandchildren. Great grandchildren might prefer the bouncy castle!

Bridewell Museum
Bridewell Alley
off Bedford Street
Norwich
0603 667228

O Monday-Saturday 10am-5pm

£ Adult £1.00, Child 50p, Under Five free, OAP/Concessions 70p

P nearby

🚌 bus to Castle Museum

& ground floor only

✕ no

This museum clusters round a quiet courtyard off Bridewell Alley and was originally a medieval merchant's house and later a prison for beggars and tramps. Now it is filled to the brim with things that Norwich people made and used in the past.

The first room you find yourself in has a delicious jumble of objects from a 1930s black perming machine with dangling elements to a two phase traffic signal control unit.

We thought the best thing here was the pharmacy. You'll walk through the door and be quite surprised not to see the pharmacist standing behind the counter. Here are the 'drug runs' or rows of mahogany drawers each labelled with their contents, the pots and jars, the pestle and mortar, the pill maker and box for silvering pills. Above the door are the carboys filled with coloured water, the symbol of the chemist's shop. Nearby are the charts for testing eyesight, one with pictures for those who could not read. Pinned up is a list of '50 Don'ts for the use of Chemists, their Assistants and Apprentices'. One of them reads 'Don't talk religion or politics in your shop', another 'Don't omit to smile when the 100th child asks for change for 6d'. 'Don't make fun of customers who ask for hikey pikey' (hiera picra, a compound of aloes and canella bark used as a laxative). Wander on and you will find displays of food, markets, textiles, printing, building and brewing, a wonderful collection of shoes and two very early fire engines.

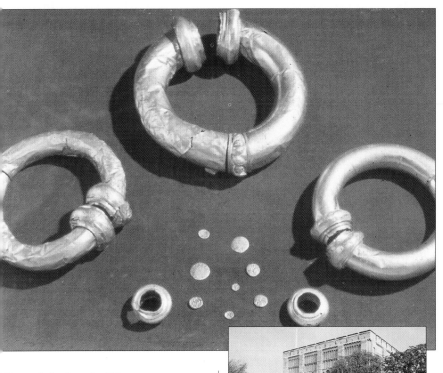

Norwich Castle Museum
Norwich NR1 3JU
Norfolk
0603 223624

○ 10am-5pm Monday-Saturday, Sunday 2-5pm.
£ Adult £1.60, Child 60p, Under Five free,
OAP £1.20
Season Ticket to Norfolk Museum Service sites
Adult £7.00, Child £1.50, Concession £4.50,
Family £14.00 allows admission to Norfolk
Museum Service sites throughout the county.
🅿 nearby
🚉 BR and bus station 10-15 minutes walk
♿ yes
✕ café and picnic area

Top: Torcs only recently discovered on view in the castle
Above: The Norwich Castle Museum.

The variety of things to see here is amazing. What other castle in Britain houses a stuffed duck-billed platypus, a mummified cat, a suit of armour, a 1930s teapot in the shape of Humpty Dumpty, a penknife belonging to Nelson, a trepanned skull, hoards of buried treasure, beautiful paintings and hundreds more?

This is a busy, humming museum with lots to see and do. Children were handling live snakes the day we were there. We found ourselves a base at one of the tables in the central café in the rotunda and spread out in all directions, returning when we needed to make contact with each other. One member of our family insisted on staying there to colour and fill in the quiz sheets nearby until she was carried away by the enthusiasm of the others. Enthusiasm did indeed grow and our initial impressions of a slightly old-fashioned, musty museum turned to surprise and delight as we made sorties from our table and plunged further in to discover more of the castle's hidden wealth.

We each chose our favourite teapot; we identified as many animals as we could; we stopped to look at a Staffordshire pottery figure of James Rush, a murderer hanged at Norwich Castle; we marvelled at the bronze and gold torcs in recently discovered treasure; we dropped coins down into the depths of the castle well and all made a wish. We loved Snapdragon, flying victoriously over the Castle's 12th century stone keep, the fearsome opponent to St George and once part of a medieval pageant of the Guild of St George. We went on the battlements and into the dungeons where we discovered some of the castle's deeper secrets. We forgot it was raining outside and that we had wanted to go to the beach.

Strangers Hall
Charing Cross
Norwich
Norfolk
0603 667229

○ Monday-Saturday 10am-5pm
£ Adult £1.00, Child 50p, Under Five free,
  OAP/Concessions 70p
P nearby
& ground floor only
✕ no

If you have some time to spend in Norwich then go to Strangers Hall. It has a wonderful atmosphere, unlike a museum. The building dates back to about 1320 with period room displays showing how people lived from Tudor to Victorian times. This is the place for anybody 'doing' the Tudors and Stuarts or the Victorians at school.

Standing in the Great Hall, climbing the staircase and peeping into bedrooms gives you a good idea of 16th and 17th century rooms. On one of the beds is a 'bed-waggon' for heating; hot embers were placed in a pan on the iron plate and the blankets were arranged over the hoops to air. Nearby is a wooden baby walker. Look out for the toys, the tiny button boots laid out by the fire in the Victorian night nursery, an 18th century sedan chair, Norwich tradesmen's signs and a box mangle, once filled with stones to press sheets wrapped round rollers.

Punch and Judy at Strangers Hall.

NORTHUMBERLAND

Border History Museum
Old Gaol
Near the Market Place
Hexham
Northumberland
0434 604011 ext 2349

○ Easter-31 October, Monday-Saturday
10am-4.30pm
May-30 September every day 10am-4.30pm
February-Easter and November Monday and
Tuesday 10am-4.30pm.
£ Adult £1.20, Child 50p, Under Five free,
OAP 50p
🅿 nearby
🚅 BR, Bus Station Hexham
♿ no
✗ picnic area nearby.

This small town, set in the rolling
Northumberland landscape, is an ideal
base should you want to go a few miles
further north to Hadrian's Wall. Follow
the signs to the excellent Tourist
Information Centre and in the same
building find the Border History
Museum.

This small museum is housed in the
Old Gaol which, in 1330, was the first
purpose-built gaol in England. It is made
of stone from the local Roman remains
and was in use until 1824. The museum
is on three floors, accessible only by
steep staircases. You will find out about
the frightening lives lived by the people
here, desperate to protect themselves
from attacks. There are lots of
reconstructed situations, models and
gory sounds.

Start on the first floor and find out
about a Border family, concerns about
cross Border marriages, their names
and weapons. Then, across the landing,
look at examples from Border castles
and gaols. There are helmets, armour
and spears on display too.

On the top floor is a reconstructed
blacksmith's shop and in the last gallery
a reconstruction of the Graham family
having a meal amidst the sounds of a
sheep stealing raid. Back downstairs
find the grid on the floor in front of the
shop. Press the button and look down at
the 'prisoner' in the dungeon. He would
have been thrown through the open grid
and left there to die; like the terrible
French 'oubliettes', there were no stairs
or means of escape. Then find another
less gruesome form of punishment, the
stocks.

The Tourist Information Centre,
across the hallway, provides invaluable
advice and information about Hadrian's
Wall and its many sites.

Hadrian's Wall
Whether you travel north up the east or
the west side of England, you cannot
avoid Hadrian's Wall. From Solway in
the west it sweeps magnificently across
eighty Roman miles of hilly terrain to
Wallsend in the east. There are twenty-
five sites along the wall and which you
visit will depend on where you are.

The wall was built by Hadrian and his
armies around AD120. The Romans first
came to Britain in 55BC and tried to
annexe it from AD43. For a considerable
time the wall was the most northern limit
of the Roman empire which stretched to
what is now Iraq and the Sahara desert.
As you drive along the road close by it,
you cannot but be impressed by its
sheer size and strength.

Roman Vindolanda
Chesterholm Museum
Bardon Mill
Hexham
Northumberland NE7 7JN
0434 344277

○ site open every day. November & February
10am-4pm, March & October 10am-5pm, April
&September 10am-5.30pm, May & June
10am-6pm, July & August 10am-6.30pm.
Museum closed November-January, early
February.
£ Adult £3.00, Child £1.75, Under Five free,
OAP/concessions £2.25
🅿 on site
♿ difficult
✗ café

Even if your children are too young to
have learnt about the Romans at school,
a visit to Vindolanda will not be wasted.
Our three year old became totally
involved, her imagination so stimulated
that she was most disappointed not to
meet a Roman here. Vindolanda is one
of the most recent sites to be excavated
and work is still going on. All around,
there are small humps beneath which
there is more 'loot' to be found.

As you begin your tour you will see
the wells and the burial tombs. In the
civil settlement, there are all types of
buildings including a house and mansio
with a latrine, kitchen and bath house.

As you go through the West Gate you enter the Roman Fort, once the headquarters. Although all the examples are ruins they are, nevertheless, quite magnificent; a big hit with children. They can touch the walls, play in the houses and rooms and really experience the scale and sophistication of the buildings.

Do find time to walk to the museum. As you clamber on the hillside you will suddenly find yourselves in the most idyllic landscaped gardens, with a stream and ducks. The museum is to one side of it.

There is a fascinating collection of Roman artefacts, found at Vindolanda, on display. Their preservation is partly due to the Roman system of putting a layer of turf on top of a building and rebuilding above it. The turf acts as a preservative and consequently much has been found intact.

There are leather sandals and shoes (evidence that women lived here as well as men), jewellery, pottery, woven fabrics, and a reconstructed Roman kitchen with a commentary giving a delicious recipe for roast duck and herbs. Older children will find the video presentation, describing the excavations and artefacts, interesting. Others might be enthralled by the scribe and may try to decipher Roman script. As there is so much still to be excavated at Vindolanda, you will no doubt find new things on display next time you go.

Morpeth Chantry Bagpipe Museum
Bridge Street
Morpeth NE61 1PJ
Northumberland
0670 519466

O March-December, Monday-Saturday
9.30am-5.30pm
January-February 10am-4pm
Closed Christmas-New Year.
£ Adult 65p, Child 35p, Under Five free, OAP 35p
P nearby
₩ bus nearby
♿ no wheelchair access. Induction loop for hearing impaired, large print size for sight impaired.
✗ picnic area nearby

If you are near Morpeth then do pay a short visit to this exciting museum full of bagpipes. Not only can you hear them but have a go yourself and listen to the difference between a rant and a reel. The history of Northumberland bagpipes is shown in relation to their development

Early Northumbrian Pipes at Morpeth.

elsewhere – in Scotland, Brittany and India.

Wallington (NT)
Cambo
Morpeth NE61 4AR
Northumberland
0670 74283

O House: 1 April-31 October 1-5.30pm, closed Tuesday.
Walled Garden: 1 April-30 September, 10.30am-7pm every day
1 October-31 March 10.30am-4.30pm.
Grounds: open all year.
£ NT members free, Adult £3.80, Child £1.90, Under Five free, OAP £3.80
P on site
₩ limited local bus service
♿ ground floor only
✗ restaurant and picnic area

This is the National Trust's answer to children and adults, addicted to dolls' houses. Among those on display in the servants' hall at Wallington, is the extraordinary Hammond House, a Victorian manor with 36 rooms, a working lift and running water in the bathroom. There are 77 members of a large family and their servants, a twelve-piece dinner service, ten clocks, 256 minute pictures, diminutive glove stretchers and dice for the backgammon game being played in the smoking room. In the upstairs nursery is a child refusing to eat her rice pudding, spoon thrown on the floor and a scolding nursery maid nearby. The master of the house lies prone in the library after too much port at lunch, while his wife is in a similar state in another room. The name Ruby Hammond is written on a tiny towel – apart from that, there is no other clue as to where the house came from or who it belonged to.

NOTTINGHAMSHIRE

Newark Castle
The Gilstrap Centre
Castlegate
Newark NG24 1BG
Nottinghamshire
0636 611908

○ 1 April-30 September 10am-6pm every day
   1 October-31 March 10am-5pm every day
£ free
🅿 nearby, Tolney Lane
🚌 BR Newark Castle, Bus Station Lombard Street,
   local bus routes.
♿ yes
✗ picnic area

Newark is situated, in what was once, a strategically important position at the crossing of the Fosse Way and the Great North Road. In the early 10th century a defensive settlement was established here to guard against Danish attack. Records show that in 1133 a castle was in existence; King John died here in 1216. During the Civil War, Newark sided with the King and controlled the road to the north and the River Trent. Newark siege pieces were minted here. With King Charles held by the Scots, the castle finally had to surrender in 1646.

The castle itself is a bishop's palace built with a courtyard. If you look at the south-west corner you will see an original tower; there used to be one at each corner of the courtyard. This one tower has four floors and a garderobe or lavatory, waste was poured down a chute into the River Trent below. There were dungeons in the basement.

The Gilstrap Centre, in the castle grounds, houses a collection of artefacts and interactive exhibits.

Brewhouse Yard Museum
Castle Boulevard
Nottingham NG7 1FB
0602 483504 ext 3600

○ Every day. Winter 10am-5pm summer 10am-
   5.30pm. Closed Christmas Day.
£ free Monday-Friday. Weekends & Bank
   Holidays Adult £1.00, Child 50p, Under Five
   free, OAP/concessions 40p
🅿 Castle Road
🚌 bus across the road
♿ to ground floor, caves and garden. No prams
   or pushchairs.
✗ picnic area nearby

Tucked away in the rock beneath the castle, a group of five 17th century cottages provides a wonderful view of all aspects of the lives of the people of Nottingham. There are period rooms and shops, even a 1930s toy shop; caves hewn out of the rock, which served as air raid shelters in World War 2.

Domestic life is shown with a rural, down-hearth kitchen, from the 17th century and a 19th century urban range. You can find out about heating and lighting. Builders tools and materials, as well as displays on back-to-back working-class and middle-class housing are covered in Nottingham Buildings.

Nottingham is famous for its Goosefair and this and other pastimes like cockfighting, bingo and pub games are documented here. In the shopping street you will find examples of ten local traders. Go into the chemist to see his old potions and processes. The 1930s toyshop in Castle Rock House has a collection of new and used toys which would have been on sale in the city. Next door is a schoolroom where you can find out what would have been taught over the last two hundred years.

Castle Museum
Nottingham NG1 6EL
0602 483504

○ 1 April-30 September 10am-5.45pm
   1 October-31 March 10am-4.45pm every day
   Closed Christmas Day.
£ free Monday-Friday. Weekends & Bank
   Holidays Adult £1.00, Child 50p, Under Five
   free, OAP/concessions 40p
🅿 city centre
🚌 city centre bus routes
♿ to most parts. Induction loops for hearing
   impaired. Exhibits to touch. A mobility car is
   available at the Gatehouse for use at the Castle
   Museum and Brewhouse Yard.
✗ café

Find out about the heroes and villains, battles and riots, inventions and discoveries which have shaped Nottingham's history. Exhibits from the permanent collection have been assembled to tell the story in an exciting and lively way.

Workshops are sometimes held, (ring for details) when children can dress up, do a quiz or touch and draw objects. Watch the 'Castle of Care' to find out why Richard III loved

Nottingham Castle so much and the anguish he suffered there and much more about its colourful history. Elsewhere in the museum are collections of Ethnography, Decorative Arts, Fine Arts and Medals.

Nottingham Industrial Museum
Courtyard Buildings
Wollaton Park
Nottingham NG8 2AE
0602 284602

O 1 April-30 September Monday-Saturday 10am-6pm, Sunday 2-6pm.
1 October-31 March Thursday and Saturday 10am-4.30pm, Sunday 1.30-4.30pm.
Closed 25 December.

£ free except for small charge on Saturday Sunday and Bank Holiday.

P on site

23 bus passes park entrance

ground floor only

café

Come here to see working steam engines, a horse gin, mining and agricultural machinery, the development of telecommunications, and much more in relation to Nottingham's industries. The harshness and grime of mining, the appalling conditions of lacemaking when young girls could go blind in this sweated trade for which Nottingham was world famous. At this museum you will find an impressive collection of lacemaking machines but much work was done by hand and often in very poor lighting condition.

There is also a very elegant pair of three hundred year old carriages, early motorcars and a collection of motorbikes. Nottingham is, after all, the home of Raleigh.

Ring up to find out about arrangements for special events like steaming and demonstrations.

Your carriage awaits! outside Nottingham Industrial Museum.

OXFORDSHIRE

Didcot Railway Centre
Didcot
Oxfordshire OX11 7NJ
0235 817200

○ Saturday & Sunday 11am-5pm,
4pm in winter.
Easter-Mid September 11am-5pm, every day.
Closed 25, 26 December.
Regular Steam Days and Rides
£ Prices vary according to events, non-steam
days are cheaper than steam days.
Steamday prices include train rides.
Adult £3.00-£5.00, Child £2.00-£5.00,
Under Five free for most events;
OAP £2.50-£4.00,
Family £8.60-£14.50.
🅿 BR car park
🚃 BR Didcot next door
♿ yes, steps at entrance only
✕ restaurant and picnic area

Isambard Kingdom Brunel began the Great Western Railway between London and Bristol. Here, at Didcot, enthusiastic volunteers are recreating the Great Western era beside Brunel's original railway track. The hub of the enterprise is the Engine Shed where you can see steam locomotives, some in the process of restoration, passenger carriages and freight wagons.

Find out how the GWR operated its signals at the Signal Box. Look at the turntable from Southampton Docks, and the Travelling Post Office which enabled mail to be put on and off trains, without stopping at the station.

On Steam Days you can take a trip on the main or branch lines. Ring for dates and times of Steam Rides.

Below: Preparing for a Steam Day

Ashmolean Museum
Beaumont Street
Oxford OX1 2PH
0865 278000

○ Tuesday-Saturday 10am-4pm, Sunday 2-4pm. Closed Monday, Christmas and Easter periods and during St Giles's fair in September.

£ free

🅿 city centre car parks

🚆 BR Oxford ten minutes walk. Bus and Coach Station, Gloucester Green three minutes walk.

♿ yes, pushchairs must be carried upstairs.

✗ no

The Ashmolean is the oldest museum in Britain and opened in 1683. It is a traditional museum and somewhat daunting. However, it is a marvellous resource for anyone doing a 'special project'. There are excellent collections of European and Egyptian archaeology, European and Tibetan ceramics, coins, sculpture and paintings from Europe, India and Tibet. You can see Guy Fawkes' lantern, King Alfred's Jewel and a model of Pliny's Villa.

Pitt Rivers Museum
Parks Road
Oxford OX1 3PP
annexe:
The Balfour Building
60 Banbury Road
Oxford
0865 270927

○ Monday-Saturday 1-4.30pm. Closed Christmas and Easter weeks.

£ free

🅿 city centre car parks

🚆 Park and Ride from city centre

♿ wheelchair users should make prior arrangements to visit the ground floor in main museum. Difficult for pushchairs. Good access for wheelchairs and pushchairs in Balfour Building

✗ picnic area in University Parks

This is a huge collection of ethnography, prehistoric archaeology and artefacts from all over the world.

Lambing season at Cogges Manor.

There are lots of skeletons, mummies, masks, a forty foot high totem pole, a witch in a bottle, armour and weapons, model boats and houses.

Everything is crammed in so that the museum feels dark and crowded, excellent conditions for exploration and discovery. Children love this place. Find out about the guided trails, demonstrations and Pitt Stop Family Activities.

Cogges Manor Farm Museum
Church Lane
Witney OX8 6LA
Oxfordshire
0993 772602

O 1 April-31 October, Tuesday-Friday 10.30am-5.30pm; Saturday and Sunday 12 Noon-5.30pm. Bank Holidays 10.30am-5.30pm.

£ Adult £2.50, Child £1.25, Under Five free, OAP £1.25, Family Ticket £6.00

P nearby

🚌 bus Oxford-Witney

♿ yes

✖ café and picnic area

Farm museums are wonderful places to take children who are used to city living. Not many of us get the chance to scratch a Tamworth pig, stroke a goat, hold a new born lamb, watch handmilking or sheep shearing or simply plod through a farmyard in our wellies, scattering ducks and chickens.

Left & above left: The totem pole and other displays at the Pitt Rivers Museum.

At Cogges Manor Farm Museum the animals are Victorian breeds, the stable where Boxer the shire horse is kept, is mid 17th century, the ox byre is 18th century and the dairy and parts of the Manor House itself date from medieval times.

The door of the house is open and an inviting smell from the kitchen welcomes you in. Inside you can find out how life was lived in an Oxfordshire farmhouse at the turn of the century. We ate cheese scones with herbs and butter made at the farm. The 'cook' tied aprons round our two children, hid their hair tidily in mob caps and put them to work. The staff here were all friendly and helpful. On another day we might have watched lacemaking, washing in the big copper or ironing with flat irons heated on the range.

From Easter to November there are daily and weekend activities such as demonstrations of farming life, local customs and crafts. Depending on the time of year you might find Easter chicks, Maypole dancing, folk singing, threshing, cider-making and preparations for Christmas. Check what is on before you go. When we were there the Toyman showed us his handmade toys from Bartholomew Babies to humming tops and dancing puppets. At the end of our visit we certainly felt we deserved home-made cakes and elderflower cordial in the museum's buttery.

SHROPSHIRE

Midland Motor Museum and Bird Garden
Stanmore Hall
Stourbridge Road
Bridgnorth
Shropshire WV15 6DT
0746 761761

O July-September, every day 10.30am-5pm. October-June, weekend only 11am-4pm
£ Adult £3.50, Child £1.75, Under Five free, OAP £2.50, Family Ticket £9.95
P on site
local bus service
&: yes
café

This museum specialises in sports and sports racing cars and motorbikes. The names of Jaguar, Ferrari, Morgan, Porsche, Aston Martin, Norton, Honda and Yamaha were chanted with awed reverence by the two boys visiting with me. 'This is a dream' was the verdict.

Two shining Bentleys at Bridgnorth.

Acton Scott Historic Working Farm
Wenlock Edge
Acton Scott
nr Church Stretton
Shropshire SY6 6QN
0694 781306

O Tuesday-Saturday 10am-5pm, Sunday & Bank Holidays 10am-6pm
£ Adult £2.50, Child £1.20, Under Five free, OAP £2.00, Family Ticket £7.50 Season Ticket-Adult £8.00, Child £4.00
P on site
BR.3 miles, bus 1/2 mile away
&: yes but it can be muddy
restaurant and picnic area

Acton Scott hums with activity as children, of all ages, take part in the working of a late 19th century farm. Suitable old clothes and boots are necessary for the outdoor work. Staff are friendly and welcome children. Telephone for details of demonstrations, children's workshops and weekend

Carthorses to be seen, touched and enjoyed by all.

events.

The hub of the farm is the large and noisy farmyard with its hens, pig sties, milking shed, dairy and blacksmith. Children can get close to and sometimes handle the great variety of livestock, which includes shire horses, Tamworth pigs, Brecon Buff geese, Dorking and Leghorn hens, Norfolk black turkeys and Aylesbury ducks. Arable crops of oats, clover, mangolds and potatoes are grown in the surrounding fields.

The blacksmith practises his craft with a roaring furnace and anvil - the sparks really do fly as he hammers a horseshoe back into shape. Watch the cows being milked in the cowshed in the farmyard, and butter being made in the spotlessly clean dairy. These quiet activities take place with the ever present noise of pigs grunting.

Country dancing and singing accompanied by tin whistles, bells and harmonica often happens in the nearby fields. There are no tractors here so shire horses really do work for their keep as they pull carts, sometimes loaded with children! If you want to get away from the bustling farm there is always the nature trail to follow around the fields.

Aerospace Museum
Cosford
Shifnal TF11 8UP
Shropshire
0902 374872/374112

O 10am-5pm every day, last admission 4pm.
   Closed 24, 25, 26 December, 1 January.
£ Adult £4.00, Child £2.30, Under Five free,
   OAP £3.00, Family £10.50
P on site
🚆 BR Cosford
♿ yes
✕ café and picnic area nearby

Four fascinating collections of aircraft and related objects are housed in hangars here. These collections include some amazing examples from research and development projects, war planes, transport aircraft and missiles. If you thought you knew a lot about aircraft be prepared for surprises.

This is a good collection and you really can stay as long as you want. If you have limited time you may like to follow our tour around, lasting about one hour. Start with the Trident then go to

Some of the variety of aircraft to be seen at Cosford.

the British Airways Hall to find out about the history of civil aviation. See the Red Arrows Gnat, two record breaking aircraft and many unusual and exotic aeroplanes in the Research and Development Hall. Then on to the World War Two hangar which houses a smart biplane trainer; the 'haunted' Lincoln; a Spitfire whose propeller turns; the first jet warplane, the Messerschmitt 262 and a very unusual 'helicopter'.

Outside you will find the Vulcan, the first jet airliner, the Comet, a Bloodhound Missile System and many more. Go to the Transport Aircraft Hangar to find the search-and-rescue helicopter and climb into the Vulcan nose. Then look for the Japanese 'suicide' plane.

Ironbridge Gorge Museum
Ironbridge
Telford TF8 7AW
Shropshire
0952 433522

O June-August 10am-6pm.
September-May 10am-5pm.

£ Passport Ticket to all sites: Adult £7.80, Child/Student £5.00, Under Five free,OAP £6.80, Family £23.50.
Entrance fees to the seven individual sites vary from 80p (adult) to the Tar Tunnel to £5.50 (adult) to Blists Hill.

P on site

🚉 BR Telford. Buses Telford and Birmingham

♿ access for wheelchairs is limited on some sites, an information leaflet is available on request. Difficulties for pushchairs in some places.

✕ restaurants and picnic areas.

I came here, with two twelve year old boys and a four year old girl; an unusual but not unsuccessful combination. I have our 'passports' on the table as I write and see that over the two days we spent here, we managed to see four of the nine possible places. This was good going as the sites are spread over nearly six square miles and there is a great deal to see at each one. Reading the small print, I notice that our passports are valid until all the museums are visited.

Our first achievement was to cross the Iron Bridge, the first structure of its kind in the world, built in 1781 by Abraham Darby over a period of four years. Bridging the Severn Gorge over Coalbrookdale was to be a revolutionary project using totally new technology. It is probably the only 18th century iron bridge which remains intact and still looks impressive to late 20th century eyes.

The boys were intrigued by the Tar Tunnel so that was to be our next port of call. We followed them nervously for half a mile into the hillside where we could peer down into wells of natural bitumen discovered in 1786. It was nice to come out again and hand back our hard hats.

We still felt fit enough to meet the demands of the Blists Hill Open Air Museum, a re-created industrial, living community of the turn of the century with its gas-lit streets of shops, cottages, railway sidings, pig sties and pubs. Our first stop was the Blists Hill Bank where I was goaded into changing decimal money into farthings, old pennies and threepenny bits. Thoroughly confused by the exchange rates (a farthing 10p; a half penny 20p; a penny 40p; threepence £1.20; sixpence £2.40; a shilling £4.80 and a pound £96.00), we still managed to blow it all on muffins from the baker's, beer from the pub, chocolate from the Victorian sweet shop and candles from the candle factory. We stopped off at the chemist to watch the pill making machine rolling out pills like pastry and to shudder at the live leeches and blood letting bowls. The children were surprised to learn that leeches are still used in certain special circumstances in modern medical practice.

From there we went on to the plasterers and watched tiny plaster roses being made and generously handed over to small children who had been patient enough to watch the demonstration; we passed the cobblers, the butchers, skirted round the slaughter house, stopped at the printers to watch printing on an early printing press and on to the candle factory where rows of thin, half-made candles hung waiting for their next dip. We bought sticky buns for lunch down by the blast furnaces. We talked to the 'residents'. 'Real people instead of labels' said one of the boys. In particular the doctor, the schoolmistress and the woman at squatter cottage feeding her chickens and making a rag rug. We walked up the steep hay inclined plane and along the Shropshire Canal and back to the car, exhausted but satisfied.

The following day we visited the Coalport China Museum. China was made here until 1926 when the company moved to Staffordshire. As we explored the museum we discovered the process of turning lumps of clay into fine porcelain. We walked right into the bottle kiln and experienced the strange sensation of being surrounded by an immense sweeping curve of blackened brick, right in the centre of which was the kiln proper where the china was fired in towering stacks of saggars or lidless fireclay boxes. In the workshops we watched potters 'throwing' clay on the wheel, turning lathes and casting from liquid clay or 'slip' in plaster-of-Paris moulds. Others were bent over fine white plates and cups, hand painting flowers or gilding elaborate decorations with fantastic concentration and intricate skill.

I recommend these four sites as suitable for families but for those with time and stamina there is much more to see at Ironbridge. The Museum of Iron and the Darby Furnace illustrates the history of iron and steel making. Abraham Darby's furnace is still here where in 1709, he pioneered the technique of smelting iron ore with coke. The Museum of the River and visitor centre has a huge model of the Gorge as it was in 1796 and displays on the way the river is managed now, revealing how we habitually take for granted the methods by which we receive fresh, clean water on tap. The Rosehill House shows the possessions and way of life of a Quaker ironmaster during the first half of the 19th century when the house was lived in by the youngest son of the builder of the Iron Bridge. The Jackfield Tile Museum has an incredible array of highly colourful wall and floor tiles attractively displayed in the original Craven Dunnill works.

SOMERSET

Cheddar Caves
Cheddar Gorge
Somerset BS27 3QF
0934 742343

O Easter-30 September 10am-5.30pm.
1 October-Easter 10.30am-4.30pm, every day.
Closed 24, 25 December

£ Adult £4.90, Child £2.90, Under Five free,.
OAP £4.90, Family Ticket £14.50.
Adventure Caving Expeditions: £6.00 per
person, minimum age 12, party size 10, hard
hat, boots etc provided.

🅿 on site

🚌 bus to Cheddar Village

♿ limited

✕ restaurant and picnic area

Three million years ago a small river
meandered across a plain that is now
the flat top of the Mendip Hills. Over
years the river cut its valley deeper and
eventually vanished underground into
caves in the limestone rocks. At the
edge of the Mendips the river cut
deeper and formed the Cheddar Gorge.
There are caves dating from the
interglacial periods 100,000 years ago.
There are more caves high in the cliffs
that are five or ten times older. Even
today new underwater caves are still
being formed.

Going deep into the ground, whether
down a mine or into an underground
grotto or cavern, is an extraordinary
experience for any child. Here the caves
begin as a large tunnel sloping down
past the Skeleton Pit, where 'Cheddar
Man', discovered in 1903, was buried
nine thousand years ago. The
'scalloped' roof looks like beaten

copper, originally formed by eddy currents in the underground river. Once out of the tunnel the stalactite chamber of St Paul's will take your breath away, with its cascade of multi-coloured stalagmites, the red of iron oxide and the blackish-blue of manganese oxide, that appears to pour over a lip from a cavern high above. In the Diamond Chamber beyond, is the strange rock formation, flowing and bubbling in perpetual stillness called the Frozen River and in the roof of Grand Passage, clustered around a lamp, are hart's tongue and other ferns, grown probably from microscopic spores brought in on the clothes of visitors. Look out for colonies of rare Greater Horseshoe Bats.

In the 1980s a tunnel was blasted and dug through to the Fantasy Grotto,

Top: Will you reach the end of the Crystal Quest and face the dragon's challenge?

Above: Richard Gough's tableau points toward the roof of Gough's Cave.

Left Above: Skeleton of Cheddar Man, nine thousand years old. The front of the skull is badly damaged, suggesting he was killed by a blow to the face. Before his ritual burial in the cave his body was exposed to the elements until only the skeleton, held together by sinews and ligaments remained.

Left: Not for those of a nervous disposition, the Crystal Quest in Cox's Cave.

a fake cave created by an eccentric local Victorian a century ago. Here children can embark on the Crystal Quest, defying Mordon, Lord of Darkness. Very small children might be scared but it might lead older ones to read Tolkein's 'Lord of the Rings'.

My twelve year old daughter went adventure caving here recently and found it a tough challenge. She admits to being terrified and excited. It certainly gave her a great sense of achievement. Cavers took her group,

The mirror maze at Wookey Hole.

(maximum ten per group, minimum age twelve) well equipped with helmets, lamps, boots, boiler suits and other equipment into the deep chambers beyond the show caves. They also climbed the Gorge to the top of the Mendips and up Jacob's Ladder, a flight of steps constructed by the same enthusiast who built Fantasy Grotto. A new exhibition there tells you that each upward step represents one million years in the history of the earth. The climb takes you from a time when Cheddar and the Mendip Mountains were part of a tropical desert, through dinosaur empires and the Ice Age to the 20th century. Human history is the thickness of a sheet of paper placed on the top step, but dinosaurs ruled the world for a hundred and fifty steps!

Wookey Hole Caves and Papermill
Wookey Hole
Wells BA5 1BB
Somerset
0749 672243

○ Summer 9.30am-5.30pm (last tour). Winter 10.30am-4.30pm (last tour). Closed 17-25 December inclusive.
£ Adult £5.20, Child £3.00, Under Four free, OAP £4.50
🅿 on site
🚌 bus from Wells to Wookey Hole
♿ wheelchair access in Mill exhibition only
✕ restaurant and picnic area

During the summer season you may well have to queue for some time before you reach the entrance to the caves, then you will have to form part of a group on a guided tour and follow a well trodden route around the site. It is well worth it! For you will also descend deep into the earth, into mysterious caverns millions of years old, dripping with stalactites and hung with curtains of shining crystalline stone. It is an unforgettable sight.

It might well be one of your own childhood memories. Yet since that time, intrepid divers have discovered new chambers, a great cavern and a vast enclosed lake. A tunnel has been blasted through the rock, opening up further chambers for all to see. The River Axe delves underground to depths that no diver has been able to reach, the 'ultimate challenge to cave explorers'.

For a child, entering these caves could be quite a challenge. The cave entrance and first four chambers, once used by Iron Age people are now homes for cave spiders and pipistrelle bats. Mosses, algae and hart's tongue ferns grow beneath the cracks of the walls.

Colours range from the vermilion of iron oxide to the black of manganese, or lead grey and golden splashes of ochre. At times you have to crouch down to get past overhanging rocks; manoeuvre round immense stalagmites, such as the 'witch of Wookey', along catwalks straddling deep ravines, listen to the sounds of water dripping from the cavern roof and the whole lit with eerie floodlights.

At the beginning of the century, Wookey Hole Mill was the largest for rag-made paper in Europe. Now you can watch demonstrations of papermaking by hand and see the giant waterwheel. Children will love the fairground animals, the magical mirror maze, the musical fountain and the vintage penny in the slot machines.

In the summer make sure you all have jumpers for the caves. Carry the pushchair underground but you will need it for the walk back.

Some of the many old fairground attractions to be seen at Wookey Hole.

Fleet Air Arm Museum

Royal Naval Air Station
Yeovilton BA22 8HT
Somerset
0935 840565

- O 10am-5.30pm, 4.30pm in winter
- £ Adult £4.80, Child £2.70, Under Five free, OAP £3.50, Family £15.00, Season Ticket £10.00
- P on site
- to Yeovil
- ♿ yes
- ✕ restaurant and picnic area

This is where to find Concorde. But there is more too at this museum of the Royal Naval Air Service, which was formed in 1914 when powered flight was in its infancy. Since then, under various names, naval aviation has played a vital part in the Royal Navy's role in both World Wars, the Falklands and the Gulf. When we see, on our television screens, those great flotillas of Royal Navy vessels neat and gleaming, they can look romantic and beautiful. Great forms on the ocean which come to life, as jump jets take off and land on these huge, floating airfields; we hold our breath as time and again we watch this happen. It all looks so exciting and unreal. The Fleet Air Arm Museum lets us and our children realize how terrifying the venture really is.

There are eight large galleries to house the forty aircraft in the collection and you can follow different routes around depending on how much time and attention span you have. Routes are clearly marked and the shortest takes about 1 hour, the longest 3-4 hours.

Hands-on displays, cockpits to climb into, interactive sets, airfield viewing galleries, a flight simulator and an aviation adventure playground combine fun with finding out about these aircraft, their history, design and development. The early history of the aircraft carrier is covered in the 1920s and 1930s gallery. There are galleries devoted to the role of the aircraft in the Falklands and Gulf Wars; in the Harrier Story is a detailed examination of how fixed winged aircraft are lifted vertically off the ground. Finally, Concorde, which arrived here in 1976 and must be one of the most beautiful aircraft ever designed.

Climb into a cockpit at Yeovilton.

STAFFORDSHIRE

Bass Museum, Visitor Centre and Shire Horse Stables
Horninglow Street
Burton upon Trent
0283 42031

○ Weekdays 10am-5pm, Saturday and Sunday 10.30-5pm

£ Adult £3.45, Child £1.85, Under Five free, OAP £2.35, Family £9.25, Season Ticket £2.50 per family.

🅿 on site

🚾 nearby

♿ yes

✗ restaurant and picnic area

Everything you have ever wanted to know about beer and brewing is here at the Bass Museum. Like many breweries this was a family concern run by the Bass Family and you will find out about their history in relation to Burton upon Trent. There are displays on hops and malt, the brewing process, casks, pulleys and cogs and brewery transport. There is an education department which runs workshops for all ages and abilities on different aspects of the brewing business. Finally a big hit for everyone is a visit to the stables to see, smell and touch the magnificent Shire horses who used to pull the heavy wagons. Find out their names and heights, look at the harnesses and rosettes. Then go and find more recent methods of transport in the yard.

The 'bottle car' at the Bass Museum.

Shugborough Estate (NT)
Milford
Near Stafford ST17 0XB
0889 881388

○ 31 March-31 October 11am-5pm.
Open all year from 10.30am on weekdays for booked parties.

£ NT Members free. Park, gardens, picnic area, walks: £1.00 per vehicle.
One ticket for all buildings
Adult £7.50, Child £5.00, Under Five free
OAP £7.50, Family Ticket £15.00

🅿 on site

🚾 BR Stafford then Chaserider bus 5, 822/3/5 Stafford-Lichfield

♿ yes

✗ café and picnic area.

Shugborough Hall was the 18th century home of the Earls of Lichfield and is now lived in by the 5th Earl, the photographer Patrick Lichfield. The house has rococo plasterwork, beautiful ceramics, silver, paintings and French furniture, but it is to the gardens and woodland walks, old servants' quarters and the Park Farm your children will want to go. The museum in the servants' quarters gives you a fascinating insight to life 'backstairs' at Shugborough during the last century. In the 1820s eighty servants lived and worked here, reducing to forty in the 1880s. The warm kitchen, with the range lit, is presided over by Leon Paul, the French chef, Emma Stearn, head kitchen maid and second and third

kitchen maids. They are very impressive, even though they are only two dimensional cut-out figures! They are surrounded by the tools of their trade: sugar loaves, sugar tongs, jelly moulds, copper pans and rolling pins. There are dirty dishes in the scullery, silver in the butler's pantry, meat, game and vegetables in the cold store and beer in the brewhouse. In the wet laundry the copper is heated by its coal-fired furnace; dolly-pegs, possers, tubs and a rocker style washing machine are put to use. In the dry laundry the rollers of the box mangle are ready 'clothed' and flat irons, presses and crimping irons await.

In the Victorian schoolroom visiting children can try out slates and slate pencils sitting up straight and silent on hard wooden benches.

At the farm there are Longhorn Cattle, Shropshire Sheep, Tamworth Pigs. There are demonstrations of hand milking and Shire horse work. In the farm dairy you might see a demonstration of butter and cheese making, while farmhouse loaves are baked in the brick bread-oven in the farm kitchen. In the working water-driven mill flour is produced and wool combed, carded, spun and woven at the fulling mill.

Look out for marvellous holiday and weekend events as varied as trimming sheep's feet, flying kites, making wigs and treasure hunting.

City Museum and Art Gallery: Stoke-on-Trent
Bethesda Street
Hanley
Stoke-on-Trent ST1 3DW
Staffordshire
0782 202173

O Monday-Saturday 10am-5pm, Sunday 2-5pm
£ free
P multi-storey car park down the road
🚌 Hanley Bus Station nearby
♿ yes
✗ restaurant

Stoke-on-Trent is the Potteries and anyone who has read Arnold Bennett will know the five towns of Burslem, Hanley, Stoke, Kidsgrove and Tunstall which make up this remarkable area. But pottery here goes back much further than the Victorians as you will find out.

This excellent museum contains the largest collection of Staffordshire ceramics in the world. It really is a vast and amazing collection of mass-

An 18th-century Toby jug from the Potteries.

produced ceramic artefacts from ornaments such as 18th century Staffordshire dogs and Toby Jugs to cauliflower shaped coffee pots and cow shaped cream jugs, (which were impossible to wash and must have caused many a stomach ache). There are functional and practical cups, saucers and plates and others beautifully decorated, like the slipware plates made by the Toft family. There is a Teapot Trail to follow through the museum. The wares of three great women of 20th century British ceramics (Suzie Cooper, Charlotte Rhead and Clarice Cliff) are displayed. This museum is a must for any child studying ceramics for GCSE who is interested in the design and manufacture of pots. Younger ones, even three year olds, need not be bored. There are good displays on the manufacturing process and firing techniques, new developments and trends. Look for Josiah Wedgwood's 'throwing room', in the factory he called 'Etruria'. Films are shown in the half-term holidays.

If you really do tire of the ceramics then visit the Natural History, Archaeology, Social History and Decorative Arts galleries, all equally fascinating. Look out for a Staffordshire wallaby, a scavenging fox, a beautiful snakeshead fritillary and a menacing stickleback. Go back to the Romans to find their big 'face' pots and forward to sixty years ago to the pub, the wash house, the chemist and the schoolroom. Compare bustles and crinolines to dungarees and tracksuits.

A truly fascinating place and worth a detour off the M6 next time you speed by.

When you have finished here you can visit Ford Green Hall.

Ford Green Hall Museum
Ford Green Road
Smallthorne
Stoke-on-Trent ST6 1NG
0782 534771

O Sunday-Thursday 1-5pm
£ free
P on site
🚌 bus to Smallthorne
♿ Ground floor only
✕ café and picnic area

This is the oldest house in the Potteries and was built in 1624 with further brick additions in the 18th century. Early music performances are held here on the second Sunday of every month.

If you can cope with more then find your way to Etruria Industrial Museum

Etruria Industrial Museum
Lower Bedford Street
Etruria
Stoke-on-Trent
0782 287557

O Wednesday-Sunday 10am-4pm
£ free
P nearby in Lower Bedford Street
🚌 Bus to Shelton New Road
♿ no
✕ picnic area

In this Grade 1 Listed building you will find the last steam powered potters mill in Britain. The 'Princess' is in steam the first weekend of every month.

Below: Ford Green Hall Museum.
Bottom: The gear room during restoration at Etruria Industrial Museum.

SUFFOLK

Long Shop Museum
Main Street
Leiston
Suffolk IP16 4ES
0728 832189

One of the more unusual steam vehicles.

○ 1 April-31 October 10am-5pm , Sunday 11am-5pm

£ Adult £1.20, Child 60p, Under Five free, OAP 60p

🅿 on site

🚌 local bus routes

♿ to most of site

✕ picnic area nearby

Come to the Long Shop to find out about the history of steam power, engineering and industry in East Anglia. The museum is in a Grade 2 listed building which was one of the earliest production assembly halls in the world.

SURREY

Hampton Court Palace
East Molesey KT8 9AU
Surrey
081 781 9500

○ Mid March-Mid October, Monday 10.15am-6pm, Tuesday-Sunday 9.30am-6pm. Mid October-Mid March, Monday 10.15am-4.30pm, Tuesday-Sunday 9.30am-4.30pm. Closed 24, 25, 26 December, 1 January.

£ Adult £5.90, Child £3.90, Under Five free, OAP £4.50, Family Ticket £17.90

🅿 on site

🚌 BR Hampton Court

♿ not in the Wolsey Rooms

✕ restaurant and picnic area.

I went to Hampton Court on a wet November day with a seven year old and a ten year old. The former wanted to spend her pocket money on the ubiquitous pencil, rubber and pencil sharpener, while the latter was 'doing' the Tudors and Stuarts and, like me, wanted to see the recently refurbished Tudor kitchens.

Throughout earlier summers we had tasted the delights of the maze, the Real Tennis court, the Great Vine, the Knot Garden, the Tilt Yard. We had walked along the towpath, across the park to the Privy Garden, past the Great Fountain and along the arbors of trees and covered ways. Now we wanted to see the State Apartments, especially those of William III, which were burnt in the fire of 1986 and are now restored to their former glory.

We admired Henry VIII's Great Hall, Watching Chamber and the Chapel Royal with its blue and gold fan vaulted ceiling. Edward VI was baptised here a few days before his mother, Jane Seymour, died of puerperal fever. We walked along the Haunted Gallery imagining the desperate spectre of the executed Catherine Howard.

We climbed upstairs to the rooms built for Cardinal Wolsey and into his beautiful closet with its ornate ceiling, paintings and oak panelling. We speculated on his reactions when Henry VIII demanded that he hand over his palace.

William and Mary chose Hampton Court as their main country residence. Christopher Wren was given orders to 'beautify and add some new building to that fabric'. He built a classical palace with cloisters around the lawn and fountain of a new court.

We wandered through the state apartments, empty but grand until we heard the sound of a spinet and wind instrument and came across a couple dressed in Georgian costume playing Handel. We looked into the King's private dining room with Sir Godfrey Kneller's 'Hampton Court Beauties' on the walls. We loved the tiny 'Queen Mary's Closet' but learnt that she had died of smallpox and never slept there.

We lost a scarf and retraced our footsteps encouraged by sympathetic and impressively dressed attendants. We still seemed to have enough energy to visit the kitchens. The youngest child and I were attached to the same tape recorder of the free audio guide, and went round exclaiming in unison. The amount of food being prepared for the feast is colossal: wild boar, deer, rich sauces, venison pies, peacocks, quantities of wine and beer. A huge fire burning in the big kitchen was a welcome sight on a cold day. Beware of crowds in the summer.

The three of us came away in a very happy frame of mind. We had managed to see everything we wanted to and more. We certainly enjoyed ourselves and all learnt something without too much effort.

Royal Botanic Gardens
Kew
Richmond TW9 3AB
Surrey
081 940 1171

○ 9.30-dusk every day.
  Closed 25 December, 1 January.
£ Adult £3.50, Child £1.30, Under Five free,
  OAP £1.80.
  Season Ticket Family £30.00, Individual
  £16.00, OAP £13.50, OAP Family £26.00
🅿 on site
🚇 Underground, BR Kew Gardens, Bus 65, 391.
♿ yes
✗ restaurant and picnic area.

Admission prices to Kew Gardens have soared over the past ten years. In 1916, the charge of one (old) penny was introduced to help with the war effort. In 1924 the then Labour Government made it free. In 1926 the Conservatives re-instated the penny charge. With every successive change of government the penny charge was removed and then re-imposed, like obstinate children playing a game, until it was raised to threepence (3d) in 1951, 1p in 1971 and 10p in 1980. Now the homeless cannot afford to come in and keep warm in the hot houses during the winter.

When you enter the gardens look out for the boards which tell you the seasonal highlights; bananas fruiting in the Palm House in November, Father Christmas and reindeer in December, drifts of crocuses in April, bluebells in May, fireworks and music in the summer.

No child, whether a reluctant toddler in a pushchair or an indifferent teenager could fail to be enthralled by any of the hot houses here. Standing inside the Palm House, the sense of green is overwhelming! Look up at the plants above you, hanging and swaying from a great height. The heat in here drops like rainfall! Climb up the spiral staircase and look down on the canopy of the tropical rainforest below. Up here, surrounded by shining glass and a fretwork of white metal, the light and air are in extraordinary contrast to the forest floor below. The Marine Display beneath the Palm House is brand new and very exciting. There are nineteen huge tanks with seaweeds from tidal rock pools, mangrove swamps and fish and coral reefs from tropical seas.

Hotter and steamier still is the Water Lily House in which the sacred lotus and papyrus rival the bottle gourd and loofah.

In the Princess of Wales Conservatory you can walk through ten climatic zones from arid desert to tropical forest. Here are banana, orange, lemon, sugar cane, cassava, pineapple, coffee and cocoa plants. There are prickly pears and aloe vera, myrrh and the disturbing carnivorous plants, fed daily with juicy insects. The Education Officer at Kew Gardens once sat her baby of six months on one of the leaves of the giant water lily. The flowers last only forty eight hours and change from white to pink to purple.

There is plenty more to see; Kew Palace and the Queen's 17th century garden, with its gazebo, herbs and medieval plants; the ice house, the pagoda, the Alpine House, Queen Charlotte's Cottage, temples and ruined arches; the Joseph Banks Building with the mandarin duck on the lake and the huge and beautiful temperate house where the Chilean wine palm is threatening to grow through the roof.

If anybody gets lost then meet at the Victoria Gate. There is a marvellous video there, comfortable seats, beautiful back-lit transparencies and a tempting shop. Word of warning: prevent your children from running over the flower beds; some time ago, when my son was small, we were ignominiously, but quite rightly, thrown out for that crime.

The Princess of Wales Conservatory at Kew.

EAST SUSSEX

Bodiam Castle (NT)
Bodiam
Robertsbridge TN32 5UA
East Sussex
0580 830 436

O 1 April-31 October 10am-6pm, last admission
5.30pm every day.
1 November-31 March 10am-sunset Tuesday-
Sunday.

£ NT Members free, Adult £2.50, Child £1.30,
Under Five free, OAP £2.50.

P on site

🚉 BR Robertsbridge 5 miles, bus Hastings-
Tunbridge Wells, Eastbourne-Rye.

♿ yes

✕ restaurant and picnic area.

Bodiam Castle was a big hit with our
friends. It is not too big, is surrounded
by a huge moat filled with water and
looks just like everybody's dream castle
should. This was one of the last
medieval castles to be built in England
and represents three hundred years of
castle building and refinement. From
the exterior it stands as complete as
the day it was finished; with its turrets,
tower and gateway still intact. People
and time have, sadly, altered the
interior. The castle's founder was a
local man, Sir Edward Dalyngrigge,
who fought the French in the Hundred
Years War, was involved in
government, made a good marriage
and was wealthy. This area of England
was made vulnerable by the French,
who had already attacked Rye and
Winchelsea, so Sir Edward built the
castle to defend his land. The castle

was never put under attack, so we shall never know if his defensive plan worked. It did, however, provide him, and future generations with a comfortable home.

During the Civil War it was attacked and fell to the Roundheads. It was then unoccupied for almost three hundred years until 1916 when it was rescued by Lord Curzon who bequeathed it to the National Trust in 1925.

Spend time inside the walls, look through windows, play games and act out fairy stories or your own dramas. Imagine what it would be like stuck here surrounded by the enemy; would you feel safe or terrified? Climb the Gatehouse Tower and peep through the gunloops, the first in England and looking like inverted keyholes. A spring feeds the well at the bottom of the south-west tower. Find where the Great Hall, kitchen and pantry are. If invaders ventured past the Great Gatehouse,

missiles would be thrown at them through 'murder holes' in the ceiling above; look up and you will see them in the vaulting.

Bluebell Railway
Sheffield Park Station
Near Uckfield TN22 3QL
East Sussex
082572 3777

O Ring talking timetable on 082572 2370 for details

£ Return Fares: Adult £6.00, Child £3.00, Under Three free, OAP £5.20, Family Ticket £16.00. Day Rover Ticket Adult £16.00, Child £8.00. Entrance includes ride on train, admission to museum, station and locomotive sheds.

P on site

BR Haywards Heath and East Grinstead.

yes

restaurant and picnic area.

Spend a day at the Bluebell Railway, have a nostalgic ride and show your children how it used to be in the good old days of steam. Make sure you show them the fireman and the engine; mine are always enthralled by this sight. The trains run throughout the year, with special attractions, like Thomas the Tank Engine weekends. Ring for details. The track operates from Sheffield Park Station through Horsted Keynes to New Coombe Bridge and it is aiming to get to East Grinstead soon!

Back at Sheffield Park Station you can wander around the collection of locomotives and carriages. Find the small 'Terrier' locomotives built in 1870 and then the huge British Railways freight engine built in 1958. Your taste buds and nostrils will be working hard inhaling all the smells and tastes of the steam shed with the bustle of the water crane, inspection pit, ash, coal and hissing steam. Then you can see how all the repairs are done.

There is an extensive exhibition of small items and ephemera relating to the railway in the museum; you will find tickets, photographs, models and much more. If you are feeling very generous then why not treat everyone to Sunday lunch on the 'Golden Arrow' Pullman, built in the 1920s and fit for the Orient Express. Stop off at Horsted Keynes and take refreshment in the 1882 station buffet; compare it with a similar experience today.

Bodiam Castle, now owned by the National Trust, is captured here on a beautiful day reflected in its moat.

WEST SUSSEX

Amberley Chalk Pits
Houghton Bridge
Amberley
Arundel BN18 9LT
West Sussex
0798 831370

O 24 March-31 October, Wednesday-Sunday,
   10am-5pm.
   Every day: 31 March-18 April, 26 May-6 June,
   21 July-6 September.
£ Adult £4.20, Child £2.00, Under Five free,
   OAP £3.30, Family £10.50
P on site
⛟ BR Amberley, bus Brighton, close to River Arun
   Cruises Boat Jetty.
& yes
✕ café and picnic area

This museum spreads over thirty six
acres of a disused chalk quarry on the
South Downs and shows the industrial
development of south-east England.
Allow plenty of time for your visit, bring
a picnic and spend a day.

You can see bottle shaped kilns
which were used to extract the lime
quarried here. Walk above them to see
how deep they are. Then go into the
bagging shed where lime was stored
and bagged. Dotted around the site
there are wind and hand water pumps,
examples of brickmaking, a concrete
exhibition showing its use from 5600 BC
a telephone exchange, vintage radios
and the history of the local electricity
board. Resident craftsmen make and
repair wooden boats, with traditional
tools, in the Timber Barn. There is a
potter in the Pottery and a working
blacksmith and printer too.

In the 1890s Locomotive, Smithy and
Bagmender's Sheds house the trains,
used on the site, now restored as well
as a collection of items from an old
cobbler's shop.

Spend time at the 1920s Southdown
Bus Garage. Find the foreman's office
and look at the range of vehicles. Then
go next door to the 1930s replica village
garage with its petrol pumps and cycle
repair shop, the interior of which was
brought from Littlehampton.

Learn about the history of narrow
gauge railways, developed to serve the
quarry. Then go into the locomotive
shed to see the 'Polar Bear' steam
engine. Follow the Nature Trail across
the railway line and through the spoil
heaps of the limeworks.

Vintage Leyland buses at Amberley.

Weald and Downland Open Air Museum

Singleton
Chichester
West Sussex
024363 348

1 March-31 October 11am-5pm every day.
1 November-28 February 11am-4pm
Wednesday and Sunday.
26 December-1 January 11 am-4pm every day.

Adult £3.60, Child £1.75, Under Five free,
OAP £3.00, Family Ticket £9.50

on site

to Singleton

limited due to uneven terrain in parts of the site

restaurant and picnic area

An open-air museum, with animals, 'hands-on' working demonstrations, empty buildings to run in and out of, and plenty of space, woods and downland to go wild in, has all the ingredients for a perfect family outing. Bring a picnic and the dog (on a lead) and follow the routes around, pushchairs and baby carriers to the fore. If you are unlucky with the weather many of the buildings have roaring fires.

The Weald and Downland Museum has rescued thirty condemned and derelict buildings from the south-east of England, miraculously dismantled them, brick by brick, and repaired and re-erected them on the site. There are more to come. This is a wonderful opportunity to go inside a medieval timber-framed hall, a 16th century farmhouse, an 18th century barn, a 19th century carpenter's workshop; all buildings you might catch a glimpse of when driving past but never get much closer to.

Give your children the map to follow the routes, first the green, then the red. If they are 'in charge' and ahead they are less likely to feel they are being dragged around on an endless excursion. You need to allow at least two and a half hours for both routes but if you are short of time you could take just one route.

Here are some of the buildings we suggest are of special interest to children. Start at the Hambrook Barn and then walk on to the tiny Toll Cottage, once at Beeding, 54 miles from London and on the last road in Sussex on which a toll was levied. Read the tollboard at the gate. The little school from West Wittering, known as Bluecoat school opened in 1712 for 'six poor children from the parish' and continued in use until 1950! Inside are the wooden desks, the slates, the abacus and the schoolmistress's cane. Outside is the stable for her horse.

The charcoal burner's camp is deep in the woods. Here are the four stages in the working of the kiln, and the hut made by Mr and Mrs Langridge, retired charcoal burners, from a pole frame covered with turf and sacking. Mrs Langridge lived in one of these till she was sixteen. Every Sunday the best clothes were taken out of a chest and the whole family went to sing with the Salvation Army.

The red route starts with the Market Hall. Under the stairs leading to what was once the town council chamber, is a 'cage' or lock-up for offenders. In the 'Joiners' shop children can feel building materials, such as thatch, brick, clay, sand and slate and try out methods of construction. End your visit with all the smells, sounds and general 'flouriness' at the Lurgashall Water Mill. Buy some flour from the museum shop if you want to make your own bread when you get home!

Below: 'Bayleaf'. An early 15th century timber-framed hall-house from Chiddingstone, Kent. Here you can warm yourself at the open fire and imagine using the 'garderobe', the french medieval equivalent of the 'cloakroom', which probably emptied into a cess pit outside the window.

TYNE AND WEAR

The Wildfowl and Wetlands Trust
District 15
Washington
Tyne and Wear NE38 8LE.
091 4165454

O Every day, Summer 9.30am-5.00pm.
Winter 9.30am-4.00pm. (Changeover depends
on clock changes.)
Closed 24, 25 December.

£ Adult £3.20, Child £1.60, Under Four free,
OAP £2.40.
Season ticket to all eight sites in the country.

P on site

🚌 bus from Sunderland or Newcastle

♿ good to most parts, but may have difficulties in
the 'wild area'.

✗ café and picnic area

This is one of the eight Wildfowl and
Wetlands sites, started by Peter Scott in
the 1940s, and is well worth a visit
especially for the under sevens. You
can buy a bag of grain for 30p (we
bought one for each child) in the shop
and feed the wildfowl as you go round.

We had not realised how many
different types of duck, geese and wild
fowl there are in the world. They have
been brought here from all parts; some
facing extinction are given a safe haven
in which to breed. Look out for the black
and white swans, the flamingoes, the
variation in colours and size of ducks
and the grace with which they coast
across the water. Many of the
domesticated fowl are very friendly and
will walk right up to you. If you have the
stamina and are good walkers take the

signed path through the woodland to look for the real wildfowl in their hideouts. You have to be very quiet to do this, but it is great fun going into the look-out posts; we managed to find some pheasants.

There is a large, well designed adventure playground. Wear boots for the irresistible puddles.

Above: A cygnet and two Trumpeter swans glide gracefully.

Left: Two of the unusual and brightly coloured mandarin ducks test the water.

Below: Grain can be bought from the shop to feed the wildfowl enabling many of the birds to be seen from very close quarters.

WARWICKSHIRE

Warwick Castle
Warwick CV34 4QU
Warwickshire
0926 495421

O 1 March-31 October 10am-6pm.
1 November-28 February 10am-5pm.
Closed 25 December.

£ Adult £6.75, Child £4.25, Under Four free,
OAP £4.75, Students £5.00 Family Ticket
£18.50/£20.50.

🅿 on site

🚉 BR Warwick, 2 miles

♿ to grounds only

✕ restaurant and picnic area

Warwick Castle stands majestically on
the banks of the River Avon and is quite
breathtaking as you walk across the
moat. William the Conqueror first began
construction here in 1068 and it has
been preserved as a medieval castle.
There are vast grounds, ramparts and
dungeons, towers and courtyards, and
inside you can get a real feel of castle
life with furnished rooms complete with
wax characters.

Take a tour around the inside and
see the Royal Weekend Party in 1898
with Lady Warwick in her boudoir and
the Prince of Wales in his bedroom; the
Great Hall with the suits of armour and
knights on horseback and the Blue
Boudoir, all very much more luxurious
than one would have imagined in a
castle.

Don't forget the Ramparts Walk; start
at the Clarence Tower walk to Guy's
Tower and through the Armoury to
Caesar's Tower and down into the
Dungeon and see the torture chamber.
Torture over, go on to the Ghost Tower
where you can have a well earned drink
in the café.

The grounds at Warwick castle are
extensive and beautiful. Follow the
nature trail, stop at the Boat House and
look up at the magnificent castle. Roam
through the Woodland Garden. Find the
Peacock Garden and take a view of the
Pageant Field. Finally, if your children will
allow, enjoy the fragrant Rose Garden.

An impressive view of Warwick Castle.

WILTSHIRE

Salisbury and South Wiltshire Museum
The King's House
65 The Close
Salisbury SP1 2EN
Wiltshire
0722 332151

O Monday-Saturday 10am-5pm. Sunday in July, August and Salisbury Festival 2-5pm

£ Adult £2.25, Child 50p, Under Five free, OAP £1.50. All tickets give unlimited visits throughout the year.

P Cathedral Close, city car parks

BR Salisbury 1/2 mile, bus to city centre.

& to most parts, wheelchair users must book in advance.

✗ café

Walk around one of the most beautiful cathedral closes in Britain and into the King's House, through the 15th century vaulted porch into a well ordered, carpeted, quiet, spacious museum for contemplative wandering. Not for the very young in your family, but good for the discerning child who is keen to find out about the secrets of Stonehenge and the burial goods of the Beaker people.

Children will like the Salisbury giant and his companion, Hob Nobs from Salisbury's medieval pageant. Well worth climbing the stairs to meet the forbidding Dr Neighbour in his surgery with his patients sitting anxiously in the waiting room, one of them having had a nasty accident at work. Apparently many of Dr Neighbour's patients, on hearing his voice through the surgery door, crept away, deciding they did not feel so ill after all. In the nearby room is a beautiful collection of costumes.

A quiet museum for a quiet family!

Stonehenge (EH)
2 miles west of Amesbury on junction of A303 with A344/A360
0980 623108

O Good Friday or 1 April, whichever is first-30 September 10am-6pm, 1 October-31 March/Maundy Thursday 10am-4pm, every day

£ EH Members free, Adult £2.70, Child £1.30, Under Five free, OAP £2.00.

P on site

BR Salisbury, then bus 3 to Stonehenge

& yes

✗ café

You may have driven past it many times and seen it, perhaps, in the sunset, at its most awe-inspiring. You may often have wondered why it is there and how it got there. If you enter the site, you cannot get right in amongst the stones, but you are very close to them as you walk around.

The stones were raised about four thousand years ago, though the site was in use a thousand years before that time. It was as ancient to the Romans as Roman remains are to the 20th century. The Saxons named it 'Stonehenge', the stone gallows. We know that the stones are bluestones, brought from the Preseli Hills in South West Wales and from the Marlborough Downs. We also know its major axis is aligned with the rising of the midsummer sun. Temple, tomb or ritual space are only a few of the theories but it still remains a mystery and will surely continue to inspire discussion for years to come.

The Salisbury Giant in all his finery.

NORTH YORKSHIRE

North Yorkshire Moors Railway
Pickering Station
Pickering
North Yorkshire YO18 7AJ
0751 72508

○ 10am-6pm. Trains run every day from 13 February-31 October
Sundays only in March
£ Return tickets from: Adult £4.80, Child £2.40, Under Five free, OAP £3.20, Family £17.00/£19.00
🅿 on site
🚃 BR Grosmont
♿ limited
🍴 restaurant and picnic area.

This railway line was built by George Stephenson and you can see locomotives of all ages and design here. You can take the LNER train from Pickering to Grosmont via Goathland, Newtondale and Levisham and get splendid views over the Moors. Explore Goathland, a village, high up on the moors, where sheep roam around freely. We have found that children, especially younger ones enjoy a train ride, parents can relax and children rest, even sleep, so it is quite a good idea to timetable the journey for a rest period in the day.

The railway traverses some extremely beautiful parts of the moors.

YORK

The City of York, like Bath, is very popular and can be unbearable in summer, so if you can, do come at another time of the year. York is steeped in history and archaeology; the Vikings came here and there is evidence of the Romans too. As you enter the city you will see the fine old city walls, with the banks covered in daffodils in the spring. Find time to walk through the Shambles, avoid the tourist shops but do look up at the timber houses and their proximity across the street to one another. Then on to the Minster, seat of the Archbishop. There is lots to do here and the city is well worth coming to for a few days' holiday, although it can be expensive.

ARC
The Archaeological Resource Centre
St Saviourgate
York YO1 2NN
0904 654324

○ 1 February-31 December Monday-Friday 10am-5pm, Saturday and Sunday 1-5pm. January, Monday-Friday 10am-5pm.
£ Adult £3.00, Child £2.00, Under Five free, OAP £2.00
🅿 nearby
🚌 BR York, bus to city centre
♿ yes
✕ picnic area

Spend time at ARC; it is a wonderful resource centre, and offers unique opportunities to learn about archaeology and to carry out real post-excavation activities. You will be able to work with original artefacts not replicas. Take this rare opportunity to handle objects and reconstruct, first hand, a picture of how our ancestors lived and worked.

York Castle Museum
The Eye of York
York YO1 1RY
North Yorkshire
0904 653611

○ 1 April-31 October, Monday-Saturday 9.30am-5.30pm (last admission), Sunday 10am-5.30pm (last admission).
1 November-31 March, Monday-Saturday 9.30am-4pm (last admission), Sunday 10am-4pm (last admission)
£ Adult £3.80, Child £2.70, Under Five £2.70, OAP £2.70, Family Ticket £10.00
🅿 St George's Field car park
🚌 BR York, local bus services
♿ Ground floor only. Free entry to wheelchair users and carers.
✕ café

To visit York Castle Museum you need lots of energy, plenty of time and be prepared to lose everybody. However

'Kirkgate' at York Castle Museum.

we do recommend it as a place for all ages to roam and explore. It is crammed from top to bottom with human paraphernalia from a witch ball to quite literally, the kitchen sink. Generations of children living in the North of England have come here, loved it and returned, years later, with their own children who are usually equally as impressed.

The museum was founded by John Kirk, a Yorkshire doctor, who was an inveterate collector. When his house overflowed with stuff his wife was greatly relieved that the City of York agreed to display the collection in the old prison. Instead of ranging his collections on shelves to gather dust in glass cases, Dr Kirk designed rooms so that objects could be in their proper places. His famous cobbled Victorian street, Kirkgate, with its horsedrawn vehicles, was a revolution in museum design. Here is a collection of real houses and shop fronts rescued by Dr Kirk from the bulldozers. Look for the leeches drug jar in the window of the apothecary, smell the tallow from the dips made of mutton fat in the candle factory and gaze at the mouth watering selection of spice pigs, togo bullets and humbugs in Joseph Terry's enticing sweetshop.

In Half Moon Court listen to music from the polyphon while the gas lamps hiss, look at the new fangled motor vehicles in Wales & Son's garage where the petrol costs sixpence (2½p) a gallon. Lean against the brass rail of the King William pub with its lead spittoon on the floor. Wander on through a staggering array of domestic equipment: vacuum cleaners like huge bicycle pumps, elaborate lavatories, early washing machines with wringers (no tumble- or spin-driers here!), and even a remarkable cumbersome apple corer.

Do find the Children's Gallery with its vast collection of clockwork toys and dolls. Then explore further down stairs and around corners until you come to the famous Saxon fighting helmet, huge two-handed swords, muskets and grenades and on to the terrible World War One trench. Plunge downwards into the prison cells, York's original Debtor's prison, past the padded cell for violent prisoners, past thumb screws and man traps, past the Execution slot machine into the condemned cell where Dick Turpin, the highwayman spent his last night on earth. Relive the story of Turpin's famous high-speed ride from London to York on his fine horse, Black Bess.

Jorvik Viking Centre
Coppergate
York YO1 1NT
0904 643211

○ 1April-31 October 9am-7pm.
1 November-31 March 9am-5.30pm.
£ Adult £3.80, Child £1.90, Under Five free, OAP £2.85
🅿 Piccadilly car park
🚌 City centre bus routes, Park and Ride
♿ yes
✗ no

Even if nobody is 'doing' the Vikings it is certainly worth joining the queue (get up early to avoid the crowds) to experience the Jorvik Viking Centre. Here you will discover intimate details about a group of people whose popular reputation is that of bloodthirsty invaders. Your children will also gain a tremendous insight into the world of archaeology and the excitement of unearthing the past. For it was very recently that archaeologists uncovered this Viking city beneath the modern Coppergate. Here were complete houses and workshops still with tools, kitchen utensils, fragments of clothing and even moss used for lavatory paper.

You travel in a four seater time car which takes you back through a

thousand years to the heart of the Viking city. You can hear the sounds of the times, catch a smattering of Scandinavian tongues, smell whiffs of baking bread and rotten fish, as your time car takes you right through the wooden walls of a Viking house with figures cross-legged by smokey fires or bending over huge looms. And on, past potters, thatchers, silversmiths, woodworkers till you reach the sights and sounds of the busy wharf. Then round a corner and you are in the archaeological dig itself, where you can see the actual Viking timber house found on the site and now recreated. Stop in the area that invitingly says 'Please Touch' and then go into the gallery where you can spend more time looking at the hoard of real Viking objects dug out of the ground.

The only disadvantage is that although the time car goes slowly, it does not go slowly enough, nor does it ever stop completely to give you time to linger. The result of this is that when you have been round once you want to go straight back to the beginning and start again. Unfortunately this will leave a gaping hole in your purse, but you might consider it worthwhile.

Below and bottom: Viking life at home and at sea as seen in the Jorvik Viking Centre.

National Railway Museum
Leeman Road
York Y02 4XJ
0904 621261

O Monday-Saturday 10am-6pm, Sunday 11am-
   6pm. Last admission 5pm.
   Closed 24, 25, 26 December, 1 January.
£ Adult £3.95, Child £2.00, Under Five free,
   OAP/Concessions £2.60, Family Ticket, up to 3
   children £11.00
P on site
BR York 5 minutes walk.
ê yes
✗ restaurant and picnic area

The recently expanded National
Railway Museum is a really exciting
place for the railway enthusiast. Find
out how two hundred years of railways
have changed the world and see the
social and technical developments in
'The Great Railway Show'. Discover
how royalty travelled by train. Wander
around the vast collection of proud,
gleaming locomotives in the Great Hall
and find a replica of Stephenson's
Rocket, the *Mallard*, the world steam
record holder; a Chinese locomotive;
the story of British Rail; footbridges and
signalling. Ask around to see who
remembers the old Euston Station and
find the gates here. Glimpse into the
future of British Rail as well as looking
at the model of the Trans Manche
Super Train which will go through the
Channel Tunnel.

Go through the subway to the South
Hall and find out about different modes
of railway travel; luxury and commuter
travel, the Royal Mail, freight, suburban
trains, dining cars, the East Coast
Express and the Channel.

In the South Yard have fun with the
locomotive operating 7 $\frac{1}{4}$ inch steam
railway.

If you really are interested in railways
and their histories then allow plenty of
time here, for you should be very
impressed. However if you just want a
brief encounter take the Express Visit
indicated on the Museum Plan.

Yorkshire Museum of Farming and Houlgate Village

Murton Park
Murton
York YO1 3UF
0904 489966

○ every day 9.30am-5.30pm.
Closed 25, 26 December

£ Adult £2.60, Child £1.30, Under Five free,
OAP £2.00, Family Ticket £6.50.
Season Tickets single person £12.00 family
£18.00

🅿 on site

🚌 York Rider Bus 10 and 20 from York

♿ yes

✕ restaurant and picnic area

Get away from the bustle of historic York at Murton Park south of the City on the A166, Bridlington Road. Take appropriate clothing and footwear for the potential young farmers.

Farming is an important industry in this area and at the museum children can find out about its history and the importance of food and livestock. Various barns house different displays on different subject areas. In the Four-Seasons Barn you can follow the arable farming year; look at machinery and demonstrations of ploughing, sowing and reaping; identify crops like oats, wheat and barley. In another barn there is a reproduction of 'James Herriot's' surgery, the most famous Yorkshire vet who practised around this area; many of the artefacts on display have been donated by the real-life vet and author. Do spend time looking at the old farming tools and implements in the Hardware Store.

Outside on the farm, animals are in pens with wire fences, so even the youngest visitor can get a good view. There are Soay and Wensleydale sheep, a Galloway cow, pigs, poultry, rabbits and a shire horse. Look into the incubator and you may see a chick being hatched. If you visit in the spring you may be able to bottle feed an orphan lamb and in summer watch the bees producing honey in a glass covered hive.

Get a glimpse of life in the Dark Ages with a visit to Houlgate Village close by. An early medieval settlement has been recreated here with buildings: a tavern, mill and Viking Hall. Staff are dressed in period costume and have names like Harald, Arinbjorn, Oswyn and Erica. There are craft making sessions in which children are encouraged to participate.

Above: Railway memorabilia from buttons and badges to model engines and an elaborate candelabra.

Left: A Midland single in the South Hall at the National Railway Museum.

SOUTH YORKSHIRE

Kelham Island Museum

Off Alma Street
Sheffield S3 8RY
South Yorkshire
0742 722106

O March-first week of December, Monday-
   Thursday 10am-4pm, Sunday 11am-4pm.
£ Adult £2.20, Child £1.10, Under Five free,
   OAP £1.10, Family £4.40
P on site
🚍 47 &48 bus
♿ yes
✖ café and picnic area

Sheffield's industrial museum stands on
an island in the River Don and is part of
a working industrial site. This is certainly
the museum to visit to find out about the
industries that made Sheffield famous
all over the world for its steel and
cutlery. Maybe take a grandparent who
worked in the city and remembers how
it used to be.

Colourful, visible information panels
present the story of the steel industry.
Go through the reconstructed die
sinker's and cutler's workshops and do
not miss the daily demonstrations of the
River Don Engine, one of the steam
engines that powered the industries.
You will find out about the social,
working and educational conditions of
the children and adults living in Sheffield
in the 19th and 20th centuries.
Master craftsmen are still at work in the
'Little Mesters' Workshops where you
will find a forger, cutler and maker of
dental and surgical tools.

Sheffield City Museum

Weston Park
Sheffield S10 2TP
0742 768588

O Tuesday-Saturday 10am-5pm, Sunday
   11am-5pm.
   Open on Bank Holiday Monday.
£ free
P on road
🚍 BR Sheffield.
   Bus 51, 52 from city centre
♿ yes
✖ café. Picnic area nearby

If you are in Sheffield it is worth paying
a short visit to the City Museum. You
will find the largest collection of
Sheffield Plate in the country there and
learn about the discovery and success
of this important industry. Don't miss the
Anglo-Saxon helmet and Bronze Age
finds in the Archaeology Gallery.

The Natural History Department runs
holiday activities as well as Wildlife
Walks. Accompanied by a friendly and
experienced member of the museum's
staff you will be able to explore the local
countryside with new eyes. These walks
are open to all ages but check in
advance the length and terrain of a
specific walk and its suitability to your
group.

Elsewhere in the museum are
displays of coins and costume
accessories. In the summer holidays
there are family related activities when
there are opportunities to handle
artefacts. There are craft activities for
the under fives and microscopic
examinations of objects and computer-
generated learning facilities for older
children and adults. These workshops
are very popular so book in advance.
There is a small fee for use of materials.

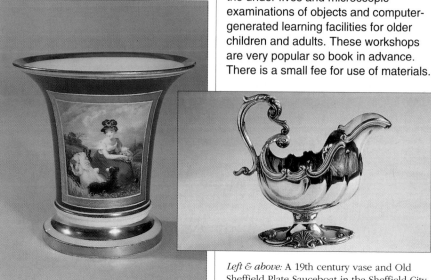

Left & above: A 19th century vase and Old
Sheffield Plate Sauceboat in the Sheffield City
Museum.

WEST YORKSHIRE

Industrial Museum and Horses at Work
Moorside Road
Bradford BD2 3HP
West Yorkshire
0274 631756

○ Tuesday-Sunday 10am-5pm.
  Open Bank Holiday Monday
£ free. Small charge for horsedrawn rides
🅿 on site
🚌 bus 614, 634 from the Tryls, 608,609 from
  Bank St to Moorside Road; 896 Micro Rider
  from Interchange
♿ to most parts
✕ café and picnic area

Come here to find out about the varied history of Bradford and its surrounding village and hamlets and you will not be disappointed. There are daily demonstrations (not between noon and 2pm on weekdays), by experienced and knowledgeable staff, of the water turbines and steam and gas engines that powered the woollen mills. In the worsted textile and spinning galleries you can see how the yarn was prepared.

Water, steam, gas and electricity were not the only source of power for all these machines; there were also horses. Go to the Horses at Work Gallery and meet them in their stables, maybe harness one for a horse-drawn ride around the site (ring in advance for details). Horses were used to power machines as well as transport goods.

The Transport Gallery houses a collection of bicycles, cars and other vehicles, with local connections. Find the tramcar and trolley bus which used to run in Bradford.

The workers and mill owners of Bradford are also remembered. The workers were highly skilled but their living conditions were cramped and poverty stricken compared to the luxury of the mill managers. Have a look at the restored one-up, one-down workers' cottages. These have one room upstairs and one down and no bathroom and were common for the mill workers of Lancashire and West Yorkshire to live in with their families. Here you can see the interior changes over the years in different cottages of the 1870s, 1920s and 1950s. Then you can look at the comparative luxury of the mill manager's home.

This is an excellent museum, displays are accessible and information well prepared and easy to read. Staff are happy to answer questions. Throughout the museum you will meet former engineers and mill operators who are delighted to offer a personal insight into the life of a factory worker in Bradford. Do allow plenty of time to enjoy your visit to the full. There are constantly changing exhibitions and holiday activities.

The National Museum of Photography, Film and Television
Pictureville
Bradford BD1 1NQ
0274 727488

○ Tuesday-Sunday 10.30am-6pm.
  Special exhibitions open until 8pm. Open Bank
  Holiday Monday. Closed around Christmas.
£ free. Admission charge to IMAX: Adult £3.65,
  Child £2.50, Under Five £2.50,
  OAP/Concessions £2.50
🅿 public car parks
🚌 BR Bradford, bus to city centre
♿ yes
✕ restaurant

We were fascinated to discover the huge impact that photography has had on our lives, this century. From early image-capturing techniques, we were transported through the medium's

The façade of The National Museum of Photography, Film and Television in Bradford.

history right up to the present with satellite surveillance of the earth. Through specialist exhibitions we were able to participate in finding out about different developments, 'The Kodak Museum' of popular photography; 'Spellbound in Darkness' and the history of the cinema; the 'Story of British Television' and 'Photography is News'. We learnt how to develop photographs in the laboratory, watched the magic lantern show and went behind the scenes of a television studio.

Then we sat in front of IMAX, the enormous, 52ft x 64ft, cinema screen and watched films on environmental issues, the natural world and space probe shots. Pictureville Cinema shows children's films daily in August and at weekends throughout the year.

Workshops are held regularly, many suitable for children of twelve years and over. The Dream Machine Summer Club runs in the summer holidays for children aged six to sixteen years and includes theatre, video and photography workshops.

The luxury new Pictureville Cinema.

Dewsbury Museum of Childhood

Crow Nest Park
Heckmondwike Road
Dewsbury
West Yorkshire WF13 2SA
0924 468171

O Monday-Friday 11am-5pm, Saturday & Sunday noon-5pm
£ free
P on site
🚌 bus 212, 214, 272, 274, 254, 255 from Dewsbury Bus Station to Crow Nest Park
♿ Limited weelchair & pushchair access

The museum is housed in a mansion in the landscaped grounds of Crow Nest Park. Its collection covers all aspects of childhood including toys and games, education and children at work. We have found it important to warn our younger children in advance, that in most museums of toys or childhood they will be able to see but not play with the toys. At Dewsbury there is a small play area, upstairs, where children can look at books.

In 'Children at Play' you will find toys from the 19th century to the 1960s. There is an Edwardian dolls' house in the middle of the gallery with lovely room settings. Also on display are cuddly animals, tin toys, die cast models, dolls and pop-up books.

In the 19th century many children in the West Riding had a very tough time. Some as young as five were sent out to work; in the 'Children at Work' gallery you will see what terrible conditions they had to contend with. There is a full scale replica of a coal mine, children were small and useful for getting into narrow gaps; they pulled coal tubs underground, worked in the mills and on the land.

Calderdale Industrial Museum

Winding Road
Halifax HX1 0QG
0422 358087

O Tuesday-Sunday 10am-5pm
£ Adult £1.50, Child 75p, Under Five free, OAP 75p, Family Ticket £3.00
P nearby
🚌 BR Halifax & bus station nearby
♿ good
🍴 restaurant

Halifax is situated in the heart of the West Riding woollen industry and this museum shows the social and working lives of the people involved in it.

Start in the pre-industrial, 18th century Piece Hall behind the main building. The history of the textile hand-working processes are explained with life-size models in contemporary costumes.

Back in the main building life in 1850s Halifax can be experienced in reconstructed streets and shops. The '100 Trades of Halifax' gallery astounds in the array of products, originating in Halifax (which we take for granted). Crawl through a mine shaft, learn about quarrying and see the working steam engine.

Eureka! The Museum for Children

Discovery Road
Halifax HX1 2NE
West Yorkshire
0422 330069.
Information Line 0426 983191

O Monday, Tuesday 10am-2pm, Wednesday
  10am-7pm, other days 10am-5pm.

£ Adult £4.50, Child £3.50, Under Three free,
  OAP £3.50, Family Ticket £13.50

P on site

BR Halifax on Calderdale Line, right next to
  station

&. yes

X café and picnic area

A cupboard of dreams, a Chinese dragon, a see-through lavatory, a friendly robot called Scoot, a tree that tells stories are all exhibits in this latest 'hands-on' museum for children. It is exactly what it says: not just a museum where there happen to be some very good things for children, but a place where everything is specially made for them.

'When you sneeze, air passes through your nose at one hundred miles an hour'. This, and other extraordinary facts, can be found in 'Me and My Body'. A giant rib cage, a walk-in mouth, a digestion pinball machine and what appears to be your own skeleton on an exercise bike all help to solve the riddles of the human body. Seek out Scoot for a real conversation on the differences between his mechanical insides and your own.

'Living and Working Together' allows children to be like grown-ups; shopping, going to the bank, filling up the car with petrol, using the fax machine. Be

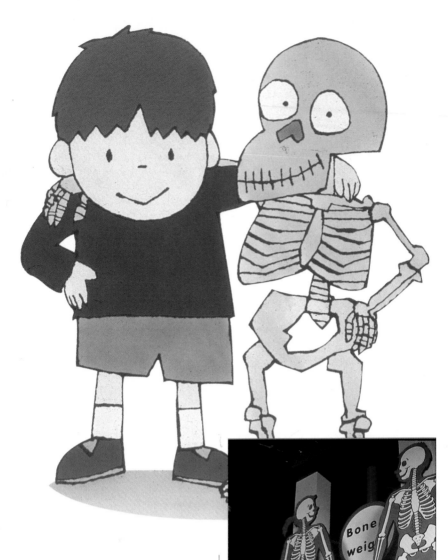

creative in a television studio or with desk top publishing facilities.

Make your own sculpture out of recycled materials with enough paints, scissors and reels of adhesive tape to make any parent happy. Guess mystery food in feely drawers and smelly boxes. Play on musical and wobbly bridges in a jungle for the under fives.

Watch out for a happily grinning Archimedes, who once cried Eureka when sitting in his bath. Here he proudly plunges in at regular intervals, displacing water which appropriately comes back up a long see-through Archimedes screw.

If you have children between the ages of two and eleven take them to Eureka! whatever part of the country you set out from. The twelve year olds we took were too blasé to 'pretend' to go shopping, too cynical to strike up friendly conversations with robots and too inhibited to put on the wonderful sixties dressing up clothes. However, teenagers are fascinated by their own bodies, they are irresistibly drawn to

Above: 'Me and My Body'.
Top: 'Me and my skeleton', one of Eureka's cartoons.
Left: 'What if I Couldn't', part of the Me and My Body exhibition.

computer screens and they still want to have a go at everything. We arrived on a wet Wednesday in August after a long drive from London and stayed for five hours until we were gently persuaded to leave, the last to go, well after 7pm on late night opening.

Keighley and Worth Valley Railway

The Railway Station
Haworth
Keighley BD22 8NJ
West Yorkshire
0535 645214.
24 hr timetable information 0535 643629

O Weekend 9am-5.30pm.
  Every day in July and August 11am-5.30pm.
  Bank Holiday Week 9am-5.30pm.
£ Train Fare: Adult £4.00, Child £2.00, Under Five free, OAP £2.00, Family £10.00
🅿 on site
🚌 BR Keighley
♿ yes
✗ café and picnic area

What better way to see the rolling Pennines than by steam train from Keighley in the east to Oxenhope, near Hebden Bridge in the west. You will go through six stations en-route, each with their individual charm and attractions. Get off and explore the Ingrow Railway Centre with its goods yard and collection of vintage carriages. Oakworth station has often appeared on television and in films such as 'Poirot' and 'The Railway Children'; its gardens are well worth seeing. Get off at Haworth if you want to visit this hilly, bleak town, home to the Brontë sisters. Look through the windows and imagine Wuthering Heights, Heathcliffe and Jane Eyre. Finally arrive at Oxenhope in the heart of the Pennines and almost in Lancashire.

There are lots of other exciting things to do throughout the year along this line – travel as they did 125 years ago. On special days, have Sunday lunch on the Pullman and a Santa Special near Christmas. Enjoy yourselves, but do check the times of trains beforehand.

American-built steam locomotive at Keighley.

Kirkstall Abbey and Abbey House Museum

Abbey Road
Leeds LS5
0532 755821

O Abbey 9am-dusk every day.
  Museum Monday-Saturday 9.30am-5pm, Sunday 2-5 pm.
£ Abbey Free.
  Museum: Adult £1.10, Child 50p, Under Five OAP 50p
🅿 nearby, signposted
🚌 bus 50 from Leeds City Centre
♿ Abbey yes Museum limited
✗ picnic area

Kirkstall Abbey and Abbey House Museum are situated on either side of the A65 Leeds-Ilkley road. They are worth a visit if you are nearby or as a stopping off place for a picnic en-route to the Yorkshire Dales.

The Abbey was completed between 1152 and 1182 and is an excellent example of Cistercian architecture. In 1147 a community of monks left Fountains Abbey to found a monastery near Barnoldswick but the cruel Pennine weather and an inhospitable local community forced them to leave. They were making their way along the Aire valley to Pontefract Castle when they found this site with lots of timber, stone and water. The ruins are extensive and still stand almost to their full height. However, due to pollution eating into the stone it is not possible to enter the church remains. The standing cloisters and excavated foundations of the dormitory can be visited.

Use the pelican crossing to get to the other side of the busy road and visit the Abbey House Museum which occupies the remains of the medieval gatehouse and the 19th century family house. Inside you will find information about the

history of the Abbey. In the 19th century extension you will find the de Lacy Room decorated in Victorian Gothic Revival style. This is a 'look-through' room with viewing limited to two at a time.

The fascinating Toy Gallery is up a steep but beautiful staircase. There are toys from 1750 to 1990 here, all displayed so even the smallest child can see them. There are jigsaws in the form of maps or covered with biblical pictures, historical and geographical themes; 19th century board games; dolls and dolls' houses; mechanical and optical toys. In most Victorian homes only toys with a religious subject could be played with on Sundays. Here you will find Sunday bricks, jigsaws, board-games and books.

Further on in the museum you will find displays of costume, cooking and cooking ranges, washing and lighting. Take care as you go down the narrow staircase to the Stephen Harding Gate which is a reconstructed 18th and 19th century street of shops. There are a 'look-through' tavern, a chemist, Burmantofts Pottery showroom, grocers and craft workshops. Look at the things in the shop windows.

Upstairs again to the restored and cluttered Victorian parlour. Throughout the museum are automata 'seaside peepshows', with figures re-enacting a day out at the circus, a murder mystery and a very revealing 'What-the-Butler-Saw' (PG).

Yorkshire Mining Museum
Caphouse Colliery
New Road
Overton
Wakefield WF4 4RH
0924 848806

O 10am-5pm every day.
  Closed 24-26 December, 1 January
£ Adult £5.25, Child £3.95, Under Five free,
  OAP £4.40. Family Ticket £17.00 Includes
  underground tour, part refund if not taken.
  Under Fives not allowed underground.
P on site
🚌 bus 263 Wakefield to Huddersfield
♿ yes
✕ restaurant and picnic area

Caphouse Colliery operated until 1985 and now forms the basis of the Yorkshire Mining Museum. It is worth spending some time here to see the history of coalmining which was a great source of employment in the region and vital to its industrial growth. The admission fee is on the high side because the pit has to be inspected for safety every day but £2.50 will be refunded if you do not go underground.

The main attraction is underground where, accompanied by former miners, you will travel 450ft beneath the surface to see coal-extracting equipment and techniques employed from the 19th century to 1960. Children under five are not allowed beneath the surface. Deep in the pit there are life-size models of the miners – men, women and children who worked long hours in appalling conditions.

In 1842 legislation prohibited women and children from working in the pits.

Back on the surface, spend time in the main exhibition building which has excellent displays on the history of mining and on the working and social conditions of the miners employed in the colliery. Watch the videos on life at Caphouse and the history of mining.

In other buildings you will find mining machinery, the Steam Winder Engine and the Lancashire Boiler. Elsewhere are the pit baths used by the miners at the end of a gruelling shift, the medical centre, waddle fan, drift mouth and Paddy haulage engine.

Pit ponies were used to transport the coal underground; after a lifetime in the dark many went blind. Here there are ponies in the stables, more healthy than their ancestors. Children can take horse and cart rides and mini-steam train rides. Under fives can enjoy themselves on their playground and older siblings can play in the adventure playground. You can round off your visit by following the nature trail around the site.

The appalling conditions suffered by men, women and children working underground are clearly shown.

Yorkshire Sculpture Park
Bretton Hall
West Bretton Wakefield WF4 4LG
West Yorkshire
0924 830579

O Summer 10am-6pm every day.
  Winter, Tuesday-Sunday 10am-4pm
£ free
P on site
⊞ BR Wakefield Westgate. Buses from Wakefield,
  Huddersfield, Holmfirth, Dewsbury and
  Barnsley
♿ yes, special sculpture trail for wheelchair users
  and the partially sighted.
✕ café and picnic area

If your children are inveterate makers of
things out of clay and papier mâché
then they may well appreciate a visit
here. Bring them on a Saturday and
they may be able to sculpt alongside the
artist in residence. The site covers one
hundred acres of rolling green
landscape with trees and a lake. Dotted
throughout, almost like a treasure trail,
are some wonderful works by 20th
century sculptors. Walk around Henry
Moore's great, hunky figures. Find the
'Monumental Horse' created by Emile
Antoine Bourdelle in 1917 and 'The First
Try' with its huge arms by Gordon
Young in 1984. Exhibits change quite
frequently so you never know what you
might meet.

Below: Dust of the Orient, Bronze 1990, by
Igor Mitoraj. Photo Jerry Hardman-Jones.

Bottom Fifteen foot leaping hare. Bronze
1990, by Barry Flanagan, from the exhibition
'The Names of the Hare', summer 1992. Photo
Jerry Hardman-Jones.

SCOTLAND

The forecourt at Holyrood House.

GRAMPIAN

Aberdeen Maritime Museum
Provost Ross's House
Shiplow
Aberdeen AB1 2BY
0224 585788

O Monday-Saturday 10am-5pm
£ free
P opposite
🚌 BR and bus to Castle St
♿ ground floor only
✗ no

The discovery of North Sea oil hit the headlines in the 1960s. At the Aberdeen Maritime Museum you can see the incredible impact it made on this area. A huge 'press-button' model of an oil rig is a good means of explaining to children, although it might need a helpful parent to point out where the helicopter lands and other useful facts. This and an audio-visual presentation all help to tell you the story of extracting oil hundreds of feet below the bed of the North Sea in one of the world's most technologically advanced industries. There is a pleasing incongruity in the fact that it is all displayed in Aberdeen's oldest surviving building, the shipping merchant, Provost Ross' house, built in 1594. Through its small windows you can look out on part of the harbour filled with strange vessels serving the offshore gas and oil industry. A cousin who lives there tells me she takes her young children to visit the harbour at night and describes the lights shining like stars, the hum of compressors and the air of expectation that hangs over it all.

Aberdeen's Maritime Museum.

This is the place for children who like beautifully and intricately made models of ships. There is the 'schip' of 1689, rigged as a fifth-rate warship, the clipper *Stornoway* built at Aberdeen in 1850 for Jardine Matheson to carry tea from China. Aberdeen was the home of one of the first clippers, the *Scottish Maid* – these were then the fastest trading ships in the world. There is even a model roll-on roll-off ferry ('Ro-Ro' ferry). Find out about *Thermopylae*, the world-beating speed ship and other famous tall ships.

Aberdeen was Scotland's biggest whaling port and busiest herring fishing port; there are rooms devoted to these trades. You can imagine only too well the hard living from the North Sea in the days of herring drifters and fisher lassies.

Grampian Transport Museum
Alford
Aberdeenshire AB33 8AD
09755 62292

O 28 March-31 October 10am-5pm every day
£ Adult £2.30, Child 80p, Under Five free,
  OAP £1.50, Family £5.00
  Season Ticket; individual £5.00, family £8.00
P on site
🚌 bus Aberdeen - Strathdon
♿ to most parts
✗ picnic area

This was the 1859 terminus for the Great North of Scotland Railway and yet another museum for the transport buff. One of the curiosities of the collection is the Craigevar Express, a strange home-made, three-wheeled, steam-driven vehicle built by the 'postie' at Craigevar to do his rounds. Everybody can dance to the Mortier Dance Organ, probably here because it is too big to fit anywhere else but quite impressive with its pipes, drums and Art-Deco facade. Bicycles to vintage cars, steam vehicles to trams, they are all here. Children can shinny up to a snow plough, clamber on a steam roller and a Saracen armoured personnel carrier. Outside is a children's adventure playground, a Grampian transport double-decker bus and a 1966 driving simulator, for budding child drivers. Take a trip on a miniature steam railway and stop off at an old GNSR village station. In the summer there are rallies, steam-up days and a children's 'mega party'.

A snow plough at Grampian Transport Museum.

North East of Scotland Agricultural Heritage Centre

Aden Country Park
Mintlaw
Peterhead
Banff and Buchan AB42 8FQ
0771 22857

O May-September every day 11am-5pm, last admission 4.30pm.
April and October weekend only 12 noon-5pm, last admission 4.30pm.

£ Adult £1.00, Child free, Under Five free, OAP £1.00

P on site

to Mintlaw

wheelchair access to ground floor only, there is a garden for the partially sighted.

café and picnic area

The story of farming in this part of Scotland is brought alive by a walk round a unique semi-circular steading with its beautiful central 'doocote'. Look for the guide making 'breid' or oatcakes in the Horseman's House and she will tell you what estate life was like in the 1920s. Explore the threshing mill, the coach house, the sawmill, the castle court and the dairy and the Grieve's house.

Children will like 'Hareshome' working farm and open-air section to the Heritage Centre. Wait at the neep shed for a guide to take you round what was once the farm of the Barron Family in the 1950s. Here are the barns, workshops, shed and stables, even an old railway carriage used as a store and the farmhouse itself.

Outside activities follow the farm year: harrowing, ploughing, sowing and harvesting. See if you can find out what 'mucking dreels', 'hyowing' and 'shimming' mean.

The Country Park has a nature trail and wildlife centre (May-September, weekends only, 2-5pm) and is a wonderful place for picnics, deep in the woods.

Former Aden Estate Home Farm, restored by Banff and Buchan District Council, now houses the award-winning N.E. Scotland Agricultural Heritage Centre.

HIGHLAND

Cromarty Courthouse

Church Street
Cromarty IV11 8XA
Highland
038 17 418

- O 1 April-31 October 10am-6pm.
  1 November-31 March 12-4pm
- £ Adult £2.50, Child £1.25, Under Five free,
  OAP £1.25, Family Ticket £7.50
- 🅿 nearby
- 🚌 buses from Inverness, ferry from Nigg
- ♿ no
- ✖ picnic area

Hugh Miller's Cottage

- O 1 April-30 September Monday-Saturday 10am-
  noon, 1-5pm. Sunday 2-5pm.

Far north on the coast of Scotland,
Cromarty is an extraordinary place. It has
not changed much since the 16th century,
and retains many of its elegant merchant
houses, as well as the Hemp Works built
in 1774, one of Scotland's first factories,
and Hugh Miller's Cottage, now run by the
National Trust for Scotland.

Below: Cromarty Courthouse.

The Courthouse has prison cells, with life-size, speaking and moving prisoners, a bewigged judge and clerks of the court. They are frightening for very young children, and certainly evoke the atmosphere of fear, tension and pomposity that the walls must have soaked in over two hundred years. You can watch the trial of a woman found guilty of theft from Cromarty's hemp factory, sentenced to be drummed round the town and exiled from the country for seven years. You will meet Sir Thomas Urquart of Cromarty, one of Scotland's greatest eccentrics and, if you like, hear the folk tales and history of Cromarty on the excellent tape tour (either 45 minutes or 1¼ hours). If this is too rigorous for you, then you can go down to the beach and look out over the Moray Firth for dolphins and porpoises between the two headlands or 'sutors', Scots for a shoemaker. There is a legend that the sutors are named after two giant shoemakers who shared their tools and threw them across from one side to another. Seals lie lazily on the sandbanks here. Scramble over the rocks, east of Cromarty, to Dripping Cave with the stalactites on the roof. The one thing you will not miss are the oil drilling platforms anchored here when not in use. The ferry north to Nigg goes right past them.

Museum and Art Gallery
Castle Wynd
Inverness IV2 3ED
0463 237114

O Monday-Saturday 9am-5pm, Sunday in July and August 2-5pm
£ free
P city centre car parks
🚍 city centre bus services
♿ yes
✗ café

The wild life of the Highlands is the best aspect of this museum. Almost the first thing you see is a huge and beautiful osprey in flight, caught in mid-air with a fish in its claws. Look for the golden

eagle and the red deer and for the bilingual labels in English and Gaelic.

The last taxidermist's shop to survive in Inverness is reconstructed here. There is a row of innocuous looking chisels and pliers but, as to their functions, perhaps it is better not to speculate further. Taxidermy was once a flourishing Victorian trade supported by highland shooting parties. Even as late as 1935, one hundred and sixty two stags' heads were mounted in this shop during the September and October of that year. The reconstructed silver shop represents another thriving Inverness trade. Here are communion cups and Christening spoons, toddy ladles and 'quaichs' once filled with whisky and passed around on festive occasions. Holiday activities for children include 'Bug Hunts' and 'Time Treks'.

Highland Folk Museum
Duke Street
Kingussie PH21
Highland
0540 661307

O Easter-31 October Monday-Saturday 10am-6pm, Sunday 2-6pm.
1 November-Easter Monday-Friday 10am-3pm
£ Adult £2.00, Child £1.00, Under Five free, OAP £1.00
P on site
🚍 BR Kingussie or bus from Inverness
♿ yes
✗ picnic area

Even thirty years ago most museums, especially in the eyes of a child, usually meant valuable or rare objects, displayed in dusty rows behind glass cases. 'Ordinary' things belonging to 'ordinary' people were not considered interesting or worthy enough. In the 1930s Dr Isobel Grant set up the first folk museum in Britain, originally on Iona and now here at Kingussie. Her aim was not only to raise the profile of people from humble origins, but also to preserve a record of a Highland way of life that was fast disappearing.

Inside you will find box beds, bagpipes, crinolines, tartans, kilts, packsaddles, fiddles, butterchurns, cheese presses, woolwinders, spinning wheels, a fire engine with a steam pump, a horse collar made of woven grass, bobbins made of cow parsley stalks, chairs made of driftwood and

Left: The Sheriff (as Scottish judges are called) passing sentence at Cromarty Courthouse.

marram grass and much, much more.

Outside is a Black House from the Isle of Lewis with a cow byre and an earth floor. It was built with an inner and outer wall to combat the unceasing Atlantic gale. A (real) Highland woman might offer you oatcakes or drop scones just baked on a griddle over the peat fire. Nearby is a 'clack' mill, a salmon smoke house made of corrugated iron or 'crinkly' tin and a kail yard for growing cabbage and broccoli.

I found a Gaelic word in the guidebook which I had never seen written before but knew exactly how to pronounce. During summer holidays in Argyll as children we always loved the music and poetry of the 'ceilidh'. In the summer at Kingussie, you might well turn up on the day the jester, the fiddler or the 'clarsach' player are there.

The blacksmith at his forge at the Highland Folk Museum.

Groam House Museum
High Street
Rosemarkie IV10 8UH
Highland
0381 20961

○ 1May-1 October Monday-Saturday 11am-5pm, Sunday 2.30-4.30pm.
Every winter weekend by arrangement with the curator.
£ Adult £1.50, Children free, OAP 75p, Season Ticket £2.00
🅿 nearby
🚌 Bus from Inverness
♿ ground floor only
✗ picnic area on beach nearby

Here is a small, friendly, informal museum where children are especially welcome. You can find out about Rosemarkie as a Pictish centre, where Christianity was brought by St Boniface in the early 8th century. The Picts are known today through their carved stones whose functions and symbols of crescents and discs, interlacing of birds, fishes and beasts, are still of unknown meaning. At Groam House is the famous Rosemarkie Cross slab and other Pictish Stones.

The museum has made award winning efforts to bring alive the magic and mystery of these Pictish Stones. Children can play on a Pictish harp designed from a carving on the Nigg stone. They can watch a cartoon video of the Brahan seer who was said to have been found guilty of witchcraft, and burnt alive in a spiked tar barrel.

Gairloch Heritage Museum
Auchtercairn
Gairloch
Ross-shire IV21 2BJ
0445 2287

○ April-September 10am-5pm, Monday-Saturday. Closed Sundays.
October-March open by prior arrangement.
£ Adult £1.00, Child 20p, Members Ticket £2.00
🅿 on site
♿ yes
✗ restaurant and picnic area

The museum was made by converting parts of an old steading and interprets past life in Gairloch. Sounds boring but it is not! It is in fact a friendly, welcoming place with a growing reputation. There are fishing boats parked outside and nobody will stop your children from climbing in them, from peering through the glass of the lantern of the old lighthouse at Rubha Reidh or looking down its foghorn. In Mr MacRae's grocery store you will find all the old favourites: Robin Starch, Epsom Salts, Robinson's Barley Water and boxes stating 'Bovril is Liquid Life'. There is a very rare portable, wooden pulpit, used by ministers of the Free Presbyterian Church during open air services in the Highlands; sometimes known as tent-preaching. Unashamedly popular with visitors is the excellent restaurant, open from 9.30am to 10pm serving food such as local crab, prawns and wild salmon.

Top: Rosemarkie Beach.

LOTHIAN

Edinburgh

When I announced that I was taking two young children to Edinburgh during the last week of August, friends thought I had lost my senses. The train did break down for an hour on the way, but we had the longest picnic ever, lasting five hours, and when we got there it rained most of the time, but it did not matter, we all had a wonderful time. Thanks to a very sympathetic friend, and her dog, we were able to stay close to the city centre. The fact that the Edinburgh Festival was in full swing added to our excitement and fun. Obviously the city is exciting throughout the year but Festival time for children is enthralling; they

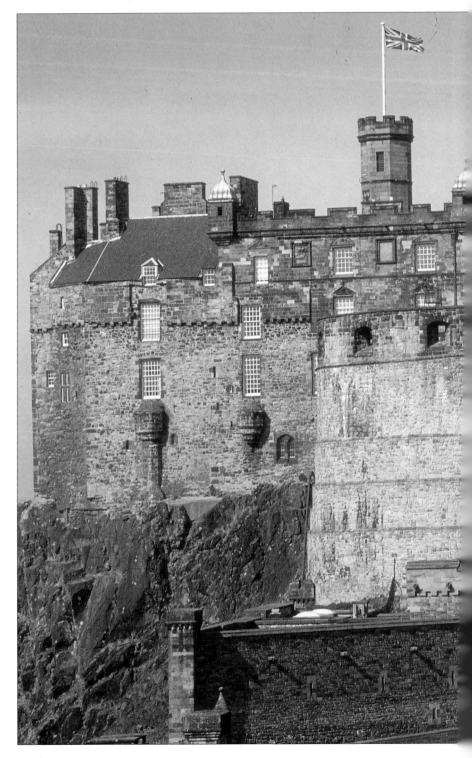

were never quite sure who or what they might bump into at the next corner: women on stilts, clowns, jugglers, fire-eaters, mime artists on the roofs of cars, rap dancers, violinists, opera singers; all young and welcoming to staring and curious children. We spent an afternoon watching and participating in the street theatre on the Mound off Princes Street. What is more, it was all free, save the odd coins thrown into a variety of hats.

Maybe Mum did not go to five theatre performances a day but she really did enjoy herself. During the Festival there are lots of morning theatre events for children; we saw Rumpelstiltskin. There is a Festival Creche if you do want to leave your children.

One day, when it poured with rain, we picked up a sightseeing bus at Waverley Station and rode around the city on a one day ticket; we could get off at various sites and get back on again in our own time as often as we wanted. Festival apart there is lots to do here.

Edinburgh Festival Information – 031 226 4001

Edinburgh Castle
Edinburgh
031 225 9846

- ○ 1 April-30 September 9.30am-5.15pm (last admission) every day.
  1 October-31 March 9.30am-4.15pm (last admission) every day.
- £ Adult £3.40, Child £1.70, Under Five free, OAP/concessions £1.70, Family Ticket £8.50
- 🅿 yes, not between 1 June and mid October
- 🚌 bus to Royal Mile
- ♿ difficult
- ✕ restaurant

Having visited many ruined castles it is marvellous to see one which is well maintained and still in use in part as a barracks for the Royal Scots Dragoon Guards. The children were delighted to see a real soldier in red and black uniform and bearskin in a sentry box at the gatehouse. It is a long trek past here and up the hill with numerous steps and our younger child, aged three and a half years had to be coaxed and carried, but once at the top she too was enthralled. We went through the massive portcullis gate, saw guns and cannon in the Half Moon Battery built in 1574, we had a wonderful view over the city and could see the docks, and trains going into Waverley Station. We imagined what it would have been like to defend the castle from here and how cold and bleak it would be in winter.

We found the oldest building in Edinburgh, the St Margaret's Chapel in the Citadel, Norman in style and built in the 12th century by David I. In Crown Square we went into the Great Hall, built by James IV, and saw many kinds of weapons. Next to it is the building in which Mary, Queen of Scots, gave birth to her son James. Then we looked at

Edinburgh Castle towers over the city.

The entrance to the Museum of Childhood.

the Scottish Crown jewels, displayed very majestically, twinkling with diamonds. Across the square we spent a sombre time in the Scottish National War Memorial, which is very moving and records the name of every Scottish serviceman and woman killed in action since 1914. Engraved in the marble walls are the names of battle grounds; the Somme, Mons, Flanders and many more. This is a place to bring older children to show them the after effects of war, as these lists of names and ages are chilling reading.

Real soldiers wander around and you can glimpse their barracks. For those really interested in the army the Scottish United Services Museum is worth a visit in Crown Square.

Archaeologists have recently found evidence of an Iron Age settlement on the Castle Rock. However, it was not until the 11th century that the present castle was begun.

Museum of Childhood
42 High Street (Royal Mile)
Edinburgh EH1 1TG
031 225 2424 ext 6645

○ 1 June-30 September, Monday-Saturday 10am-6pm.
   1 October-31 May 10am-5pm. Sunday 2-5pm during the Edinburgh Festival.
£ free
🅿 city car parks
🚉 BR Edinburgh Waverley. Buses to Royal Mile
♿ yes
✗ no

This must be the best museum of its kind in the world. I have watched it grow over twenty five years and, whilst enlarging its premises, it still retains a magical intimacy which I was delighted my children enjoyed. Unlike many other museums of toys and childhood there is lots for children to do here; they can put money in the automata, make the Nickelodeon work, play old board games, ride a huge wooden rocking horse, get on their hands and knees and look into the display cases at the quantities of toys, games, children's shoes and clothes. They can find out how rich and poor children lived. When we visited, the place was packed and very noisy as children and adults alike enjoyed themselves.

The museum has a colourful history. It began by chance when Patrick Murray, an Edinburgh councillor with a small collection of childhood related objects, persuaded the council to find a home for them. This was an immediate hit, the collection quickly grew and Murray became its curator. He publicised the museum widely and put about the rumour that he did not like children much, though many think this was a myth. Do look for some of the amusing notices Murray put up in the museum. However he was always adamant that this was to be a museum about childhood, not for children; maybe it is a measure of his success in amassing this marvellous collection that it is loved by both parents and children and boasts of being one of the noisiest museums in the world.

In Gallery 1 on the ground floor look for the Shoe Doll; an old shoe with a face carved into the bottom of the heel and a dress made out of old rags, by a child from London's East End in the last century. I find this doll both sad and highly creative; sad because the family was so poor they could not afford a real doll and this was all they could find,

imaginative because you can make anything into a doll as long as it has a face. Then gape at the huge Nickelodeon and listen to its percussion instruments bashing away. Look at the smart sit-in cars, 'nasty' Punch and Judy and a range of nursery clothing.

Have you ever seen so many, dolls' houses and shops, toy circuses, Noah's Arks, gramophones and train sets as there are upstairs? Did you know that many children were only allowed to play with toys with religious subjects on Sundays, hence the large number of 19th century Noah's Arks. Then go into Gallery 3 for the most amazing collection of dolls from all over the world, dotted amongst them you will find tea sets and tea parties. Some have wax, porcelain or cloth heads, others are newer and made of plastic. Others are huge or tiny, there are girl and boy dolls, baby dolls and fashion dolls. Some are in exquisite clothes and they look as if they have never been played with, whilst others have clearly been loved for many years.

In Gallery 4 there is a huge 1930s Meccano wheel, roller skates, old games like diabolo and marbles. Finally at the very top you can see room settings of a nursery, schoolroom and birthday party. If you are feeling somewhat out of touch with current toy trends do spend time here to see what a wealth of toys there are. The really good, classic toys, may reappear as something new, but underneath they are just the same; their purpose for play, fun and enjoyment. I had to drag my children away and each time we passed the museum again, they wanted to go back for more.

Palace of Holyrood House
Edinburgh EH8 8DX
031 556 7371,
031 556 1096 information line

○ The Palace is closed at certain times of the year so ring in advance to find out if it is open.
£ Adult £3.00, Child £1.50, Under Five free, OAP £2.50, Family Ticket £7.50
🅿 Holyrood Park
🚉 Bus to Royal Mile
♿ limited, wheelchair users should ring in advance
✗ café

This is HM The Queen's official residence in Scotland and to visit you will have to join a guided tour lasting about forty minutes. It can get very crowded here so we suggest taking

older children only, if they are interested.

The palace is situated at the eastern end of the Royal Mile, Edinburgh Castle being at the other. The ruined abbey, on the site, was founded by King David I in 1128 and over the centuries generations of royalty have added to and changed the buildings. It was here that Mary Queen of Scots lived and her favourite Rizzio was murdered.

Your tour will take you through the 17th century State Rooms full of tapestries and paintings, into the Mary Queen of Scots apartments, the King's Bedchamber and the Royal Dining Room. Outside wander through the courtyards and into the gardens.

The People's Story
Canongate Tolbooth
163 Canongate
Edinburgh EH8 8BN
031 225 2424 ext 6638

O Monday-Saturday 10am-5pm.
   10am-6pm in June
£ free
P parking meters in Royal Mile
🚌 buses to Royal Mile
♿ to ground and first floor only.
✗ no

Wander down the Royal Mile to Canongate and you will come upon 'The People's Story'; do go in. My children were fascinated, they came across the histories of 'real' people for the first time and older children were obviously engrossed in these stories. This is a marvellous concept: instead of showing the lives of the wealthy the city lets us see the lives of the people who actually made that wealth, a bit like one of the open air museums, but here totally within the context of Edinburgh. The building is cramped so you do get a feeling of the constraints of city living.

At the beginning you will be introduced to two families: an 18th century scavenger and a 20th century refuse collector. Compare their living accommodation, wages, educational and health expectations for their children. Find the town crier and the prison cell.

On the first floor look at all the beautiful Trades Union banners, displays about the Co-operative Movement, and suffragettes. Explain to your daughters how recent it was that women were allowed to vote and relate this to the fact that few people in Edinburgh were allowed to vote in the

Top: The imposing Palace of Holyrood House from the West front.
Above: The imposing four-poster in the King's Bedchamber.
Left: The elegant quadrangle is seen here unusually empty.

Tam Docherty in his cubicle at the Artisan's Lodging House, Grove Street, Edinburgh, 1978

last century. Find the domestic servant who, in 1933 got up at 5.30am every morning to scrub the grates of some wealthy merchant's house. Go up to the bus conductress, the fisherman and fishwife and the printer.

On the second floor smell the wash house and steam drier, look at the notice on the wall demanding that it remain open in 1960. I found out later that there is still one operating in Edinburgh. Look at the wartime kitchen and then peep into the Artisan's Lodging House and see Tam Docherty sitting on his bed with all his worldly possessions around him. Go into the 1933 Fergusons' Tea Rooms and listen to two women talking about their husbands, and in the Empire Bar hear what those husbands say about their wives!

If you have time go and watch the video on the top floor and see old film footage of people at work and interviews with some of them, now retired, about their living and working conditions.

This is an excellent place to visit as children are never too young to be introduced to social history. Labelling is good, the background information very readable and the displays excellent.

Royal Museum of Scotland

There are two parts to the Royal Museum of Scotland, one in Chambers Street, the other in Queen Street.

**Royal Museum of Scotland
Chambers Street
Edinburgh EH1 1JF
031 225 7534**

O Monday-Saturday 10am-5pm, Sunday 2-5pm. Closed 25,26 December, 1 January and a Monday in May.
£ free
P meters nearby
🚌 city cenyre buses
♿ yes
✗ restaurant

You could certainly spend a day here as there are so many different subjects on display and just the right amount of each. The building is light and airy and the staff very helpful. We loved the staircases, the fountains and the galleried walkways to look over. There are galleries of natural history, geology, transport and engineering, costume, ceramics, glass and ethnography.

We started by watching a very good fourteen minute audio-visual presentation 'The World in our Hands' in G11 on the ground floor. It told us about the first life on earth and into the future; we learnt about the Ice Age, volcanoes, the depletion of the ozone layer and current global issues. In the gallery we saw examples of extinct wildlife, endangered species and saved animals. Glass cases filled with rubbish and computer data bases helped to explain about the depletion of resources and recycling. I suddenly had a 'green' daughter. Meanwhile the three year old was wandering around the next gallery entranced at the huge, stuffed lions, bears and anaconda. We drank juice in a rather surreal café surrounded by cases of stuffed birds which we later inspected and found out about the bird life of Edinburgh and the rest of Scotland.

We spent time in the Victorian Engineering, Power and Transport galleries and were particularly impressed by the huge lights from a lighthouse. We wandered up the beautiful winding staircases to the Ethnography department, peeped at the Egyptian mummies and their coffins and then at the Costume Gallery before going upstairs again to the Tribal Art Gallery to see the array of costumes, masks and sculptures from all over the world. Do spend time here looking at how they are all put together and the materials like grass, straw, beads and metal used. We enjoyed looking at the fossils, minerals and gems.

Royal Museum of Scotland
Queen Street
Edinburgh EH4 3DR

O £ P ₩ As for Chambers St site except:
✗ café

This part of the museum is devoted to the history of Scotland. You can see artefacts from the Dark Ages, relics of the early Saints and Mary Queen of Scots' jewels. Then find out about the archaeology of Scotland including the St Ninian's Isle Treasure, Pictish silverwork, a hoard of Viking silver and crafts from Orkney. The Romans came to Scotland and here you can find out what they left behind.

Scottish National Gallery of Modern Art
Belford Road
Edinburgh EH4 3DR
031 556 8921

O Monday-Saturday 10am-5pm, Sunday 2-5pm
£ free, admission charge for special exhibitions
P on site
₩ bus to Belford Road
&. yes
✗ restaurant and picnic area

Set in beautiful gardens this 19th century neo-classical building houses a fascinating collection of 20th century painting, graphics and sculpture. Many children relate to the imagination of modern artists and enjoy their work. Come here to show them paintings by Picasso, Matisse, Hockney and many more. There are fine examples of sculpture including the slim, elongated figures by Giacometti and great chunky, beautiful forms of Henry Moore. How much better to see it all for real than in postcards or not at all. There are talks and lectures for children of all ages so ring for details

Museum of Flight
East Fortune
North Berwick
East Lothian EH39 5LF
0620 88308

O 1 April-30 September 10.30am-4.30pm every day
£ Adult £2.00, Child £1.00, Under Five free, OAP £1.00, Disabled visitors free, Family Ticket £5.00. Free entrance all day Friday.
P on site
₩ BR Drem
&. yes
✗ café and picnic area

Come to this airbase and see a collection of over thirty aeroplanes, rockets and aero-engines. In 1919 the R34 Airship took off from East Fortune to make the first east-west air flight to the USA. Find the relics of this airship in the collection inside the hangar. You will also see a 1930 de Havilland Puss Moth, a 1934 Weir W-2 autogiro, a Supermarine Spitfire and a Messerschmitt Me163 'Komet'. Inspect the aero-engines, seven of which were built before 1914, whilst others are from Concorde and Blue Streak. Then sit in a cockpit and try your hand at piloting.

Cadell's *Lady in Black* (detail) in the National Gallery of Modern Art.

STRATHCLYDE

Auchindrain Township/ Open Air Museum
By Inveraray
Argyll PA38 8XN
0499 5235

O Easter-30 September 10am-5pm every day.
April, May and September closed on Saturday

£ Adult £2.20, Child £1.40, Under Five free,
OAP £1.70, Family Ticket £6.80

P on site

Inveraray 5½ miles

& to some parts

✕ café and picnic area.

Inveraray Jail
Inverary
Argyll PA31 8TX
0499 2381

O 1 April-31 October 9.30am-6pm, last admission
5pm, every day.
1 November-31 March 10am-5pm, last adm 4pm.

£ Adult £3.60, Child £1.75, Under Five free,
OAP £1.90, Family Ticket £9.85.

P nearby

BR Arrochar or Dalmally, then bus to Inverary.

& limited

✕ picnic area nearby

'We like exploring all the little houses and running about making a frightful noise.'

So say my brother's children who come here regularly and love it. There cannot be many museum staff who would not shudder with horror at that remark. Far out in the wilds of Argyll, with nobody to be disapproving except some shaggy highland cattle, this must be the perfect place to do just that.

Once the children have got all that out of their system, then there are marvellous things to appreciate at Auchindrain. It was a little community of six West Highland families and has survived for centuries on its original site. The last man to work here was Eddie MacCallum who retired in 1962. Walk into the houses and you step into another world, that of the crofters of 'the old days'. Would you like to be MacCallum, the proud owner of the only sink in the township, to nod off by the peat fire in Bell Pot's house, to sleep in one of the box beds in Munro's house? Can you imagine working in the smiddy, the byre, the stables? Spending your days out in all weather tending sheep and cattle, spinning and weaving? As you wander through the houses and ruined cottages it is not hard to imagine the hard life of a Highland Crofter.

Queen Victoria brought her children here so make sure you follow her excellent example. My brother gives it a three star rating and points out that a positive attitude is needed for Scottish rain and suggests you use the golfing umbrellas, thoughtfully provided by the Royal Bank of Scotland. I am proud to add that my grandfather's tweed suit is on display here as well as the knife cleaner from the house that he lived in nearby.

This is one of the most fascinating places in Scotland, full of the atmosphere of prison life a century ago. Here are the cells complete with 'live' prisoners picking oakum, mending nets while the waves of the loch outside still crash against the prison walls.

After you have braved the exhibition on the 'Fortune, Death and Damnation' of medieval crime and punishment in Scotland, take a seat on the public benches of the Courtroom. You can stare rudely at the other occupants of the room; the judge, the jury, the lawyers, the witness, the accused and the policeman. Did that person next to you move slightly? Fibreglass is incredible material! Settle back comfortably once you have recovered from the shock, and listen to recordings of some of the trials held here.

Leave the Courtroom and begin your prison sentence, down the steep steps into the courtyard. Walk down the cage-like exercising yard and imagine the solitary hour's exercise, locked behind the iron gates, pacing relentlessly back and forth, dimly aware of the fellow prisoner on the other side of the stone wall!

Being behind bars in the Old Prison, built in 1820 before prison reforms were brought in, it was cold and damp, with little food and hours of inactivity. Up to twenty-four men, women, children and lunatics were confined in eight small cells.

The new prison, of 1849, was a model of its time, with well heated cells, water closets and a washroom. Talk to the prisoners here, meet the warder and the prison matron. Turn the hard labour crank machine, try out the whipping table, birch and thumb screw and then recover in the hammock.

Our visit to Inveraray Jail was on a wild, stormy, winter's day. The experience was unforgettable.

Above: The lifelike models debating the case in the Inveraray Courtroom.

Left: Inveraray Jail, showing the height of its surrounding wall.

Summerlee Heritage Trust
West Canal Street
Coatbridge ML5 1QD
0236 431261

Riding a single-deck tram at Summerlee.

O every day 10am-5pm.
  Closed 24 December-2 January.
£ free
P nearby
🚉 BR Coatbridge Central, Coatbridge Sunnyside
♿ yes
✗ café and picnic area.

In the 1830s workers at Summerlee Iron Works, endured long hours, usually in appalling conditions, to produce steel for Britain. By the 1920s all this was forgotten as the works became derelict. Ten years ago they were rediscovered and now you can visit them to get a glimpse of what life there was once like.

Children always enjoy the ride on the electric tram, which was used to transport people to work. Drop by the Tram Shed to see the renovation work on other vehicles. Through the summer they can watch steam rollers in operation (ring for details) and elsewhere find the steam locomotives and steam cranes.

In the exhibition hall there is a spade gorge, brass finishers' shop and a Victorian trade exhibition with lots of working machines. Find out about coalmining, other local industries and brickmaking. Go underground in the newly reconstructed shallow coal mine.

Look at the communities which developed around these industries. Room interiors show the public wash house, co-op and temperance society. The steelworks and other industries of the Monklands district created much pollution and here you can find out about the campaigns for clear air and pure water. Poor housing, poverty and disease contributed to worse living conditions.

Have a picnic by the playground next to the canal.

Glasgow

Glasgow has every right to be proud of its museums; they are all free and devote lots of time and energy to serving the needs of all their visitors, especially children. There really is plenty to do here.

Art Gallery and Museum
Kelvingrove
Glasgow G3 8AG
041 357 3929

O Monday-Saturday 10am-5pm, Sunday 11am-5pm.
Closed 25 December, 1 January.
£ free
P on site
♨ Undergound Kelvinhall; bus to Argyle Street, Dumbarton Road
& to most parts
✕ restaurant and picnic area nearby

The Art Gallery and Museum was founded in 1888 and generously endowed by the wealthy city fathers who believed implicitly in the education of the young. Today it is a lively place where everyone is welcome. You will find Sir Thomas Lipton's collection of silverware and Tiffany Glass which this famous Glasgow grocer bequeathed to the museum. Find out about endangered species and threats to the planet in the Natural History Galleries where you will see skins of animals, confiscated locally by HM Customs, and the destruction caused by beer cans and other rubbish.

There is a good collection of paintings and sculpture by Scottish artists here too. Find some of the witty constructions by Eduardo Paolozzi where it seems he has amalgamated anything and everything he could lay his hands on to create a work of art. Try for yourself when you get home. Have fun making sense of work by the Surrealist Salvador Dali. Then look at pieces by Glasgow's best known designer, Charles Rennie Mackintosh.

Elsewhere there are artefacts from Ancient Egypt, Melanesia, Ethiopia, China and India. It is worth spending time here looking at these collections of objects which include masks, hats, shields, axes and much more. The museum offers a range of activities and is constantly changing its displays, so find out in advance what is on. The Museum of Transport is also close by.

Glasgow Art Gallery and Museum.

The Burrell Collection
Pollok Country Park
Glasgow G43 1AT
041 649 7151

O Monday-Saturday 10am-5pm, Sunday
   11am-5pm.
   Closed 25 December, 1 January

£ free

P on site

🚇 BR Pollokshaws West, Shawlands; bus to
   Pollokshaws Road

♿ yes

✕ restaurant, picnic area nearby

We took our whole family here when the youngest was still in a pushchair. It was pouring with rain and we had driven down from Argyll and across Glasgow. At the mention of the word 'museum', there was virtually a riot from the back seat and vociferous demands to stop at the nearest fish and chip shop. However, for once, parents held sway and we found ourselves running out of the rain and through the great 16th century doors and carved stone archway from Hornby Castle, Yorkshire, into a modern building, both dynamic and peaceful. We were obliged to head straight for the restaurant, where coffee, French bread and camembert, eaten at long pine tables in a large, light space, with the rain teeming down, seen through the glass as a blur of trees, grass and raindrops, was pure joy.

Stained glass in the Burrell Collection.

Now in the right frame of mind we wandered happily through this marvellous building of white stone floors, light grey walls and tubular concrete pillars supporting a roof of glass and timber. We all gravitated to the green glazed Boddhisatva sitting cross-legged in smiling meditation against a background of trees; green in summer, golden in autumn, bare in winter, reminding us of impermanence. Objects from ancient civilizations are here, from Sumeria, Phoenicia, Iraq, Egypt, the Indus Valley, China, Greece and Rome; objects so venerable and beautiful that we all, even the youngest of us, felt humbled.

Hanging tapestries and carpets, china, lace, paintings, oriental art, stained glass, Roman helmets are all part of the huge collection, over eight thousand items, of Sir William Burrell, a Glasgow ship owner. He only bought objects he considered to be beautiful, and insisted in his will that they be displayed in a beautiful building. Even our children were aware of a light-headed sensation of moving in and out of spaces that work so perfectly for the objects they hold. Posters of Degas ballet dancers and the Boddhisattva were brought home and hung on the wall as a constant reminder to cultivate inner peace and appreciate beauty.

Pollok House
Pollok Country Park
Glasgow G43 1AT
041 632 0274

O Monday-Saturday 10am-5pm, Sunday
  11am-5pm.
  Closed 25 December, 1 January.

£ free

P on site

BR Pollokshaws West, Shawlands; bus to
  Pollokshaws Road

access for disabled by arrangement

restaurant, picnic area nearby

Set in the same park as the Burrell
Collection, Pollok House is yet another
endowment to the city by one of its long
established families. From the outside it
looks cold and unwelcoming but this is
deceptive, for inside it is awash with
flamboyant, 18th century plasterwork. If
you are rethinking a piece of cornicing
at home, come here to see it on a grand
scale. The house, thought to have been
designed by William and John Adam
around 1750, was lived in by the
Maxwell family until 1966. Go through
the large entrance hall and see the
grandeur of their lives. Look into the
business room, the morning and
drawing rooms and then the library;
houses of this size had their own
libraries. Wander into the dining room
and see the porcelain and china and
then on to the billiard room. On your
tour look out for a fine collection of
Spanish paintings including works by El
Greco and Goya and some English
works by William Blake and others
collected by Sir William Stirling Maxwell.
There is a very intricate astronomical
clock and much elegant furniture.

It is fascinating to visit a house like
this to see the taste of the wealthy
owner. However it is also pertinent to
discuss with your children, what it would
have been like living here, how they got
so rich, who helped them do it, the living
and working conditions of the servants
and where they came from. Maybe you
can link it up with an open air museum
you have visited. There is an education
department here so find out about
workshops and talks for children.

The bleak exterior of Pollok house hides an
extravagant interior.

Haggs Castle
100 St Andrews Drive
Glasgow G41 4RB
041 427 2725

O Monday-Saturday 10am-5pm, Sunday
   11am-5pm.
   Closed 25 December, 1 January

£ free

P nearby

🚃 BR Maxwell Park; bus to St Andrews Drive

♿ access for the disabled by arrangement

✗ picnic area nearby

Haggs Castle is a museum for all
children between about four and eleven
years old. A cottage in the grounds of
the park has been converted specifically
for their use. They can make butter,
cheese, oatcakes and sweets, learn
crafts like weaving and doll making and
explore the more energetic pastimes of
croquet and archery or discover some
of the street games played by their
grandparents. Ring up to find out what
events are taking place.

The actual castle was once home of
the Maxwell Family who lived here in
the 16th and 17th centuries before
moving out (see Pollok House their later
home). The castle then fell into ruin but
has been restored so that now you can
see period room settings and get an
idea of life in a castle. The original
kitchen has been reconstructed with a
huge range, cauldron, quern stone and
utensils. Meet Sir John and Lady
Maxwell getting ready for dinner in their
rooms upstairs.

Find out about the life styles of
children one hundred years ago in the
Victorian Nursery.

Spend time in the gardens smelling
the lavender, mint, sage and rue, grown
for medicinal purposes in the herb beds.

Haggs Castle's un-castle like appearance
conceals a fine children's museum.

Museum of Transport
Kelvin Hall
1 Bunhouse Road
Glasgow G3 8DP
041 357 3929

○ Monday-Saturday 10am-5pm, Sunday 11am-5pm.
Closed 25 December, 1 January
£ free
P nearby
▥ Underground Kelvinhall, bus to Argyle Street, Dumbarton Road
♿ yes
✗ restaurant

Everything to do with transport in Scotland is here in this noisy, bustling place. Do go, it is well worth the trip. Horse-drawn vehicles, bicycles, motorcars, buses and trams, ships and anything else to do with transport are here.

Walk along a reconstructed Art Deco street, past the underground station, look at the shops and the delivery boy's bicycle. Go down the alleyway and see Merkland Street Station from the Glasgow Underground, the third oldest in the world. Into the car showroom to see the vast array of mass produced motorcars. On the railway platform you will see the Saloon of the King George VI train and lots of big locomotives including the *Fort William*. Look for the commercial vehicles, the fire engines, buses and trams and the Glasgow and London Royal Mail horse-drawn coach. Look at the beautiful vintage cars and

The railway platform inside Glasgow's Museum of Transport with *Fort William* in the foreground.

trace their evolution from the horse-drawn carriage; the similarity of their running boards and mudguards and their tiny windscreens; I remember my grandfather having one which opened on hinges.

Go up to the mezzanine and into the Clyde Room and find out about the history and importance of Glasgow's famous river. Its shipbuilding yards, sadly depleted, produced some of the finest craft in the world. You can see models of all kinds of ships made here, from the great liners and warships to paddle steamers and yachts.

Find the oldest surviving pedal cycle in the world here and then look at all those gleaming motorbikes waiting to throb into action.

People's Palace
Glasgow Green
Glasgow G40 1AT
041 554 0223

○ Monday-Saturday 10am-5pm, Sunday 11am-5pm.
Closed 25 December and 1 January
£ free
P on site
▥ bus to London Road
♿ to most parts
✗ café and nearby picnic area.

When you have finished seeing the wealth of the original owners of Pollok

The striking redbrick exterior of the People's Palace in front of the Winter Garden.

House and Haggs Castle, come here to find out about the lives of the people who were foremost in making Glasgow a large industrial city. Situated near the Gorbals, in the oldest park in Glasgow, in an area where much of the British Trade Union movement began, this museum is carrying out the function of its Victorian founder-it is a museum for the people. It is proud of its Winter Garden where you can now relax in the elegant restaurant. Children are most welcome and can learn about cities, industry, work, skill, hardship and poverty. There is an education department so ring up in advance to find out if there are any workshops.

Start with the origins of the city in 1175 and the people who lived here, then follow life from the medieval period to the reign of Mary, Queen of Scots. Look at the sculpture and crafts of the times.

By the 18th century Glasgow was beginning to be a commercial centre. See the Glasgow Tobacco Lord's office. Tobacco brought trade with America which was important to the city's growth. Look at the pieces of Delft pottery, candles, clay pipes and muslin produced here for the home market and the export trade. Glasgow has long been associated with the book trade and publishing, and here you will see the first printing press of *The Glasgow Herald* and various other books and magazines.

In 'Victorian Glasgow' there are wooden machines for the textile industry, Turkey Red materials, carpets and Arab headdresses. There are fireplaces, stoves, ironwork, sewing machines, mangles, glass bottles and pottery to show the variety of manufacture.

Look at the history of the trade union movement with its colourful banners and regalia. Find out about the co-operative movement and changes brought by the suffragettes.

With all this hard work the people of Glasgow deserved entertainment, so go and see the theatrical, music hall, cinema and football memorabilia. Find the 1959 jukebox and admire the costume of Glasgow's most famous, modern-day, funny man, Billy Connolly.

WALES

Slate splitting demonstration at the Welsh
Slate Museum.

DYFED

The Wildfowl and Wetlands Trust
Ymddiriedolaeth Adar y Gwylptir

Penclacwydd
Llwynhendy
Llanelli
Dyfed SA14 9SH
0554 741087

○ Summer, 9.30am-5pm.
Winter 9.30am-4pm.
Closed 24, 25 December

£ Adult £3.20, Child £1.60, Under Four free,
OAP £2.40, Family £8.00.
Season Ticket to all sites available.

P on site

🚌 bus to Llwynhendy

♿ yes

✗ café and picnic area

In 1946, Sir Peter Scott, son of Captain Scott of Antarctic fame, founded the first of eight centres, to care for wetland birds. Today these are thriving places and have done much to protect and preserve endangered species from all over the world as well as introducing them to countless children and adults in a relaxed environment. We had a lovely time feeding the birds, which include ducks, swans, flamingoes, geese and pheasants. We watched them swim and dive, then waddle towards us. Our four year old was enraptured by them, and not at all afraid. We roamed through rough terrain to find the wilder creatures, curlews, oystercatchers and redshanks, we had to be very quiet so as not to scare them, and we hid ourselves in little hideouts to catch a glimpse. Pheasants appeared and were grateful for our food. As we wandered round we were amazed at the numbers of birds here, the variety in shape, size, colour and friendliness. They really do come from everywhere; there are Hawaiian geese, Caribbean flamingoes and wood ducks who are refugees from the rain forests. Information is well displayed and you can find out about migration, why flamingoes are pink and stand on one leg, how deep ducks dive.

This centre is situated on the Burry Inlet which has been designated as a wetland of international importance. One final word; it is wet, so do have boots on hand (or feet!).

Below: The wildfowl roam freely at Penclacwydd and as can be seen many are not in the least afraid of the visitors.

SOUTH GLAMORGAN

National Museum of Wales
Amgueddfa Genedlaethol Cymru
Cathays Park
Cardiff
0222 397951

○ Tuesday-Saturday 10am-5pm, Sunday 2.30-5pm

£ Adult £2.00, Child £1.00, Under Five free, OAP £1.50, Season Ticket available to National Museums in the Cardiff area.

🅿 nearby

♿ yes

✗ restaurant

Do not be put off by this grand and imposing building; it isa good national museum where children are very welcome. We enjoyed the Natural History galleries, finding out about local animals and rock formations, seeing the leather backed turtle, hump-back whale and, of course, the dinosaur skeleton. Find out about the early people of Wales, the influence of religion and chapel life. Then look at the paintings, many by Welsh artists or with a Welsh subject matter. Find the portrait of Dylan Thomas by Augustus John and then the sculpture of the painter's head by Jacob Epstein. There is a good collection of Impressionist paintings here including Monet's 'Rouen Cathedral' and studies of waterlilies and works by Cezanne, Daumier and Rodin. Let your children see them and look at the uses of paint, colour and light. The museum has handling sessions, videos and special exhibitions for children; ring up for details.

The splendid exterior of the National Museum of Wales.

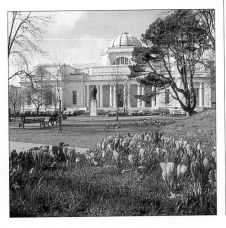

Cardiff Bay

Welsh Industrial and Maritime Museum
Amgueddfa Diwydiant a Môr Cymru
Bute Street
Cardiff Bay
Cardiff CF1 6AN
0222 481919

○ Tuesday-Saturday 10am-5pm, Sunday 2.30-5pm.
Closed 24, 25, 26 December and 1 January

£ Adult £1.00, Child 50p, Under Five free, OAP 75p, Season Ticket available to National Museums in the Cardiff area.

🅿 nearby

🚌 No 7 bus stops outside

♿ yes

✗ picnic area

Cardiff Bay was once a thriving dock, exporting coal, from the nearby valleys, all over the world. The Welsh Industrial and Maritime Museum now runs five sites on the dock to show the development of industry, transport, power and science in various parts of the bay area.

Begin your visit at the main building of the Museum where you can see and touch the huge engines which powered the heavy industries, horse-drawn trams and buses, a pennyfarthing, vintage motor cars, steam rollers, traction engines, buses and a Sinclair C5 car. Spend time on the hands-on and interactive exhibits on the ship's bridge and air-sea rescue video game. Visit the lifeboat, pilot cutter, tugboat, locomotives, cranes and helicopters outside. Find the working replica of Trevithick's Penydarren locomotive of 1804 which was the first railway locomotive. Then wander into the 'Q-Shed', once the booking office for the local pleasure steamers and now a changing exhibition area. Take stock of what it must have been like when this was a busy port and the role this area of Wales played in the industrial revolution worldwide.

Further along the dock you will come across Techniquest which is a hands-on science centre for children, of all ages, and adults to have fun but also to learn about science. At 126 Bute Street you will find Joseph Frazer's ship - chandlery business which has been

Children work on a ship at the Welsh Industrial and Maritime Museum.

renovated to display an exhibition about the history of Cardiff as a port. You will meet people, from all over the world, who came here to make Cardiff well known as a seafaring and cosmopolitan city. Then in a reconstructed dockland scene you can find out about the rise and fall of the coal mining and export industries in South Wales.

Take note of all the buildings as you go around this fascinating area; many of them played an important part in the functioning of the docks.

Welsh Folk Museum
Amgueddfa Werin Cymru
St Fagans
Cardiff CF5 6XB
0222 569441

○ 10am-5pm every day.
  Closed Sundays November-April
£ Adult £3.50, Child £1.75, Under Five free,
  OAP £2.60, Family £8.75, Season Ticket
  available to National Museums in the Cardiff area..
P on site
🚌 bus from Cardiff City Centre
♿ yes
✗ restaurant and picnic area

If ever you meet anyone who has been to St Fagans you will be told,

emphatically, that you must go there. This is an open-air museum of Welsh life, to which buildings and objects have been brought from all over the country. I know someone, from Merthyr Tydfil who visited with a friend to find her grandmother's cottage here, miles from where it had originally stood. We really do recommend a visit. Places like this convey, extremely well, the harshness and poverty of the lives endured by working people in the surrounding communities.

Here you can see life over the centuries. There is a Celtic village, castle, farmhouses and a Victorian schoolhouse. In the six Rhyd-y-Car iron workers' cottages you will see life over a period of 180 years, each one has been decorated in styles from 1805 to 1985. Compare the life style of 1895 with that of 1985. How many people lived in each cottage? Where did they work? What kitchen gadgets did they have? Where was the toilet?

The working smithy at St Fagans, one of the many trades to be seen in action here.

GWENT

Big Pit Mining Museum
Amgueddfa Gloddfa Pwll Mawr
Blaenavon
Gwent NP4 9XP
0495 790311

○ March-November first tour starts at 10am, last tour starts at 3.30pm, Museum open until 5.00pm.
Ring for details at other times.

£ Adult £4.75, Child £3.50, Under Five not allowed underground, OAP £4.50, Family Ticket £15.00
Surface only Adult £1.75, Child £1.00, OAP £1.50

P on site

♿ yes, but contact the museum in advance if you want to go underground.

✕ restaurant and picnic area

My daughter came here on her school journey; over a year later she was still able to describe it vividly. They all wore safety helmets and cap lamps, with belt, battery and 'self-rescuers', and began their tour with a 90m/300ft descent down a mineshaft in a pit cage. Their guide was an ex-miner who had worked in mines in South Wales all his life. He took them along underground roadways in which at first they were able to walk upright and then were forced to crouch and creep along. As they passed the air doors she was horrified by the guide's description of the small children or 'trappers' who opened those doors in the 19th century, squatting alone for hours in total darkness. They passed hundred year old coal and ironstone workings and reached the coal face where their guide explained methods of extracting coal. They saw the underground stables where pit ponies were kept and the mine's stationary haulage engines. On the surface they saw the blacksmith's forge, the tool workshops, the pithead baths and the original miners' canteen.

The future of coalmining in this country is threatened and might soon become a 'museum industry' only. The shaft at Big Pit was sunk to its present level in 1880 and the mine was used as a working colliery for exactly one hundred years. On 3 February 1980 it was closed. Now it is a museum piece.

It is dark and damp down there and, insists my daughter, not for the timid or claustrophobic. Children under five are not allowed down and children in school groups must be over seven. Disabled visitors can go underground but need to contact the museum in advance.

A group of children pose for the camera having emerged from the black depths of Big Pit.

GWYNEDD

Museum of Childhood
Amgueddfa Dyddiau Ieuenctid
1 Castle Street
Beaumaris
Anglesey
Gwynedd LL58 8AP
0248 712498

○ Easter-1 November, Monday-Saturday 10am-6pm, Sunday 1-5pm
£ Adult £2.00, Child £1.00, Under Five free, OAP £1.00, Family Ticket £5.00
🅿 in town car parks
🚌 bus to town centre
♿ no
✖ no

This small, privately owned museum contains over two thousand toys, games, pieces of nursery furniture and childhood ephemera from the last one hundred and fifty years. There is a room full of dolls, dolls' houses and games, there are teddy bears, toy money boxes and machines, tin plate toys, ships and aeroplanes, music boxes and polyphons. Look at the educational toys to discover the learning aspect of play. Even the paintings, prints, samplers, pottery and glass, have childhood as their subject matter.

Ffestiniog Railway
Rheilffordd Ffestiniog
Harbour Station
Porthmadog
Gwynedd LL49 9NF
0766 512340

○ Mid March-November every day.
£ Fares vary depending on journey chosen. Basic round trip: Adult £11.40 (+1 child free), Children ½ fare, OAP ¾ fare.
🅿 on site
🚌 BR Blaenau Ffestiniog, Porthmadog
♿ yes, trains have wide doors for wheelchairs, ring up in advance.
✖ restaurant and picnic area

Travel by steam train through the beautiful Snowdonia National Park from Porthmadog to Blaenau Ffestiniog. Most trains have a buffet service and you can get off at Boston Lodge, Plas Halt, Dduallt and Tanygrisiau, though do inform the guard before you start your journey. To get on again, stand on the platform and hail the train as it comes into the station.

Merddin Emrys departs Tan-y-bwlch on the Ffestiniog Railway.

Snowdon Mountain Railway
Trên Bach yr Wyddfa
Llanberis
Caernarfon
Gwynedd LL55 4TY
0286 870223

○ 15 March-1 November. First train at 9am, 8.30 at peak times, then up to every 30 minutes, depending on demand.
£ Adult £12.50 return, Child £9.00, Under Four free, OAP £12.50
🅿 on site
🚌 BR Bangor, bus to Caernarfon then to Llanberis
♿ yes
✖ restaurant and picnic area

I remember the thrill of going up Snowdon, on this railway, when I was a child. Some friends, and their parents, recently enjoyed their trip up the mountain on the only rack and pinion railway in the country. It was first opened in 1896 and its steam and diesel engines pull their carriages three thousand feet to the summit. The carriages are divided into compartments seating eight people on wooden slatted seats. It takes about one hour to get to the top where you can spend thirty minutes before you come down again. Our travellers were disappointed at the mist on the mountain but they did enjoy waving at the walkers and climbers and the views lower down.

We are assured that on clear days you can see Anglesey, the Wicklow Mountains in Ireland and the Isle of Man from the summit.

Llanberis Lake Railway
Rheilffordd Llyn Padarn
Padarn Country Park
Llanberis
Gwynedd LL55 4TY
0286 870549

○ 2 March-29 October, running times variable
£ Adult £3.40, Child £1.00, £2.00 if travelling alone, Under Five free, OAP £3.40
🅿 on site
🚉 BR Bangor, bus to Caernarfon then to Llanberis
♿ yes in station but wheelchairs will not fit in trains.
✕ café and picnic area.

Travel on one of the 'Great Little Trains' of Wales and see glorious views across the lake, and the summit of Snowdon, if it is not shrouded in mist. The return trip to Penllyn takes about forty minutes which includes a short stop at Cei Llydan where you can get off and return on a later train.

Welsh Slate Museum
Amgueddfa Lechi Cymru
Padarn Country Park
Llanberis
Gwynedd LL55 4TY
0286 870630

○ Easter Saturday-30 September 9.30am-6.30pm
£ Adult £1.50, Child 80p, Under Five free. OAP/Concessions £1.20, Family Ticket £3.80
🅿 on site
🚉 bus 80 from Caernarfon, 77 from Bangor, 19 from Llandudno, 11 from Beddgelert
♿ to most parts
✕ café and picnic area

The Dinorwig Slate Quarry was one of the largest quarries in Wales. Three thousand men quarried tens of thousands of slates every year to be exported all over the world. It closed in 1969 and has since become a museum.

Most of the machinery and buildings remain for you to see how the slate was quarried then sawn, split and trimmed to become roofing material. There is a blacksmith at work, a foundry, a water-wheel which once powered all the machines, and 'Una' the locomotive used around the site.

Talyllyn Railway
Rheilffordd Talyllyn
Wharf Station
Tywyn
Gwynedd LL36 9EY
0654 710472

○ 1 April-31 October, 26 December-1 January, every day, running times of trains vary.
£ fares vary depending on journey chosen. Basic round trip: Adult £6.50, Child £3.25, Under Five free, OAP £5.50
🅿 nearby
🚉 BR Tywyn Station 300 yds away. Bus S28/29/30
♿ yes, wheelchair users should ring up in advance
✕ café and picnic area

This 'Great Little Train of Wales' was first opened in 1865 and saved from closure in 1951. Its steam engines run on narrow gauge track from Tywyn through the Snowdonia National Park to Nant Gwernol. Various stations along the track are open for you to get off and explore. Start a mountain walk at Rhydyronen, look at the waterfalls at Dolgoch Falls as well as riding across valleys on great arched viaducts. Nant Gwernol, the terminus, is inaccessible by road and situated in a ravine. There are wonderful forest walks around here. Back at Tywyn you can wander around the museum and discover the full history of this enchanting railway.

Tom Rolt at Nant Gwernol terminus.

POWYS

Centre for Alternative Technology
Canolfan y Dechnoleg Amgen
Machynlleth
Powys SY20 9AZ
0654 702400

O 10am-5pm every day

£ Adult £2.95, Child £1.40, Under Five free, OAP £2.70, Family Ticket £11.70

P on site

🚌 bus from Machynlleth

♿ restaurant and picnic area

✗ to most parts. Difficult for pushchairs in some parts

Ten years ago, on a cold, wet day, I trudged along a muddy path from the car park to the centre and wondered what I was letting myself in for. Within minutes of my arrival I was transfixed; there were so many fascinating things and so much to learn and do. This was the early days of public awareness of environmental and ecological issues and I was impressed at the simplicity of explanation of highly complex issues. Now, years later, I am delighted that our young visitors also found it exciting. I can think of nowhere else quite like it as every aspect of alternative technology is explored in a living environment.

Here you can see wind and solar power generation, the hydraulic ram (a water pump using no external energy supply), learn about organic gardening, and enjoy the small holding with its animals and fish culture. The cliff railway made out of green oak and recycled pine runs around the site. Elsewhere there are examples of small scale manufacture which keep costs to a minimum and use local resources. Look at the economic house and see how resource conscious you are at home; can you do better? Then see how methane gas is produced.

Our children loved this place and we certainly recommend it for anyone doing CDT or interested in Green issues. Do wear boots as the centre is rather muddy, being on the site of a disused slate quarry.

The Organic Gardens at Machynlleth.

INDEX

ACKNOWLEDGEMENTS

The authors and publisher would like to thank the staff of the various establishments featured in this book for their assistance in compiling information. All of the illustrations reproduced were kindly supplied by the relevant museum.The photographs of the various royal establishments are Crown Copyright and reproduced by gracious permission. Additional picture credits are as follows: Fotek(p9), Mike Williams (p21), Ron Wells (p26), Joe Blossom (p41), Barry Lewis (p74), Rick Hogben (p81), J Brooks/Jarrold Publishing (p94), N Jinkerson/Jarrold Publishing (p103), P Grand (p140).